PENGUIN CLASSICS

EARLY GREEK PHILOSOPHY

ADVISORY EDITOR: BETTY RADICE

JONATHAN BARNES is Professor of Ancient Philosophy at the University of Oxford. He was born in 1942 and educated at the City of London School and Balliol College, Oxford. From 1968 to 1978 he was a Fellow of Oriel College, Oxford; since then he has been a Fellow of Balliol College, Oxford.

His visiting appointments have taken him to the University of Chicago, the Institute for Advanced Study, Princeton, the University of Massachusetts at Amherst, the University of Texas at Austin and the Wissenschaftskolleg zu Berlin. He has published numerous articles in learned journals and his books include *The Presocratic Philosophers* (1979, second edition 1982) and, in the Past Masters series, *Aristotle* (1982). Jonathan Barnes has also written the introduction to Aristotle's *Ethics* in the Penguin Classics.

JONATHAN BARNES

EARLY GREEK
PHILOSOPHY

PENGUIN BOOKS

PENGUIN BOOKS

Published by the Penguin Group
Penguin Books Ltd, 27 Wrights Lane, London W8 5TZ, England
Penguin Books USA Inc., 375 Hudson Street, New York, New York 10014, USA
Penguin Books Australia Ltd, Ringwood, Victoria, Australia
Penguin Books Canada Ltd, 10 Alcorn Avenue, Toronto, Ontario, Canada M4V 3B2
Penguin Books (NZ) Ltd, 182–190 Wairau Road, Auckland 10, New Zealand

Penguin Books Ltd, Registered Offices: Harmondsworth, Middlesex, England

Published in Penguin Books 1987
9 10

Copyright © Jonathan Barnes, 1987
All rights reserved

Printed in England by Clays Ltd, St Ives plc
Filmset in Linotron 202 Baskerville

CONTENTS

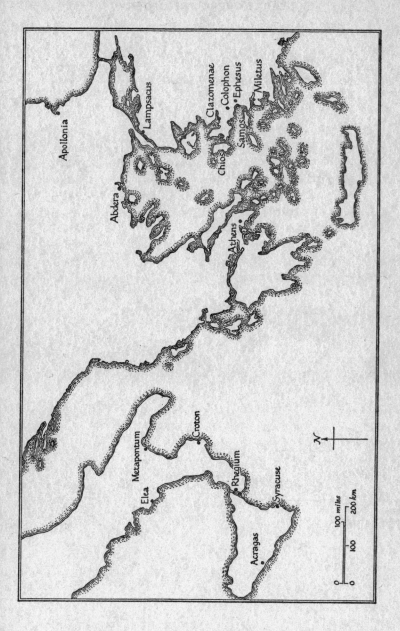

INTRODUCTION

I *The First Philosophers*

According to tradition, Greek philosophy began in 585 BC and ended in AD 529. It began when Thales of Miletus, the first Greek philosopher, predicted an eclipse of the sun. It ended when the Christian Emperor Justinian forbade the teaching of pagan philosophy in the University of Athens. The tradition is a simplification: Greeks had entertained philosophical thoughts before 585 BC, and Justinian's edict, whatever its intention, did not bring pagan philosophy to a sudden stop. But the traditional dates stand as convenient and memorable boundaries to the career of ancient philosophy.

The thousand years of that career divide into three periods of unequal duration. First, there were the salad years, from 585 until about 400 BC, when a sequence of green and genial individuals established the scope and determined the problems of philosophy, and began to develop its conceptual equipment and to fix its structure. Then came the period of the Schools – the period of Plato and Aristotle, of the Epicureans and the Stoics, and of the Sceptics – in which elaborate systems of thought were worked out and subjected to strenuous criticism. This second period ended in about 100 BC. The long third period was marked in the main by scholarship and syncretism: the later thinkers studied their predecessors' writings with assiduity; they produced commentaries and interpretations; and they attempted to extract a coherent and unified system of thought which would include all that was best in the earlier doctrines of the Schools.

9

The present book is concerned with the first of the three periods, with early Greek philosophy. This period is commonly called the 'Presocratic' phase of Greek thought. The epithet is inaccurate, for Socrates was born in 470 BC and died in 399, so that many of the 'Presocratic' philosophers were in fact contemporaries of Socrates. But the label is well entrenched and it would be idle to attempt to evict it.

The Presocratic period itself divides into three parts. There was first a century of bold and creative thought. Then the early adventures were subjected to stringent logical criticism: the dawn they had heralded seemed a false dawn, their discoveries chimerical, their hopes illusory. Finally, there were years of retrenchment and consolidation, in which thinkers of very different persuasions attempted each in his own way to reconcile the hopes of the first thinkers with the rigorous criticisms of their successors.

These schematisms impose a fixity on what was in reality fluid and irregular. The Greeks themselves, when they came to write the history of their own thought, were even more schematic. They liked to talk about 'Schools' and about 'Successions', in which each thinker had a master and a pupil, and each philosophy a set place. These constructions, artificial though they are, supply an intellectual framework without which the history of thought cannot readily be comprehended. Moreover, it is at least approximately true that the Presocratics form a unitary group, that they differ in fundamental ways both from their unphilosophical predecessors and from their great successors, and that within the era which their fortunes span three main periods can be distinguished.

Such naked abstractions require a covering of decent historical robes. When we think of Greece we habitually think first of Athens, supposing that the city of Pericles and the Parthenon, of Socrates and Aristophanes, was the centre and focus of the Greek world, artistically, intellectually and politically. In fact none of the earliest philosophers was Athenian. Philosophy bloomed first on the eastern shores of the Aegean, in small independent city-states which had at that time no political ties with Athens. The Greek states of Ionia, on the south-west

coastal strip of Asia Minor (modern Turkey), were torn by
internal strife and threatened by external enemies. Yet for a
century and a half, from about 650 to 500 BC, they enjoyed a
remarkable efflorescence: they burgeoned economically, they
bloomed politically, in art and in literature they flourished,
producing majestic architecture, noble sculpture, exquisite
poems, elegant vase-paintings.

It was at Miletus in the south of Ionia that Greek philosophy
was born. The Milesians were an uncommonly vigorous lot.
Internally, their politics were turbulent – they knew faction,
strife and bloody revolution. Externally, they were neigh-
boured by two powerful empires, first the Lydians, with whom
they maintained an uneasy symbiosis, and after 546 the Persians, by whom they were eventually destroyed in 494. Despite
these unpropitious circumstances, the Milesians were commer-
cially indefatigable. They traded not only with the eastern
empires but also with Egypt, establishing a trading emporium
at Naucratis on the Nile delta. In addition they sent numerous
colonies to settle in Thrace, by the Bosphorus and along the
coast of the Black Sea; and they also had connections with
Sybaris in south Italy. It was in this gifted township that Thales,
Anaximander and Anaximenes, the first three philosophers,
lived and worked.

How soon and how widely their own work became known
we cannot say. But the intellectual activity which they pion-
eered soon spread. Heraclitus came from the city of Ephesus,
a prosperous state some miles to the north of Miletus. Xenophanes came from nearby Colophon. Pythagoras was born
on the island of Samos, which lies close to the mainland half-
way between Ephesus and Colophon. Later, Anaxagoras came
from Clazomenae, Melissus from Samos and Democritus from
Abdera in the north-east.

The west too made its contribution. Pythagoras emigrated
from Samos to the Greek colony of Croton in south Italy.
Alcmaeon was a native of Croton. Parmenides and Zeno were
born in Elea on the west coast of Italy. Empedocles came from
Acragas in Sicily.

This geographical diversity did not mean that the Presocratics were independent workers, writing in ignorance of one another's thoughts. Although communications were slow and frequently dangerous, many of the early philosophers were itinerant. Pythagoras, as I said, migrated from the east to the west. Xenophanes and Empedocles both tell us that they travelled. Parmenides and Zeno are supposed by Plato to have visited Athens. Anaxagoras spent much of his life in Athens before he retired in exile to Lampsacus in the Troad. It is true that there is little direct evidence of fruitful intellectual converse among the various philosophers, and the influences and interactions which scholars commonly assume are speculative. But the speculations are plausible. For much in the history of Presocratic thought is most intelligible on the hypothesis of mutual contact.

One particular case is worth mentioning. Melissus came from Samos in the eastern Aegean, Parmenides from Elea in west Italy. Melissus was working at most a decade or so after Parmenides. Yet it is quite certain that Melissus knew Parmenides' work intimately: either he had met Parmenides, or he had discovered a copy of his work, or he had learned of it from some third party. There was no Eleatic 'School': Parmenides, Zeno and Melissus did not meet regularly, discuss their thoughts together, give lectures, have students, hold seminars. Nonetheless, they were not working and thinking in isolation.

Thus far I have spoken of the Presocratics as 'philosophers' or 'thinkers'. It is time to be a little more precise. 'Philosophy' is a Greek word, the etymological meaning of which is 'love of wisdom'. The Greeks themselves tended to use the term in a broad sense, to cover most of what we now think of as the sciences and the liberal arts. The School philosophers of the second period regularly divided their subject into three parts: logic, ethics and physics. Logic included the study of language and meaning as well as the study of thought and argument. Ethics included moral and political theorizing, but it also embraced topics which would now fall under the head of sociology and ethnography. Physics was defined very generously:

it was the study of nature and of all the phenomena of the natural world.

In terms of this later threefold distinction, the Presocratics were regarded primarily as 'physicists'. There are ethical and logical parts to some of their works, but their chief interest was physics: Aristotle calls them the *phusikoi* and their activity *phusiologia*; they were 'students of nature' and their subject was the 'study of nature'. To the modern reader that may sound more like science than philosophy – and indeed our modern subject of physics derives its content no less than its name from the Greek *phusikoi*. But the modern distinction between empirical science and speculative philosophy is not readily applied to the earliest phase of western thought, when academic specializations and intellectual boundaries had not been thought of.

Thales, then, was the first *phusikos*, the first 'student of nature' or 'natural philosopher'. The written works of the early thinkers frequently bore the title *On Nature* (*Peri Phuseos*); and although the titles were bestowed not by the authors but by later scholars, they were largely appropriate. For the general enterprise of the early philosophers was to tell the whole truth 'about nature': to describe, to organize, and to explain the universe and all its contents. The enterprise involved, at one end of the scale, detailed accounts of numerous natural phenomena – of eclipses and the motions of the heavenly bodies, of thunder and rain and hail and wind and in general of 'meteorological' events, of minerals and of plants, of animals – their procreation and growth and nourishment and death – and, eventually, of man – of the biological, psychological, social, political, cultural and intellectual aspects of human life. All this we might justly count as 'science'; and we should regard the Presocratics as the first investigators of matters which became the special objects of astronomy, physics, chemistry, zoology, botany, psychology and so on. At the other end of the scale, the Presocratic enterprise involved much larger and more obviously 'philosophical' questions: did the universe have a beginning? And if so, how did it begin? What are its basic constituents? Why does it move and develop as it does?

What, in the most general terms, is the nature and the unity of the universe? And what can we hope to learn about it?

Not all the Presocratics asked all these questions, and not all of them wrote in such comprehensive terms 'about nature'. But they all wrote within that general framework, and they all deserve the honorific title of *phusikos*. Whether we should now call them philosophers or scientists or both is a matter of no importance.

The sequence of *phusikoi* who are the heroes of this book were not the only intellectual adventurers of early Greece – indeed, they were not the only thinkers to engage in *phusiologia*. The didactic poets of the age sometimes indulged in philosophical reflection. The playwrights of the fifth century indicate a widespread interest in philosophical matters: the tragedian Euripides shows a keen awareness of Presocratic speculation, and the comic poet Aristophanes will parody philosophical and scientific notions. The great historians, Herodotus and Thucydides, are touched by philosophical thought. Several of the early medical writings associated with the name of Hippocrates are thoroughly Presocratic in their concerns. In the second half of the fifth century the so-called 'Sophists' – men such as Protagoras, Gorgias, Hippias – who professed to teach rhetoric, virtue and practical success, were closely allied to the philosophical tradition. Thus a history of Presocratic *phusiologia* is not a history of early Greek thought in its entirety. Nonetheless, as Aristotle saw, the Presocratics are the most important and influential representatives of the early period: it was they who began philosophy, they who prepared the way for Plato and for the great philosophical schools of the following generations.

Presocratic philosophy did not spring into existence *ex nihilo*. The commercial and political relations between Ionia and the Middle East brought cultural connections along with them. Not all observers approved of these ties.

The Colophonians, according to Phylarchus, originally practised a tough mode of life, but when they contracted ties of friendship and alliance with the Lydians they turned to luxury, growing their hair long and adorning it with gold ornaments. Xenophanes says the same:

> Learning useless soft habits from the Lydians
> when they were free from hateful despotism
> they went to the town square in purple robes,
> not less than a thousand of them in all,
> haughty, with elegant hair-styles,
> drenched in the perfume of synthetic ointments.
>
> (Athenaeus, *Deipnosophists* 526A)

But effeminacy was not the only Lydian gift. There are clear lines of contact between Ionian pottery and sculpture on the one hand and Lydian art on the other. The Lydian language had some influence on Ionian poetry. And scholars both modern and ancient have supposed that there were also connections between the earliest Greek thought and the intellectual concerns of the eastern empires.

The advanced astronomy of the Babylonians, for example, must surely have become known on the shores of Asia Minor and have stimulated the Ionians to study astronomy for themselves. Thales' knowledge of the eclipse of the sun of 585 BC must have been derived from Babylonian learning. Other, more speculative, parts of Presocratic thought have parallels, of a sort, in eastern texts. In addition, there was the Egyptian connection. The Greeks themselves later supposed that their own philosophy owed much to the land of the Pharaohs. But although some eastern fertilization can scarcely be denied, the proven parallels are surprisingly few and surprisingly imprecise. What is more, many of the most characteristic and significant features of early Greek thought have no known antecedents in eastern cultures.

The Greek philosophers also had Greek predecessors. Earlier poets had written about the nature and the origins of the universe, telling stories of how Zeus married Earth and produced the world of nature, and offering mythical histories of the human race. There are similarities between certain aspects of these early tales and certain parts of the early philosophers' writings. But Aristotle made a sharp distinction between what he called the 'mythologists' and the philosophers; and it is true that the differences are far more marked and far more significant than the similarities.

Just as the early thinkers sought for the origins of the universe, so later scholars have sought for the origins of these first thoughts about the universe. It would be silly to claim that the Presocratics began something entirely novel and totally unprecedented in the history of human intellectual endeavour. But it remains true that the best researches of scholarship have produced remarkably little by way of true antecedents. It is reasonable to conclude that Miletus in the early sixth century BC saw the birth of science and philosophy. That conclusion does not ascribe any supernatural talent to Thales and his associates. It merely supposes that they were men of genius.

II First Philosophy

In what did their genius consist? What are the characteristics that define the new discipline? Three things in particular mark off the *phusikoi* from their predecessors.

First, and most simply, the Presocratics invented the very idea of science and philosophy. They hit upon that special way of looking at the world which is the scientific or rational way. They saw the world as something ordered and intelligible, its history following an explicable course and its different parts arranged in some comprehensible system. The world was not a random collection of bits, its history was not an arbitrary series of events.

Still less was it a series of events determined by the will – or the caprice – of the gods. The Presocratics were not, so far as we can tell, atheists: they allowed the gods into their brave new world, and some of them attempted to produce an improved, rationalized, theology in place of the anthropomorphic divinities of the Olympian pantheon. But they removed some of the traditional functions from the gods. Thunder was explained scientifically, in naturalistic terms – it was no longer a noise made by a minatory Zeus. Iris was the goddess of the rainbow, but Xenophanes insisted that Iris or the rainbow was in reality nothing but a multicoloured cloud. Most importantly, the Presocratic gods – like the gods of Aristotle and even of that arch theist Plato – do not interfere with the natural world.

The world is orderly without being divinely run. Its order is intrinsic: the internal principles of nature are sufficient to explain its structure and its history. For the happenings that constitute the world's history are not mere brute events, to be recorded and admired. They are structured events which fit together and interconnect. And the patterns of their interconnections provide the truly explanatory account of the world.

In the first book of his *Metaphysics* Aristotle wrote a short account of the early history of Greek philosophy. He discussed the subject exclusively in terms of explanations or causes. He himself held that there were four different types of explanation (or 'four causes') and he thought that the four had been slowly discovered, one by one, by his predecessors. The history of philosophy was thus the history of the conceptual understanding of explanatory schemes. Aristotle's account of this history has been criticized for bias and partiality. But in essence Aristotle is right; at any rate, it is in the development of the notion of explanation that we may see one of the primary features of Presocratic philosophy.

Presocratic explanations are marked by several characteristics. They are, as I have said, *internal*: they explain the universe from within, in terms of its own constituent features, and they do not appeal to arbitrary intervention from without. They are *systematic*: they explain the whole sum of natural events in the same terms and by the same methods. Thus the general principles in terms of which they seek to account for the origins of the world are also applied to the explanations of earthquakes or hailstorms or eclipses or diseases or monstrous births. Finally, Presocratic explanations are *economical*: they use few terms, invoke few operations, assume few 'unknowns'. Anaximenes, for example, thought to explain everything in terms of a single material element (air) and a pair of co-ordinated operations (rarefaction and condensation). The natural world exhibits an extraordinary variety of phenomena and events. The variety must be reduced to order, and the order made simple – for that is the way to intelligibility. The Presocratics attempted the most extreme form of simplicity. If their attempts sometimes look comic when they are compared with the elaborate structures of modern science, nonetheless the same desire informs both the ancient and the modern endeavours – the desire to explain as much as possible in terms of as little as possible.

Science today has its own jargon and its own set of specialized concepts – mass, force, atom, element, tissue, nerve, parallax, ecliptic and so on. The terminology and the conceptual equipment were not god-given: they had to be invented. The Presocratics were among the first inventors. Plainly, the very attempt to provide scientific explanations presupposes certain concepts; equally plainly, the prosecution of the attempt will bring other concepts to birth. The process will not – or not often – be a self-conscious one. The scientists will not often say to themselves: 'Here is a curious phenomenon; we must elaborate new concepts to understand it and devise new names to express it.' But concept formation, and the consequent development of a technical vocabulary, is a constant corollary of scientific struggle.

Let me illustrate the point briefly by way of four central examples.

First, there is the concept of the universe or the world itself. The Greek word is *kosmos*, whence our 'cosmos' and 'cosmology'. The word was certainly used by Heraclitus, and it may perhaps have been used by the first Milesian philosophers.

It is remarkable enough that these thinkers should have felt the need for a word to designate the universe – everything, the whole world. Normal conversation and normal business do not require us to talk about everything, or to form the concept of a totality or universe of all things. Far more noteworthy, however, is the choice of the word *kosmos* to designate the universe. The noun *kosmos* derives from a verb which means 'to order', 'to arrange', 'to marshal' – it is used by Homer of the Greek generals marshalling their troops for battle. Thus a *kosmos* is an orderly arrangement. Moreover, it is a beautiful arrangement: the word *kosmos* in ordinary Greek meant not only an ordering but also an adornment (hence the English word 'cosmetic'), something which beautifies and is pleasant to contemplate.

The cosmos is the universe, the totality of things. But it is also the *ordered* universe, and it is the *elegant* universe. The concept of the cosmos has an aesthetic aspect. (That, indeed, it is sometimes said, is what makes it characteristically Greek.) But also, and from our point of view more importantly, it has an essentially scientific aspect: the cosmos is, necessarily, ordered – and hence it must be in principle explicable.

The second term is *phusis* or 'nature'. The Presocratics, as I have said, were later regarded as *phusikoi*, and their works were generally given the title *Peri Phuseos*. They themselves used the term *phusis*: it is present in several of the fragments of Heraclitus, and it is plausible to suppose that it was also used by the Milesians.

The word derives from a verb meaning 'to grow'. The importance of the concept of nature lies partly in the fact that it introduces a clear distinction between the natural and the artificial world, between things which have 'grown' and things which have been made. Tables and carts and ploughs (and perhaps societies and laws and justice) are artefacts: they have been made by designers (human designers in these cases) and they are not natural. They have no nature, for they do not grow. Trees and plants and snakes (and perhaps also rain and clouds and mountains), on the other hand, have not been made: they are not artefacts but natural objects – they grew, they have a nature.

But the distinction between the natural and the artificial (in Greek, between *phusis* and *techne*) does not exhaust the significance of the notion of nature. In one sense the word 'nature' designates the sum of natural objects and natural events; in this sense to discourse 'On Nature' is to talk about the whole of the natural world – *phusis* and *kosmos* come to much the same thing. But in another, and more important, sense the word serves to denote something within each natural object: in the first fragment of Heraclitus, the term *phusis* designates not the cosmos as a whole but rather a principle within each natural part of the cosmos. When the Presocratics inquired into 'nature', they were inquiring into 'the nature *of things*'.

Any natural object – anything that grows and is not made – has, it was assumed, a nature of its own. Its nature is an intrinsic feature of it, and it is an essential feature – not an accidental or chance fact about it. Moreover, it is an explanatory feature: the nature of an object explains why it behaves in the ways it does, why it has the various accidental properties it does.

All scientists are interested, in this sense, in the *phusis* of things. A chemist, investigating some stuff – say, gold – is concerned to find out the underlying or basic properties of gold, in terms of which its other properties can be explained. Perhaps the basic properties of gold are those associated with its atomic weight. These properties will then explain why gold is, say, malleable and ductile, why it is soft and yellow, why it dissolves in sulphuric acid, and so on. The chemist is looking for the 'fundamental properties' of gold, for its 'essence' – for its 'nature' or *phusis*. This indispensable scientific concept was first established by the Presocratics.

Nature is a principle and origin of growth. The notions of principle and origin introduce us to a third Presocratic term: *arche*. The word, we are told, was first used by Anaximander. It is a difficult term to translate. Its cognate verb can mean either 'to begin', 'to commence', or else 'to rule', 'to govern'. An *arche* is thus a beginning or origin; and it is also a rule or a ruling principle. (*Arche* is in fact the normal Greek word for an office or magistracy.) Writers on ancient philosophy often use the word 'principle' or the phrase 'first principle' to render *arche*, and I shall follow the practice. The term is apt, providing that the reader keeps in mind the Latin etymology of the English word: a principle is a *principium* or a beginning.

The inquiry into the natures of things leads easily to a search for principles. Nature is growth: what, then, does growth start from? What are the principles of growth, the origins of natural phenomena? The same questions were readily asked of the

cosmos as a whole: how did it begin? What are its first principles? What are the fundamental elements from which it is
made and the fundamental operations which determine its
structure and career?

The inquiry into *archai* was in this way closely associated with
cosmology, and also with abstract physics or chemistry. The
'principles' of the universe will include its basic stuff or stuffs.
But evidently everything must be made out of the basic stuff
or stuffs of the universe. Hence inquiring into the principles
of the cosmos means inquiring into the fundamental constituents of all natural objects. The Presocratic inquiries were inevitably crude. Thales, if we are to believe the later testimony,
held that everything is made of water. The *arche* of the cosmos
is water (or perhaps liquid), so that everything in the cosmos
is, at bottom, made of water. (Cucumbers are 100 per cent
water, not 99 per cent as modern culinary pundits say.) The
different stuffs we see and feel are, in Thales' view, merely
modifications of water – much as we now think coal and dia-
monds to be modifications of carbon. Thales' suggestion is
false in fact; but it is not foolish in principle – on the contrary,
it is thoroughly scientific in spirit.

The fourth of my illustrative examples is the concept of
logos. The word *logos* is even harder to translate than *arche*. It
is cognate with the verb *legein*, which normally means 'to say'
or 'to state'. Thus a *logos* is something said or stated. When
Heraclitus begins his book with a reference to 'this *logos*', he
probably means only 'this statement' or 'this account': my *logos*
is simply what I am going to say. But the word also has a richer
meaning than that. To give a *logos* or an account *of* something
is to explain it, to say *why* it is so; so that a *logos* is often a reason.
When Plato says that an intelligent man can give a *logos* of
things, he means not that an intelligent man can *describe* things,
but rather that he can *explain* or *give the reason* for things.
Thence, by an intelligible transference, *logos* comes to be used
of the faculty with which we give reasons, i.e. of our human
reason. In this sense *logos* may be contrasted with perception,
so that Parmenides, for example, can urge his readers to test
his argument not by their senses but by *logos*, by reason. (The

English term 'logic' derives ultimately from this sense of the word *logos*, by way of the later Greek term *logike*.)

It cannot be said that the Presocratics established a single clear sense for the term *logos* or that they invented the concept of reason or of rationality. But their use of the term *logos* constitutes the first step towards the establishment of a notion which is central to science and philosophy.

The term *logos* brings me to the third of the three great achievements of the Presocratics. I mean their emphasis on the use of reason, on rationality and ratiocination, on argument and evidence.

The Presocratics were not dogmatists. That is to say, they did not rest content with mere assertion. Determined to explain as well as describe the world of nature, they were acutely aware that explanations required the giving of reasons. This is evident even in the earliest of the Presocratic thinkers and even when their claims seem most strange and least justified. Thales is supposed to have held that all things possess 'souls' or are alive. He did not merely assert this bizarre doctrine: he argued for it by appealing to the case of the magnet. Here is a piece of stone – what could appear more lifeless? Yet the magnet possesses a power to *move* other things: it attracts iron filings, which move towards it without the intervention of any external pushes or pulls. Now it is a noticeable feature of living things that they are capable of producing motion. (Aristotle later took it as one of the defining characteristics of things with 'souls' or living things that they possess such a motive power.) Hence Thales concluded that the magnet, despite appearances, has a soul.

The argument may not seem very impressive: certainly we do not believe that magnets are alive, nor should we regard the attractive powers of a piece of stone as evidence of life. But my point is not that the Presocratics offered *good* arguments but simply that they offered *arguments*. In the thinkers of the second Presocratic phase this love of argument is more obvious and more pronounced. In them, indeed, argument becomes the sole means to truth, and perception is regarded as fundamentally illusory. The writings of Parmenides, Melissus and Zeno were nothing more than chains of arguments.

The Presocratic achievement here is evident in their language. Greek is ideally suited for rational discourse. It is rich in particles, and it can express nuances and niceties of thought which in Latin or English are normally conveyed by the tone of voice or the manner of delivery. The Greek particles – which are part of the natural language and not devices peculiar to academic writers – make explicit and obvious what other languages normally leave implicit and obscure. Little words like 'so', 'therefore', 'for', which English customarily omits (or includes at the cost of tedious pedantry), are normally expressed in a Greek text. The fragments of Melissus, for example, are peppered with such inferential particles. Presocratic writing wears its rationality on its sleeve.

It is important to see exactly what this rationality consisted in. As I have already indicated, the claim is not that the Presocratics were peculiarly good at arguing or that they regularly produced sound arguments. On the contrary, most of their theories are false, and most of their arguments are unsound. (This is not as harsh a judgement as it may seem, for the same could be said of virtually every scientist and philosopher who has ever lived.) Secondly, the claim is not that the Presocratics *studied* logic or developed a *theory* of inference and argument. Some of them, it is true, did reflect on the powers of the mind and on the nature, scope and limits of human knowledge. But the study of logic was invented by Aristotle, and Aristotle rightly boasted that no one before him had attempted to make explicit and systematic the rules and procedures which govern rational thought.

Nor, thirdly, am I suggesting that the Presocratics were consistently *critical* thinkers. It is sometimes said that the essence of science is criticism, inasmuch as science lives by the constant critical appraisal of theories and arguments. Whether or not that is so, the Presocratics were not avid critics. Although we may talk of the *influence* of one Presocratic on another, no Presocratic (as far as we know) ever indulged in the exposition and criticism of his predecessors' views. Parmenides urged his readers to criticize his views, but his urgings went unanswered. Critical reflection did not come into its own until the fourth century BC.

What, then, is the substance of the claim that the Presocratics were champions of reason and rationality? It is this: they offered reasons for their opinions, they gave arguments for their views. They did not utter *ex cathedra* pronouncements. Perhaps that seems an unremarkable achievement. It is not. On the contrary, it is the most remarkable and the most praiseworthy of the three achievements I have rehearsed. Those who doubt the fact should reflect on the maxim of George Berkeley, the eighteenth-century Irish philosopher: All men have opinions, but few think.

III The Evidence

A few Presocratics wrote nothing, but most put their thoughts to paper. Some wrote in verse and some in prose. Some wrote a single work, others several – Democritus, whose works were arranged and catalogued by a scholar in the first century AD, apparently composed some fifty books. All told, the collected works of the Presocratic thinkers would have made an impressive row on the library shelves.

Of all those works not one has survived intact for us to read. Some of them endured for at least a thousand years, for the scholar Simplicius, who worked in Athens in the sixth century AD, was able to consult texts of Parmenides, Melissus, Zeno, Anaxagoras, Diogenes of Apollonia and others. But Simplicius himself remarks that Parmenides' book was a rarity, and it is not difficult to imagine that by his time many other Presocratic works had actually disappeared. The Presocratics were never bestsellers. Books were easily destroyed.

Our knowledge of the Presocratics, then, unlike our knowledge of Plato or Aristotle, is not gained directly from the books they wrote. Rather, it depends upon indirect information of two different types.

First, there are numerous references to Presocratic thought

in the surviving works of later authors. Some of these references are brief and casual allusions, mere embellishments to a text whose chief aim was not the transmission of historical information about early philosophy. Many of the references are embedded in later philosophical texts – for example, in Aristotle's *Metaphysics* and in his *Physics*. These accounts have a historical purpose and they are written with a philosophical intention; but they are not, properly speaking, 'histories of philosophy'. Finally, there are genuine attempts at the history of philosophy. We can now read such histories in brief handbooks (for example, in the *History of Philosophy* which goes under Galen's name), in the ambitious but uncritical *Lives of the Philosophers* by Diogenes Laertius, in several works of Christian polemic (such as the *Refutation of All Heresies* by Hippolytus), in scholarly writings of late antiquity (most notably in the commentary on Aristotle's *Physics* by Simplicius).

These histories – or 'doxographies', as they are commonly called – have been the subject of subtle scholarly investigation. In themselves they are of uncertain value. They were written centuries after the thought they chronicle, and they were written by men with different interests and different outlooks. If Bishop Hippolytus, for example, ascribes a certain view to Heraclitus, we should not believe him before answering two important questions. First, from what source did he draw his information? For the channel which winds from Heraclitus to Hippolytus is long, and we must wonder if the information flowing down it was not sometimes contaminated with falsehood or poisoned by inaccuracy. Secondly, what were Hippolytus' own philosophical predilections, and what were the aims of his own book? For these may have biased him – consciously or unconsciously – in his reporting. The arguments on these issues are intricate. They rarely issue in certainty.

In addition to later references and reports, we still possess some actual fragments of the original works of the Presocratics. The word 'fragment' perhaps suggests a small scrap of paper, torn out of a Presocratic book and surviving by some fluke of time. That suggestion is inappropriate here, where the word 'fragment' is used in a more generous sense: it refers to passages from the Presocratics' own writings – words, phrases, sentences, paragraphs – which have been preserved as *quotations* in the writings of later authors. These 'fragments' constitute our most precious testimony to the views of the Presocratics. Their number and their extent vary greatly from one thinker to another. Sometimes they are short and sparse. In a few cases we possess enough fragments to form a tolerably determinate idea of the original work. The fuller the fragments, the less we need to rely on the doxographical material. But even in the most favourable cases, the doxographies are of importance: they provide indirect evidence where direct evidence is missing, and they give invaluable aid in the interpretation of the fragments themselves.

For it should not be thought that these fragments are readily extracted from their contexts or readily understood and interpreted. There is a sequence of difficulties of which every serious student of early Greek philosophy becomes quickly aware. It is necessary to say a little about these difficulties here – and they have, in any case, an intrinsic interest of their own. Let us consider the general issues through the medium of a particular example. Take the following passage (which will reappear in the chapter on Anaxagoras):

> In the first book of the *Physics* Anaxagoras says that uniform stuffs, infinite in quantity, separate off from a single mixture, all things being present in all and each being characterized by what predominates. He makes this clear in the first book of the *Physics* at the beginning of which he says: Together were all things, infinite both in quantity and in smallness . . .
>
> (Simplicius, *Commentary on the Physics* 155.23–27)

Simplicius was born in Cilicia in the latter part of the fifth century AD. He studied philosophy first at Alexandria and then at Athens, where he became one of the leading figures of the Neoplatonist school. After Justinian's edict he left Athens and went, with some of his associates, to the royal court in Persia, but the eastern life proved unattractive and he returned to Athens about 533. There he continued his

case I do not think that scepticism is justified; but the possibility of such error demands contemplation.

Suppose, now, that we have a genuine quotation of Anaxagoras before us: the next questions concern its contents – and first, its contents in the most literal sense of the term. What words did Anaxagoras use? For there is no reason to assume that *Simplicius'* words must accurately represent *Anaxagoras'* words. On the contrary, there is every reason to think that they do not. Simplicius may be quoting from memory – and misremembering; or he may be quoting from a text he has in front of his eyes – and miscopying. Errors of both sorts are easy and common. More importantly, even if Simplicius is accurately transcribing the text he himself has in front of him, there is no guarantee that his text is faithful to the original. During the millennium separating Simplicius from the Presocratics, the works of Anaxagoras must have been copied many times over. Just as we read copies of copies of Simplicius' autograph, so Simplicius will have read copies of copies of Anaxagoras' autograph. The probability that Simplicius read a pure text of Anaxagoras is zero.

What can a modern scholar do about this? Some Presocratic passages are quoted more than once. The first phrase of the quotation in our illustrative text became the 'To be, or not to be' of Presocratic thought: it is cited some sixty times by some twenty authors. In such cases there are always variant versions of the text, but there is often reason to prefer one version to another. For example, an author who quotes a brief passage was probably quoting from memory, and he is therefore more likely to have made an error than an author who quotes a long portion of the original and was presumably transcribing it from his copy of the text. Or again, we may be able to construct a plausible story to account for the different readings in the different citations, and hence to establish the genuine Presocratic text. In our illustrative case we can, by these means, be reasonably confident that we know what words Anaxagoras himself wrote.

But most surviving fragments are quoted only once. Here there is less chance of getting back to the original text. Various philosophical tests and techniques can be applied. Sometimes, for example, a linguistic anachronism will betray itself, and we may suspect that an explanatory note or gloss has insinuated itself into the text. Sometimes we may conjecture that the old text was retailored to fit its later context – and plausible guesses may sometimes hit upon the original readings. The case is rarely hopeless, but it always requires expert diagnosis and sometimes demands subtle therapy. Most often we must be content with something less than certainty.

Once we have before us the words of Anaxagoras, or as close an approximation to them as we can reach, we must next try to understand them. This task has two distinct but closely connected aspects. First, and most obviously, there is the elementary matter of grasping the sense of the words and phrases which the text contains. Sometimes this is surprisingly hard. Anaxagoras is, it is true, on the whole an intelligible author; but the same cannot be said for all the Presocratics – and some of them (Heraclitus and Empedocles, for example) are often highly obscure. Their obscurity for us is due in part to the ravages of time: had more Greek of the early period survived, we should possess more comparative material and so experience less difficulty in understanding the Presocratics. But in part the obscurity is intrinsic to the texts themselves: the Presocratics were writing in a new idiom on a new subject – it is only to be expected that they should sometimes have been less than pellucid.

Secondly, even if we can grasp what, at a literal level, the words of a fragment mean, we may still be far from understanding the passage. Sentences taken out of context are often hard to interpret, and isolated phrases, which are sometimes all we have, may be virtually senseless. We need, in other words, to ask what sense the fragment had in its original context, what contribution it made to the general economy of the philosopher's work, how it fitted into his argument or into the exposition of his views.

This is the point at which serious philosophical interpretation begins. It is a testing and an elusive business. There are some external aids. In particular, there is the context in which the fragment is cited. Sometimes, it is true, this context is of little use: for the fragments cited by John Stobaeus, for example, all we have to go on are the section headings under which he arranged them in his anthology. Sometimes the context may be actually misleading. Clement of Alexandria, for example, cites the Presocratic pagans for his own Christian ends, and he does not purport to preserve the original settings of the passages he adduces (why should he?). Nonetheless, the context is sometimes helpful – especially so, I think, in the case of Simplicius, who was an able scholar of great learning. (A good example of this is the long passage from the commentary on Aristotle's *Physics* which contains all the surviving fragments of Zeno.) At the very least, the context of citation will give us an idea of how a fragment *could* have functioned in its original home.

Again, comparison of one fragment with another, and comparison of the fragments with the doxographical tradition, will yield further evidence. The collocation of fragments is often a risky matter: it is too easy to imagine that we have enough bits and pieces to reconstruct the original picture when in fact we may well possess only enough to give one small part of the original. (This is certainly true of Anaxagoras, where almost all the surviving fragments appear to come from the early part of his book.) The dangers need to be acknowledged. They can sometimes be overcome.

In sum, the task of interpretation is full of difficulty. (That is one reason why it is full of excitement.) Sometimes we may fairly claim success. Frequently we should be content with a Scottish verdict: *non liquet*, 'It is not clear'. But these questions take us beyond the scope of the present book, whose function is not to offer an exegesis of Presocratic thought but to exhibit the material on which any exegesis must be based.

IV The Texts

This book contains English translations of all the surviving philosophical fragments of the Presocratic thinkers. In each chapter the fragments have been supplemented by extracts from the doxographical material. The surviving doxography is vast (and very repetitive). A comprehensive translation would fill several tedious and confusing volumes. The selection of texts here does not pretend to convey *all* we can glean from the doxography, but it is intended to include all the most important items and to give a fair sample of the unimportant items.

The main chapters of the book thus present a partial view of their subjects relative to the evidence we possess. They also, and inevitably, present a partial view relative to the sum total of the original evidence; for it is not to be supposed that the surviving information represents a balanced account of the original works. Some parts of the Presocratic writings happen to have been well reported; others were only sketchily described; still others were entirely forgotten. We can do little to redress things.

The information which we do possess is contained in a large number of different and disparate texts, and it cannot readily be set out in a manner which reveals the general drift and tenor of the philosophies it describes. From the material exhibited in the chapter on Heraclitus, for example, it is no easy business to form a general impression of the overall shape and intention of his thought. The next chapter is designed to mitigate this difficulty. It contains a sequence of brief synopses of the main views of each thinker, insofar as they can be known. The synopses are not substitutes for the texts in the main chapters, nor do they claim to convey definitive interpretations or incontestable truths. Rather, they are intended to provide a moderately intelligible framework within which the texts may first be read. I hope that the reader will forget them as soon as he has found his own way through the texts. They are fixed ropes on a difficult rock face, placed there for the inexperienced climber. Use them once or twice and then climb free.

The fragments are presented in the contexts in which they have been preserved. This mode of presentation, which is not customary, has certain disadvantages: it makes for occasional repetition, and it means that the texts appear in a different order from that of the standard modern editions. But those disadvantages are, I think, decisively outweighed by the advantages. A presentation of the texts shorn of their contexts gives a wholly misleading impression of the nature of our evidence for Presocratic philosophy. Translation in context avoids that erroneous impression, and at the same time it enables the English reader to see how difficult it often is, especially in the case of prose fragments, to distinguish genuine citations from paraphrases or mere allusions. In addition, as I have already remarked, the context of a quotation often helps us to understand the fragments better – or at least to see how the ancient authors understood them. And in any case, the contexts are, or so I believe, interesting in their own right.

Every translator, and in particular every translator of philosophical texts, has two desires. He wants to be faithful to his original: he wants to convey all and only what it conveys, and he wants to reproduce something of the form, as well as the content, of the original. But he also wants to produce readable and tolerably elegant sentences of his own language. These two desires usually conflict; for different languages have different idioms and different modes of expression. Fidelity, if pressed to the limit, will result in barbarous, or even unintelligible, English. Elegance will disguise the sense and the argumentative flow of the original. Moreover, the first desire is essentially unsatisfiable. It is a commonplace that 'something is lost in translation' – a commonplace which applies to prose no less than to poetry. It is equally true that any translation will add something to the original, if only by virtue of the different resonances and overtones of synonymous expressions in different languages.

In the face of these difficulties a translator must adopt some working principle. On the whole I have chosen to give more weight to the first desire than to the second. I have put fidelity above elegance, being more concerned to transmit the *sense* of the Greek texts than to provide an aesthetic feast for the English reader.

My translations are in consequence sometimes obscure or ambiguous. But I should stress that these infelicities are not invariably faults in the translation. Presocratic Greek is sometimes contorted, and it is often obscure or ambiguous. It is no duty of a translator to polish his authors' work. On the contrary, fidelity demands that the translation be as uncouth as the original.

The translated texts are linked together by brief bridge passages, and each chapter is introduced by a short paragraph or two. But I have tried to keep such editorial matter to a minimum. There are numerous commentaries and interpretations in print: this book is not an addition to that large literature.

The source of each translated passage is given. The Appendix supplies some elementary information about the dates and the chief interests of the authors to whom we owe our surviving knowledge of the Presocratic texts.

The fragments are also equipped with 'Diels-Kranz' references (these are the ciphers which appear in square brackets after the texts). These references key the passages to the standard collection of the Greek texts, edited by Hermann Diels and Walther Kranz, *Die Fragmente der Vorsokratiker* (Berlin, 1952 [10th edition]). I add these references because they are invariably used by scholars who write about early Greek philosophy: anyone who wants to follow up one of the fragments in the modern literature will find his task simplified if he notes the the pertinent Diels-Kranz number.

Readers of this book will, I suspect, be frequently perplexed and sometimes annoyed. It is as though one is presented with a jigsaw puzzle (or rather, with a set of jigsaw puzzles) in which many of the pieces are missing and most of the surviving pieces are faded or torn. Or, to take a closer analogy, it is as though one were looking at a museum case containing broken and chipped fragments of once elegant pottery. Many of the pieces are small, some of them do not seem to fit at all, and it is difficult to envisage the shape and form of the original pot.

But the vexation which this may produce will, I hope, be accompanied and outweighed by other, more pleasing, emotions. Fragments of beautiful pottery may, after all, be themselves objects of beauty; and certainly many of the Presocratic texts are fascinating and stimulating pieces of thought. Moreover, fragments are challenging in a way that wholes are not: they appeal to the intellectual imagination, and they excite the reader to construct for himself, in his own mind, some picture of the whole from which they came.

For my part, I find the Presocratic fragments objects of inexhaustible and intriguing delight. I hope that the reader of this book may come to find a similar pleasure in contemplating the battered remains of the first heroes of western science and philosophy.

SYNOPSIS

I

Greek philosophy began with the three men from Miletus.
THALES was a practical statesman, and perhaps also a
geometer. What he did in philosophy is uncertain: he is said
to have argued that magnets 'have souls' (that they are alive),
and that everything is full of gods. He suggested that the earth
floated on a vast water-bed. Most famously, he conjectured
that everything was made from water – or even that everything is made of water, that water is the 'material principle' or
arche of everything. Whether or not he inquired further 'into
nature' we do not know.

ANAXIMANDER was certainly a full-blooded *phusikos*, and he
certainly spoke of the principle or *arche* of all natural things.
But he did not identify this basic principle with any familiar
sort of stuff: the *arche* was described simply as 'the infinite' –
infinite in extent and also indefinite in its characteristics. From
this 'infinite' the familiar stuffs of the world – earth, air, water,
and so on – were generated by a process in which the twin
notions of heat and cold played some part. The generated
stuffs encroach on one another and have in the course of time
to pay compensation for their 'injustice'. (We may think of the
alternating encroachments of summer and winter, of the hot
and dry and the cold and wet.) Thus the world is law-governed.
Anaximander also gave a detailed account of natural phenomena. The two most remarkable features of his account lie in
biology (where he speculated on the origins of mankind)
and in astronomy (where he developed an ingenious account

of the celestial system and offered the suggestion that the earth remains unsupported in mid-universe because it is equidistant from every part of the outer heaven).

ANAXIMENES is a pallid reflection of Anaximander. He too provided a detailed account of nature, in which he ventured to correct Anaximander on certain points; and he also proposed a cosmogony. His *arche* was infinite, like Anaximander's, but it was not indeterminate: rather, it was infinite air. And Anaximenes maintained that a pair of operations – rarefaction and condensation – was sufficient to generate all the familiar things of the world from the original and underlying air.

A different tradition was initiated by PYTHAGORAS. He had indeed a reputation for vast learning, but he seems not to have concerned himself particularly with nature. His interest was the soul: he held that the soul was immortal, and that it undergoes a sequence of incarnations in various types of creatures (this was later known as the theory of 'metempsychosis'). Moreover, this process – and the whole history of the world – is endless and unchanging, the same things repeating themselves in cycles of eternal recurrence. The theory of metempsychosis suggested that all creatures were fundamentally the same in kind, inasmuch as they are hosts to the same souls: Pythagoras probably made this the ground for certain dietary recommendations.

Pythagoras was also a political figure of some importance, and he attracted a band of disciples who followed a 'Pythagorean way of life' and who formed a sort of secret society. What else he did we do not know. Scholars are now generally sceptical of the ancient tradition which associates him with various mathematical and musical discoveries.

ALCMAEON had Pythagorean connections. He held that the soul was immortal, and he advanced a new argument for this belief. He was a doctor with an interest in nature, and especially in human nature – he speculated, for example, on the structure and functioning of the sense-organs. He seems to have held that all things – or at least all things in human life – are to be explained in terms of pairs of opposites: hot and cold, light and dark, wet and dry, etc.

37

The poet XENOPHANES knew something about Pythagoras and his other Presocratic predecessors. He himself engaged in inquiries into nature, even if he did not speculate 'On Nature' in the thorough-going Milesian way. He may possibly have held that the material *arche* of things is earth. But his most original ideas concern other matters. Reflecting on the pretensions of the new science of the *phusikoi*, he was led to ponder the possible limits on human knowledge. Later tradition held him to have been a sceptic, and one fragment does appear to entertain a highly sceptical position; but other texts suggest that he was a gradualist: knowledge is doubtless difficult to come by, but it is not beyond all endeavour.

Xenophanes' second claim to originality lies in the field of natural theology. He criticized the immoral gods of Homer and the poets; more generally, he regarded customary religious beliefs as groundless and foolish. In the place of this folly he offered a rational theology. The later tradition ascribes to him a highly articulated system: the tradition may exaggerate, but the fragments show that Xenophanes believed in a single god, who was moral and motionless, all-knowing and all-powerful. Nor was the god anthropomorphic: rather, he was an abstract and impersonal force; not a god from the Olympian pantheon, but a god accommodated to the new world of the Ionian philosophers.

The major figure in the first phase of Presocratic philosophy is HERACLITUS. He is in some respects a baffling thinker, whose writings won him an early reputation for obscurity. Not all his work was newfangled or riddling. He stood in the Ionian tradition, making fire the *arche* of the universe, and offering an account of nature and the natural world. The account included a novel astronomy, and it made much use of 'exhalations'; but it followed the Milesian model – and, like Anaximander, Heraclitus stressed that the universe of nature was law-governed. He also had what might be called a Pythagorean side: the fragments betray an interest in the soul and in human psychology, and some of them hint at an existence for the soul after death. He advanced some moral and political notions which are perhaps connected with this. Again, Heraclitus, like

Xenophanes, criticized received religious practices and offered the world a new and more scientific god, now identified with the cosmic fire. And, again like Xenophanes, Heraclitus reflected on the possibility of knowledge: he thought that knowledge about the nature of things was not easy to come by, that most of his contemporaries were ignorant and stupid, that most of his predecessors had been arrogant and misguided. But he believed that he himself had attained to truth, and he supposed that the book of nature could be read by men provided that they made proper use of their senses and their understanding.

The novelty of Heraclitus lies in what we may call his metaphysical views. Here three features are worth emphasizing. First of all, he rejected cosmogony: the Milesians had told stories about the origins of the world; Heraclitus held that the world had always existed, and that there was no cosmogonical story to tell. Secondly (his most celebrated notion), he held that 'everything flows': the world and its furniture are in a state of perpetual flux. What is more, things depend on this flux for their continuity and identity; for if the river ceases to flow it ceases to be a river. Finally – and most strangely – Heraclitus believed in the unity of opposites. The path up is the same as the path down, and in general, existing things are characterized by pairs of contrary properties, whose bellicose coexistence is essential to their continued being.

The fundamental truth about nature is this: the world is an eternal and ever-changing modification of fire, its various contents each unified and held together by a dynamic tension of contrarieties. This truth is the account in accordance with which everything happens, and it underlies and explains the whole of nature.

II

The early philosophers had taken the first tottering steps down the road to science. The sceptical suggestions of Xenophanes perhaps cast a small shadow over their inquiries, but the sun of Heraclitus soon burned it away. In the second phase of philosophy, a thicker and darker cloud loomed: it threatened to cut off all light from empirical science, and it must have seemed almost impenetrable. The cloud blew in from Elea – from Parmenides, Melissus, Zeno.

PARMENIDES himself actually wrote at some length on nature. He developed a novel system invoking two principles or *archai*, and he spoke in detail on biology and on astronomy. (He was the first Greek to say that the earth was spherical, and perhaps also the first to identify the evening and the morning star.) But the discourse on nature occupied the second half of his great poem, which described the Way of Opinion and which was self-confessedly false and 'deceitful'. The first part of the poem was a guide to the Way of Truth, and that Way led through strange and arid territory.

Parmenides began by considering the possible subjects of inquiry: you can inquire into what exists, or you can inquire into what does not exist. But in fact the latter is not a genuine possibility – for you cannot think of, and hence cannot inquire into, the non-existent. So every subject of inquiry must exist. But everything that exists must, as Parmenides proceeds to argue, possess a certain set of properties: it must be ungenerated and indestructible (otherwise it would, at some time, not exist – but that is impossible); it must be continuous – without spatial or temporal gaps; it must be entirely changeless – it cannot move or alter or grow or diminish; and it must be bounded or finite, like a sphere. Reason – the logical power of ineluctable deduction – shows that reality, what exists, *must* be so: if sense-perception suggests a world of a different sort, then so much the worse for sense-perception.

MELISSUS rewrote the Parmenidean system in plain prose. But he was not without originality. First, he produced some new arguments for Parmenides' old positions – most notably, he argued that the existence of a vacuum was not logically possible, that the world was therefore full or a *plenum*, and that motion through a *plenum* was manifestly impossible. Secondly, he differed on two important points from his master. For whereas Parmenides' world was finite, Melissus held that whatever exists must be *infinitely* extended in all directions.

Moreover, he inferred that there can be at most *one* thing in existence. Melissus also presented an explicit argument to show that sense-perception is illusory, and that the world is utterly different from the way it appears to our senses.

ZENO produced no systematic philosophy. He contrived a series of arguments (forty in all, we are told), each of which concluded that plurality is paradoxical: if more things than one were to exist, then contradictions would follow. Two of the forty arguments survive: in them Zeno argues that if more things than one exist, then they must be both large and small, and that if more things than one exist, then they must be both finitely and infinitely many. Zeno also devised four celebrated arguments proving the impossibility of motion: it is not clear whether these are to be numbered among the forty arguments against plurality.

Zeno's puzzles are both entertaining and serious. His arguments may seem at first sight merely jocular; but they all involve concepts – notably the concept of infinity – which continue to perplex and exercise philosophers. Zeno's own aim in devising his puzzles is uncertain. Plato regarded him as a supporter of Eleatic monism: Melissus had argued that there existed only one thing, Zeno denied that there existed more than one – two sides of the same coin. Others have suspected that Zeno was an intellectual nihilist.

III

The third phase of Presocratic philosophy is best understood as a reaction against the Parmenidean position. If the Eleatics were right, then science was impossible. The post-Eleatics tried in their different ways to do justice to the force of Parmenides' arguments while retaining the right to follow the pathways of science. The period produced three major figures (Empedocles, Anaxagoras, Democritus) and some interesting minor characters.

EMPEDOCLES promised his readers knowledge, and with it some strange powers. He insisted, against the Eleatics, that the senses, if properly used, were routes to knowledge. He agreed with Parmenides that nothing could really come into existence or perish, and he agreed with Melissus that vacuums could not exist. The universe was full of eternal stuff. But nonetheless, Empedocles argued, motion was possible, and hence change too was possible; for the eternal stuffs could move and intermingle with one another, thereby effecting the changes we observe.

The basic stuffs of the universe, according to Empedocles, were four: earth, air, fire, water. Everything in the world is made up from these four 'roots' or elements. In addition there were two opposing powers, love and strife, or attraction and repulsion, whose operations were aided by, or manifested in, the natural powers of the stuffs themselves and governed, without intention or providence, by the forces of chance and necessity. The powers determined the development of the universe, which development was cyclical and eternal. In the battle between love and strife each warrior periodically dominated: under the dominion of love, all the elements came together into a unity, a homogeneous sphere. As strife regained power, the sphere broke up, the elements separated, and (after a complex series of stages) our familiar world came to be articulated. Then the process reversed itself: from the articulated world, through the several stages, back to the homogeneous sphere again. The infinite alternations between sphere and world, world and sphere, mark the eternal and never changing history of the universe.

Much of Empedocles' poem *On Nature* gave detailed description of the articulated world we live in. But a notorious feature was his account of the various monstrosities which, he believed, come into existence in an early stage of cosmic history, before the world attains its present state. The description of the present world was rich – it covered every subject from astronomy to zoology. Long accounts of the structure of the eye and of the mechanism of breathing survive. Empedocles' major originality here lies less in matters of detail than in one general and unifying notion. He believed that all things always give off 'effluences', and that they are all perforated by channels or pores of various shapes and sizes. These effluences and pores are Empedocles' fundamental explanatory concepts: that effluences fit, or fail to fit, pores of a particular type accounts for physical and chemical reactions, for biological and psychological phenomena – for perception, for magnetism, for the sterility of mules.

In addition to his poem on nature, Empedocles wrote a work which was later called *Purifications*. The story of the poem was the story of the Fall: originally the spirits enjoyed a life of bliss; then they erred (the error is unspecified, but it is usually supposed to have been bloodshed); and their punishment is a sequence of mortal incarnations. We are all such fallen spirits, clothed temporarily and punitively in human flesh. Animals and some plants are also fallen spirits. (Empedocles himself, he says, has already been a bush, a bird, and a fish. But he has now reached the highest point in the cycle of incarnations – he is not only a human, but a seer and a god.) For Empedocles, as for Pythagoras, metempsychosis had moral implications: the animals (and certain plants) are our kin; eating them is therefore cannibalism, and must be assiduously avoided. The Fall was tragic, and our life here is painful; but the future shines: if we follow Empedocles' advice we too may hope to become fellow feasters at the table of the gods.

It is much disputed whether *Purifications* is consistent with *On Nature*, and the question is complicated by the fact that many fragments cannot be securely assigned to either poem. The two poems were probably very different in spirit and in content. But they certainly employed the same general ideas. Whether or not they were strictly consistent with one another, it seems clear that the ancient commentators – and probable that Empedocles himself – thought of them as twin parts of a single scientifico-mystical system.

Empedocles is sometimes called a Pythagorean, and his views have Pythagorean connections. Pythagoras' followers soon divided into two groups, the Aphorists and the Scientists. The Aphorists have little claim on our attention: they appear to have believed that wisdom – and by that they meant the wisdom of Pythagoras – could be captured in gnomic utterances, and they had no desire to inquire or to reason. Their aphorisms were for the most part religious or ritualistic in content – they concerned diet, or sacrifice, or burial: most of them are either bizarre or silly. The Scientists fell into different factions; but they were united by a belief in the scientific and philosophical importance of mathematics. They were not themselves technical mathematicians, but they hypothesized that the world was, in some sense, fundamentally composed of numbers: numbers, or rather the principles of numbers, were the principles of all things. Such a view can degenerate into nonsense; it can also represent the insight that science is essentially applied mathematics. In the case of the Pythagoreans sense and nonsense were present in equal measure.

The only Pythagorean of this period who has a face is PHILOLAUS (for HIPPASUS is little more than a name). If the surviving fragments are genuine (and their authenticity has often been doubted), then it seems that Philolaus was attempting to produce a Pythagorean version of natural science, a version which would be invulnerable to the Eleatic objections.

Philolaus holds that we can know little about the world. But we can see that it must have been made up out of two types of thing – unlimited things and limiters. (Roughly, these are stuffs and shapes: a pond, for example, consists of unlimited stuff, water, determined by a limiter, its shape.) Something – we cannot tell exactly what – was required to harmonize limiters and unlimiteds in order to generate the world. So far the scheme is essentially Milesian in form. Pythagorean elements enter when Philolaus introduces numbers: the world when generated is determined by numbers, in the sense that it is describable in quantitative terms – otherwise it could not be known by us. On these foundations Philolaus hoped to erect the structure of natural science. Few details of his views are reported: we know, however, that he had theories in biology (including an account of the nature of diseases), and that he embraced the theory of the 'counter-earth' (another planet, balancing the earth, and bringing the heavenly bodies up to the perfect number, ten). In addition, he expressed an opinion about the nature and future of the soul.

Like Empedocles, ANAXAGORAS accepted the Eleatic argu-

44

ments to the effect that generation and destruction were impossible, but maintained that motion was nonetheless possible, and hence that change could take place in the world. Again like Empedocles, he believed that our faculties, if properly used, would yield reliable information about the natural world. But in his conception of the nature of things he differed fundamentally from Empedocles.

Anaxagoras believed that *every* substance or stuff was eternal: he had no theory of basic stuffs, no 'elements'. As Parmenides had shown, nothing can come from nothing. Hence everything always existed. In the beginning 'everything was together' in an infinite gaseous tohu-bohu, wherein everything was present and nothing was clear. (By 'everything' Anaxagoras probably meant 'all stuffs and all qualities' – stuffs such as earth, gold, flesh, cheese; qualities, themselves conceived of as stuffs, such as the hot and the cold, the sweet and the bitter.) The cosmos formed when stuffs and things gradually separated out from this undifferentiated mass. And here come Anaxagoras' two most original and influential doctrines.

First, he held that the original cosmogonical force was mind. Mind, he said, although different from all other things and not mixed with them, nonetheless pervaded everything and was responsible for everything. Later thinkers saw this as a great leap forward: Anaxagoras, they believed, had seen that the universe was planned by an intelligent designer. But they then found fault with Anaxagoras and complained that he had not invoked mind at the level of particular scientific explanations – there he had remained content with the standard Ionian explanations in terms of material forces. It is in any case uncertain to what extent Anaxagoras' mind was thought of as a personal, planning faculty which determined the history of the world in a benevolent, or at least an intentional, fashion: perhaps it was an impersonal force, comparable to the love and strife of Empedocles.

Anaxagoras' second innovation concerns his conception of stuffs. As stuffs separate out, none is ever *entirely* segregated, no *pure* stuff ever comes into being. Indeed, every piece of stuff always contains a portion of every other stuff. What we call 'gold' is not wholly golden: rather, 'gold' is the name we give to lumps of stuff which are *predominantly* gold. Anaxagoras' grounds for holding this doctrine are disputed; two of its consequences are clear. Anaxagoras himself drew the first consequence: there is no smallest piece of stuff of any sort – however small a piece of gold you may take, there is always a smaller; for within your piece of gold there is a portion of, say, blood – and that blood will itself contain a smaller portion of gold. The second consequence is not explicitly present in the fragments: stuffs cannot consist of particles or be 'in' one another in the way in which different sorts of seeds may be mixed in a packet; rather, Anaxagoras' view demands that stuffs be mixed through and through – that they be associated in something more like chemical combination than physical juxtaposition.

Anaxagoras' views were largely adopted by ARCHELAUS, who stood to him as Anaximenes to Anaximander. But Archelaus has the reputation of being the first philosopher to reflect on ethics: he maintained – we no longer know on what grounds – that moral qualities were conventional and not natural.

In the long run, the physics of Anaxagoras proved infertile. Far more influential were the views of LEUCIPPUS and DEMOCRITUS, the two Atomists. They tackled Parmenides head on. For they denied that what does not exist cannot be thought of – indeed, they maintained, paradoxically enough, that what does not exist is no less real than what does exist. What does not exist is void, empty space. What exists are bodies, the things which occupy space and move through its emptinesses. The void is infinite in extent, the bodies are infinite in number. Bodies, in the proper sense, are atomic or indivisible. The Atomists argued that there *must* be indivisible bodies, for they thought that the supposition that bodies can be divided *ad infinitum* led to paradox. These indivisibles were very small, solid, and without any 'qualities': they have size and shape and hardness or solidity, the so-called 'primary' qualities, but they lack the 'secondary' qualities – colour, smell, taste, etc. The atoms exist for ever and are unchangeable. To this extent each atom is a Parmenidean entity. But atoms move – indeed, they move constantly and have been moving for all eternity.

Atomic movements create the world. For atoms sometimes collide, and after some collisions they stick together, when the hooks on one atom may happen to lock with the eyes on another. In this way compound bodies are eventually formed. Everything happens by mechanical chance; but given infinite space and infinite time, it is only to be expected that the complex structure of the world about us will somewhere and some-when be formed.

Democritus was an enthusiastic and prolific scientist. He wrote on a wide variety of topics, and in some cases at least he attempted to apply his atomism to detailed scientific explan-ations. The best examples of this come in his account of per-ception and the objects of perception. Of his remaining scientific writing little remains. Perhaps the most interesting portion of his work was that which dealt with anthropology – the history and description of the human race as a social and cultural object. Democritus discussed, among other things, the origins of religion and the nature of language. His remarks here are almost entirely speculative (and they have little con-nection with atomism), but his speculations began a long tra-dition of armchair anthropology.

More interesting from a philosophical point of view are Democritus' opinions on the possibility of human knowledge. Despite his scientific ambitions, he appears to have entertained an extreme form of scepticism. His reasons for this are mostly missing, but some of them at least were closely connected with his atomism. The only real things are atoms and void, and neither void nor atoms can be coloured. Hence colours – and all other secondary properties – are illusory. Hence the world is very different from the way our senses take it to be, and our senses are fundamentally misleading. But if we distrust our senses, how can we say anything about the structure of reality? The atomist theory itself, though largely an *a priori* construc-tion, seemed to presuppose the validity of sense-perception and to gain its support from its capacity to explain the phenomena of perception. If atomism is right, perception is illusory; but if perception is illusory, why embrace atomism? Democritus was aware of this puzzle. How he attempted to solve it we do not know.

Finally, Democritus wrote at length on matters of moral and political philosophy. Some scholars have attempted to find connections between his ethics and his atomism, but there is probably none. Some scholars have attempted to discern a moral system behind the fragments. It is clear that Democritus was a hedonist of sorts: the goal of life is contentment, or imperturbability, and this is somehow equated with joy or pleasure. Democritean pleasures, however, are on the whole somewhat dry and severe, mental rather than physical in their objects: Democritus was no advocate of a life of Riley. It is perhaps a mistake to look for anything more systematic than that in the fragments. They are presented as maxims or aphorisms, and aphorisms do not typically communicate systematic thought. Of the maxims, some are sane, some are amusing, some are banal, some are outrageous – they are, in fact, a typical collection of moralistic aphorisms.

The last of the Presocratics was DIOGENES of Apollonia. His was not an original genius, and he is often, with some justice, described as an eclectic. His treatment of nature was in many respects close to that of the early Milesians: he took a single *arche*, in his case air, and generated the world from it by rarefaction and condensation. He explained the various natural phenomena by reference to this original stuff and its manifold modifications. And he adopted Anaxagoras' cosmogonic mind. But in Diogenes' system, mind was identified with eternal, all-knowing air, and it was the controlling and governing force of the universe. Diogenes certainly held that the world was well designed. If he can claim originality in his physics it must lie in his attempt to justify the positing of a *single* underlying stuff or *arche*: unless all things were fundamentally the same, he argued, the changes which we observe in the world could not come about.

The most remarkable fragment of Diogenes' work is a detailed description of the blood vessels of the human body.

Here we can read at first hand what in the case of the other Presocratics we know of only indirectly: an attempt to describe in scientific detail the structure and organization of the physical world. The Presocratics were philosophers, and they concerned themselves with the most general questions about the nature and origins of the universe. But they were also scientists. The abstractions of their cosmogonical thought are complemented and completed by the concrete detail of their particular descriptions and explanations. In this way they were the forerunners of Aristotle – and through him of modern science and philosophy.

NOTE TO THE READER

The main chapters of this book employ a variety of typographical devices.

Italics, in addition to marking stress and identifying booktitles, perform two special functions: (1) all purported citations from the Presocratics and (2) all editorial comments are set in italics. Citations are typographically distinguished from comments inasmuch as they are invariably indented.

Roman type marks all quotations from ancient authors *except* purported citations from the Presocratics. Thus the contexts of citations will be set in roman, and so too will allusions to and paraphrases of Presocratic views.

Brackets of three different styles appear in the quoted material. (1) Ordinary parentheses, '(. . .)', are used in the normal way as punctuation signs. (2) Square brackets, '[. . .]', enclose trivial editorial *alterations* to the quoted texts. (For example, an unspecific pronoun, 'he', in the original is sometimes replaced by the appropriate proper name.) They also enclose editorial *comments*. (For example, they enclose the modern equivalent of the ancient system of dating by Olympic years.) (3) Pointed brackets, '<. . .>', mark lacunae in the Greek text — i.e. places where the ancient scribes have accidentally omitted something. Where the pointed brackets enclose words, these represent what we may guess to have been omitted.

Asterisks, '*. . .*', surround passages where either the translation or the text itself is wholly uncertain. Words between the asterisks are at best an optimistic guess.

References follow each quoted passage. They are of two sorts.

(1) To each text quoted there is appended the author's name, the title of the work, and sufficient auxiliary information to enable the passage to be located in any standard edition. Square brackets about an author's name are a sign of spuriousness. (E.g. '[Aristotle], *Problems*' refers to the book called *Problems* which the manuscript tradition falsely ascribes to Aristotle.) (2) To each Presocratic fragment quoted there is appended a 'Diels-Kranz' reference, enclosed in square brackets. This normally consists of the letter 'B' followed by a number. The number is the number of the fragment in H. Diels and W. Kranz, *Die Fragmente der Vorsokratiker* (Berlin, 1952 [10th edition]). The first Diels-Kranz reference in any chapter prefixes a number to the letter 'B'. This is the number of the relevant chapter in Diels-Kranz. Thus '[59 B 1]' refers to fragment 1 in chapter 59, the chapter on Anaxagoras, of Diels-Kranz. A subsequent '[B 21a]' refers to fragment 21a in the same chapter. In principle, the 'B' passages in Diels-Kranz are genuine fragments (in contrast to paraphrases and allusions which appear in separate sections labelled 'A'). In fact Diels-Kranz often include passages among their 'B' texts which are certainly not fragments. When the reader finds a Diels-Kranz reference for a passage which is not set in italic type, he should infer that Diels-Kranz falsely present the passage as a fragment.

PART
I

1
PRECURSORS

Thales, the first of the canonical line of Presocratic philosophers, no doubt had his predecessors, and scholars have speculated on the sources and influences behind him. Two varieties of influence have been discerned.

First, there are native Greek antecedents. Homer's poems, the earliest surviving works of Greek literature, contain occasional references to what were later to become scientific and philosophical topics. The poems presuppose a certain vague conception of the nature and origins of the universe (how could they not?), and that conception finds echoes, both verbal and substantial, in Presocratic thought. More influential, because more explicit, was the view of the universe expressed by the seventh-century poet Hesiod. A short passage from his Theogony — *'The Birth of the Gods' — merits quotation.*

Hail, children of Zeus, grant a sweet song
and celebrate the holy race of the immortals who exist forever,
those who were born of Earth and of starry Heaven
and of dark Night, and those the salt Sea reared.
Tell how first gods and earth came into being,
and rivers and the boundless sea with its seething swell,
and shining stars and the broad sky above,
and tell how they divided their wealth and shared out their
    honours
and how first they gained Olympus with its many glades.
Tell me this, you Muses who have your home on Olympus,
from the beginning, and tell which of them first came into
    being.
First of all came the Chasm; and then

55

wide-bosomed Earth, the eternal safe seat of all
the immortals who hold the heights of snowy Olympus,
and murky Tartarus in the recesses of the wide-pathed land,
and Love, who is fairest among the immortal gods,
loosener of limbs, by whom all gods and all men
find their thoughts and wise counsels overcome in their breasts.
From the Chasm came black Darkness and Night;
and from Night came Ether and Day
whom she conceived and bore after mingling in love with
    Darkness.
Earth bore first, equal to herself,
starry Heaven, to veil her all about
that there might be an eternal safe seat for the blessed gods.
And she gave birth to tall Mountains, the graceful haunts of
    the goddesses –
of the Nymphs who dwell on the wooded mountains.
And she also bore the restless deep with its seething swell,
Sea, without desirable love; and then
she lay with Heaven and bore deep-eddying Ocean
and Coius and Creius and Hyperion and Iapetus
and Theia and Rheia and Right and Memory
and golden-crowned Phoebe and lovely Tethys.
And after them, the youngest, wily Cronus, was born,
most terrible of her children; and he hated his strong father.

                                (Hesiod, *Theogony* 104–138)

*All this is myth, not science; but it is, as it were, scientific myth: many
of Hesiod's gods are personifications of natural features or phenomena,
and in telling the birth of 'the gods' Hesiod is telling, in picturesque
form, the origins of the universe.*

*The Greeks themselves were well aware of this. The Sicilian comic
poet Epicharmus, who wrote at the beginning of the fifth century,
presents a mock philosophical criticism of Hesiod's story in a little
dialogue preserved by Diogenes Laertius:*

– The gods were always there: they were *never* yet missing;
and these things are always there, the same and in the same
    way always.

– But the Chasm is said to have been the first god to be born.
– How could that be? He had nothing to come from and
   nowhere to go to if he was the first.
– Then didn't *anything* come first? – No, nor anything second,
by Zeus,
   of the things we're now talking about: they existed always.
                    (Diogenes Laertius, *Lives of the Philosophers* III 10)

A story from a later century is also worth retelling:

The poet who writes

> First of all came the Chasm; and then
> wide-bosomed Earth, seat of all . . .

refutes himself. For if someone asks him what the Chasm came
from, he will not be able to answer. Some people say that this
is the reason why Epicurus turned to philosophy. When he
was still very young he asked a schoolmaster who was reading
out

> First of all came the Chasm . . .

what the Chasm came from if it came first. The schoolmaster
replied that it wasn't his job, but the job of the so-called philosophers, to teach that sort of thing. 'Well, then,' said Epicurus,
'I must go along to them, if they are the ones who know the
truth about the things that exist'.
                    (Sextus Empiricus, *Against the Mathematicians* x 18–19)

In the final book of his Metaphysics *Aristotle discusses the place of
'the good and the beautiful' in the world. Some thinkers, he says, hold
that goodness and beauty only make their appearance as the world
progresses,*

and the early poets say something similar insofar as they hold
that it is not the first comers – Night and Heaven, or the Chasm
or Ocean – who rule and hold sway, but Zeus. But they in fact
say this because their world-rulers change: the *hybrids* among

them, who do not say everything in a mythical vein – I mean Pherecydes and some others – do make the first generating principle the best thing.

(Aristotle, *Metaphysics* 1091b4–10)

Pherecydes of Syrus, whom Aristotle here distinguishes from Hesiod and his fellows, is probably to be dated to the early sixth century BC. He was therefore a contemporary of the first Presocratic philosophers.

Aristotle's judgement that he was a hybrid, part mythologist and part natural philosopher, is scarcely borne out by the surviving remnants his writings. Here are the two most 'philosophical' pieces:

The book which Pherecydes wrote has been preserved; it begins like this:

Zas and Time always existed, and so did Chthonie; and Chthonie acquired the name Earth when Zas gave her the earth as a bridal gift. [7 B 1]

(Diogenes Laertius, *Lives of the Philosophers* I 119)

Pherecydes of Syrus says that Zas and Time and Chthonie existed always as the three first principles (the one before the two, I say, and the two after the one). Time from his own seed created fire and air and water (I take this to be the threefold nature of the intelligible): they were divided into five nooks and from them were constituted the rest of the numerous race of the gods which is called the race of the five nooks (meaning, perhaps, of the five worlds).

(Damascius, *On First Principles* 124)

The other reports of Pherecydes' work contain nothing but fanciful mythology.

Many of the Greeks themselves believed that philosophy began among 'the barbarians' – in Egypt, in Persia, in Babylonia. They credited the early Presocratics with journeys to Egypt and the Near East, and supposed that they returned with philosophy among their souvenirs.

It is plausible to suppose that there was some intellectual contact between the Greeks and their eastern neighbours. But in philosophy, or the theoretical approach to science, it is difficult to find a single clear case of influence. (It should be said that where some scholars see striking parallels between a Greek and an eastern text, others see no more than superficial coincidence.) Here, for what they are worth, are two brief passages from eastern creation stories, one from Babylonia and the other from Egypt.

The Enuma Elishu, *the Babylonian creation epic, was probably composed early in the second millennium* BC. *It begins as follows:*

When on high the heaven had not been named,
firm ground below had not been called by name,
naught but primordial Apsu, their begetter,
and Mummu-Tiamat, she who bore them all,
their waters commingling as in a single body:
no reed hut had been matted, no marsh land had appeared,
when no gods whatever had been brought into being,
uncalled by names, their destinies undetermined –
then it was that the gods were formed within them.
Lahmu and Lahamu were brought forth, by name were
    they called.
Before they had grown in age and stature,
Anshar and Kishar were formed, surpassing the others.
They prolonged the days, added on the years.
Anu was their heir, of his fathers the rival;
yea, Anshar's first-born, Anu, was his equal.
Anu begot in his image Nudimmud.

(James B. Pritchard, *Ancient Near Eastern Texts*, third edition,
Princeton, 1969, p. 61)

(The text is written in Akkadian, and the translation of the lines is in many places uncertain – at all events, different scholars have produced remarkably different versions.) Anu and Nudimmud are the sky and the earth; Apsu and Mummu-Tiamat are primordial waters, the fresh waters and the sea. The identities of the other divinities are uncertain.

The Egyptian creation myth is known in a number of variant forms. The following text probably dates from about 2,000 BC:

I am he who came into being as Khepri. When I had come into being, being came into being, and all beings came into being after I came into being. Many were the beings which came forth from my mouth, before heaven came into being, before earth came into being, before the ground and creeping things had been created in this place. I put together some of them in Nun as weary ones, before I could find a place in which I might stand. It seemed advantageous to me in my heart; I planned with my face; and I made every form when I was alone, before I had spat out what was Shu, before I had sputtered out what was Tefnut, and before any other had come into being who could act with me.

I planned in my own heart, and there came into being a multitude of forms and beings, the forms of children and the forms of their children. I was the one who copulated with my fist, I masturbated with my hand. Then I spewed with my own mouth: I spat out what was Shu, I sputtered out what was Tefnut. It was my father Nun who brought them up . . .

Then Shu and Tefnut brought forth Geb and Nut. Then Geb and Nut brought forth Osiris, Horus Khenti-en-irti, Seth, Isis, and Nephthys from the body, one of these after another; and they brought forth their multitudes in this land.

(Pritchard, *Ancient Near Eastern Texts*, p. 6)

Khepri, the speaker, is the morning sun-god; Nun is the primordial water; Shu and Tefnut are the air-god and the moisture-goddess; Geb and Nut are earth and sky.

Both the Babylonian and the Egyptian stories bear comparison with Hesiod as examples of mythical cosmogony. Many scholars compare the stories more directly with Greek philosophy, suggesting (for example) that Thales' ideas about the importance of water may derive from the primordial significance of Mummu-Tiamat and Nun. They may be right; but to me Thales seems to live in a different and a more luminous world.

2
THALES

According to Aristotle, Thales of Miletus was 'the founder of natural philosophy'. *He is dated by the eclipse of the sun which he allegedly predicted and which modern astronomers place on 28 May 585 BC. The other known facts about his life suggest that he was born in about 625 and died in about 545. Simplicius reports that*

Thales is said to have been the first to introduce the study of nature to the Greeks: although many others preceded him, as Theophrastus himself admits, yet he so far excelled them as to eclipse all his predecessors. But he is said to have left nothing behind in writing except the so-called *Nautical Astronomy*.

(Simplicius, *Commentary on the Physics* 23.29–33)

Other sources ascribe other writings to him, and there were certainly books circulating under his name in antiquity. But it seems most probable that he wrote nothing – or at least nothing which survived even to the time of Aristotle. For our knowledge of his views, then, we depend entirely on later reports; and those reports must themselves have been based on oral tradition.

Thales was not simply, or even primarily, a philosopher. He was a man of practical wisdom, one of the so-called Seven Sages of early Greek history, and he was regarded by posterity not only as an original contributor to science and philosophy, but also as an astute statesman. Herodotus, the fifth-century historian, tells several stories which illustrate his political sagacity.

Useful advice had been given, even before the destruction of Ionia, by Thales, a Milesian whose family originally came from

Phoenicia: he urged the Ionians to establish a single council-chamber, saying that it should be located in Teos, which was the centre of Ionia, and that the other cities should continue to be inhabited but should be treated as though they were parishes.

(Herodotus, *Histories* I 170.3)

When Croesus came to the River Halys, then – according to my account – he crossed his army by way of the existing bridges; but according to most of the Greeks, Thales of Miletus crossed the army for him. For it is said that Croesus was at a loss how his army should cross the river, since these bridges did not yet exist at that time, and that Thales, who was in the camp, made the river which flowed on the left of the army flow on the right too, and that he did so in the following way. Beginning upstream of the camp, he dug a deep channel which he drew in the shape of a crescent so that it ran round the back of where the camp was sited, being diverted from its original course down the channel, and then, having passed the camp, debouched again into its original course. Thus as soon as the river was divided it became fordable in both its parts.

(*ibid* I 75.4–5)

Herodotus also reports the famous eclipse:

The war [between the Lydians and the Persians] was equally balanced, until in the sixth year an engagement took place in which, after battle had been joined, the day suddenly turned to night. This change in the day had been foretold to the Ionians by Thales of Miletus, who had fixed as its term the very year in which it actually occurred.

(*ibid* I 74.2)

(Modern scholars conjecture that Thales had learned something of Babylonian astronomy; even so, it is generally doubted that he could actually have predicted *the eclipse.)*

Of Thales' philosophico-scientific doctrines, the most celebrated concern water. First, he held that the earth rests upon water (a notion which has some Egyptian antecedents). Here is Aristotle's critical report:

Some say that [the earth] rests on water. This in fact is the oldest view that has been transmitted to us, and they say that it was advanced by Thales of Miletus who thought that the earth rests because it can float like a log or something else of that sort (for none of these things can rest on air, but they can rest on water) – as though the same must not hold of the water supporting the earth as holds of the earth itself.

(Aristotle, On the Heavens 294a28–34)

(Note Aristotle's non-committal 'some say' and 'they say': this cautious approach to Thales is yet more pronounced in the next few passages.)
In addition, and more strikingly, Thales held that everything was made from water, or that water, in Aristotle's later jargon, was the 'material principle' of the world. Aristotle again is our best source:

Most of the first philosophers thought that principles in the form of matter were the only principles of all things. For they say that the element and first principle of the things that exist is that from which they all are and from which they first come into being and into which they are finally destroyed, its substance remaining and its properties changing . . . There must be some nature – either one or more than one – from which the other things come into being, it being preserved. But as to the number and form of this sort of principle, they do not all agree. Thales, the founder of this kind of philosophy, says that it is water (that is why he declares that the earth rests on water). He perhaps came to acquire this belief from seeing that the nourishment of everything is moist and that heat itself comes from this and lives by this (for that from which anything comes into being is its first principle) – he came to his belief both for this reason and because the seeds of everything have a moist nature, and water is the natural principle of moist things.

(Aristotle, Metaphysics 983b6–11, 17–27)

Aristotle elsewhere reports something about Thales' views on the nature of the soul:

Some say that \<soul\> is mixed in the whole universe. Perhaps that is why Thales thought that everything was full of gods.

(Aristotle, *On the Soul* 411a7–8)

Thales, judging by what they report, seems to have believed that the soul was something which produces motion, inasmuch as he said that the magnet has a soul because it moves iron.

(*ibid* 405a19–21)

There is also some evidence that Thales made geometrical discoveries. The source, Proclus, wrote in the fifth century, but he is relying on the work of Eudemus, a pupil of Aristotle. Nonetheless, scholars have been reluctant to credit Eudemus' reports. Here, for what they are worth, are the four passages in question.

They say that Thales was the first to demonstrate that a circle is bisected by its diameter.

(Proclus, *Commentary on Euclid* 157.10–11)

We are indebted to old Thales for many discoveries and for this theorem in particular; for he is said to have been the first to have recognized and stated that in every isosceles triangle the angles at the base are equal, and to have called the equal angles 'similar' in the archaic style.

(*ibid* 250.20–251.2)

This theorem proves that when two straight lines intersect with one another the angles at the vertex are equal – according to Eudemus, it was first discovered by Thales.

(*ibid* 299.1–4)

Eudemus in his *History of Geometry* ascribes this theorem [*that a pair of triangles with one equal side and two equal angles are equal*] to Thales; for he says that he must have made use of it in the procedure by which he is said to have determined the distance of ships at sea.

(*ibid* 352.14–18)

I append part of the discussion of Thales in Diogenes Laertius' Lives of the Philosophers. Some of the statements in this discussion certainly false, and many are at best dubious: it should be read not as a reliable guide to the views of Thales but rather as a specimen of the sort of material which we now depend on for our knowledge of the philosophy of the Presocratics. The passage is a good illustration of the complex and controversial nature of much of our evidence for the Presocratics – and it does also contain some important and trustworthy pieces of information.

Thales' father (according to Herodotus, Duris and Democritus) was Examyes and his mother was Cleobulina, from the family of Theleus (they are Phoenicians, the most noble of the descendants of Cadmus and Agenor). <He was one of the Seven Sages,> according to Plato, and he was the first to be called a Sage – during the archonship of Damasias at Athens [582–580 BC], at which time, according to Demetrius of Phaleron in his *List of Archons*, the Seven Sages were in fact named. He was enrolled as a citizen at Miletus when he came there with Neileus who had been expelled from Phoenicia – but most authorities say that he was a native Milesian of a famous family.

After his political activities he turned to scientific speculation. According to some he left no writing behind; for the *Nautical Astronomy* ascribed to him is said to be by Phocus of Samos. But Callimachus knows him as the discoverer of the Little Bear and writes as follows in his *Iambi*:

And he is said to have measured out
the little stars of the Wain by which the Phoenicians sail.

According to others, he wrote just two works, *On the Solstice* and *On the Equinox*, *judging that everything else was unknowable*.

He is thought by some to have been the first to study

astronomy and to have predicted eclipses of the sun and sol-
stices, as Eudemus says in his *History of Astronomy* – that is why
Xenophanes and Herodotus admire him. Heraclitus and
Democritus also give a good report of him. Some (among them
the poet Choerilus) say that he was also the first to say that
souls are immortal. He was the first to discover the period from
one solstice to the next, and the first, according to some, to
state that the size of the sun is a seven hundred and twentieth
part <of the solar orbit, just as the size of the moon is a seven
hundred and twentieth> of the lunar orbit. He was the first
to call the last day of the month the thirtieth. And he was the
first, according to some, to discourse about nature.

Aristotle and Hippias say that he ascribed souls to lifeless
things too, taking the magnet and amber as his evidence.

Pamphila says that he learned geometry from the Egyptians
and was the first to inscribe a right-angled triangle inside a
circle, for which he sacrificed an ox. (Others, including
Apollodorus the calculator, ascribe this to Pythagoras, who
developed to their greatest extent the discoveries which Callimachus in his *Iambi* attributes to Euphorbus the Phrygian – for
example, 'scalenes and triangles' and what belongs to the study
of geometry.)

He is also thought to have given excellent advice in political
affairs. For example, when Croesus sent envoys to the
Milesians to make an alliance he prevented it – and that saved
the city when Cyrus came to power. But he himself actually
says, as Heraclides recounts, that he lived a solitary life as a
private citizen. Some say that he married and had a son, Cybis-
thus, others that he remained a bachelor but adopted his
sister's son – so that when he was asked why he had no children
he replied, 'Because I love children'. And they say that when
his mother pressed him to marry he said, 'It's too early', and
that then, when he had passed his prime and she insisted again,
he said 'It's too late'. Hieronymus of Rhodes, in the second
book of his *Miscellanies*, says that, wanting to show how easy it
is to be rich, he foresaw that there was about to be a good crop
of olives, hired the olive presses, and made a huge sum of
money.

He supposed that water was the first principle of all things, and that the world has a soul and is full of spirits. They say he discovered the seasons of the year and divided it into three hundred and sixty-five days.

No-one taught him, although he went to Egypt and spent time with the priests there. Hieronymus says that he actually measured the pyramids from their shadows, having observed the time when <our shadows> are the same size as we are. He lived with Thrasybulus, the ruler of Miletus, according to Minyes.

There is a celebrated story about the tripod which was discovered by the fishermen and sent round to the Sages by the people of Miletus. They say that some young men from Ionia bought a net from some Milesian fishermen. When the tripod was fished up there was a dispute until the Milesians sent to Delphi. The god gave this oracle:

Offspring of Miletus, do you ask Apollo about a tripod?
I declare that the tripod belongs to him who is first in
    wisdom.

So they gave it to Thales. But he gave it to one of the other Sages, and so it was passed on until it reached Solon, who said that the god was first in wisdom and sent it to Delphi. [There follow a number of different versions of the tripod story.]

Hermippus in his *Lives* ascribes to Thales what others say of Socrates. He used to say, they report, that he thanked Fortune for three things: first, that I am a human and not a beast; secondly, that I am a man and not a woman; thirdly, that I am a Greek and not a foreigner.

He is said to have been taken from his house by an old woman to look at the stars, and to have fallen into a ditch: when he cried out, the old woman said: 'Do you think, Thales, that you will learn what is in the heavens when you cannot see what is in front of your feet?' Timon too knows him as an astronomer and praises him in his *Silli* in the following words:

Such was Thales of the Seven Sages, a sage astronomer.

Lobon of Argos says that his writings stretched to two hundred lines and that the following epigram was inscribed on his statue:

> This is Thales whom Ionian Miletus bred and showed
> an astronomer, the highest of all in wisdom.

He adds that his poems include these verses:

> It is not many words which show an intelligent opinion:
> search out one wise thing,
> choose one good thing;
> for thus you will stop the ceaseless tongues of babbling
> men.

The following aphorisms are ascribed to him. Of existing things, god is the oldest – for he is ungenerated. The world is the most beautiful – for it is god's creation. Space is the greatest – for it includes everything. Mind is the swiftest – for it runs through everything. Necessity is the strongest – for it controls everything. Time is the wisest – for it discovers everything. He said that death is no different from life. 'Then why don't *you* die?' someone asked him. 'Because it makes no difference,' he replied. When someone asked him which came first, day or night, he answered, 'Night came first – by a day.' When someone asked him whether a man can escape the notice of the gods if he does wrong, he replied: 'Not even if he *thinks* of doing wrong.' An adulterer asked him if he should swear that he had not committed adultery: he replied, 'Perjury is no worse than adultery.' When asked what is difficult, he said, 'To know yourself'; what is easy, 'To give advice to someone else'; what most pleasant, 'Success'; what divine, 'What has neither beginning nor end'. When asked what was the strangest thing he had seen, he said: 'An old tyrant'. How can we bear misfortune most easily? – If we see our enemies faring worse. How can we live best and most justly? – If we do not ourselves do the things we blame others for doing. Who is happy? – One who has a healthy body, a well-stocked soul, and an educable nature. He says that we should remember our friends both present and absent, and that we should not beautify our faces but be beautiful in our practices. 'Do not be rich by evil means,' he says, 'and let not words estrange you from those who have shared your trust.' 'Expect from your children the same benefits that you gave to your parents.'

He said that the Nile floods when its streams are checked by the contrary etesian winds.

Apollodorus in his *Chronicles* says that he was born in the first year of the thirty-ninth Olympiad [624 BC]. He died at the age of seventy-eight (or, as Sosicrates says, at ninety); for he died in the fifty-eighth Olympiad [548–545 BC], having lived during the time of Croesus, whom he undertook to transport across the Halys without a bridge by diverting its course.

There were other men called Thales – five, according to Demetrius of Magnesia in his *Homonyms*: an orator from Callatis, who had a poor style; a painter from Sicyon, of great talent; the third is very early, a contemporary of Hesiod, Homer, and Lycurgus; the fourth is mentioned by Duris in his work *On Painting*; the fifth, more recent and obscure, is mentioned by Dionysius in his *Critical Essays*.

The Sage died of heat and thirst and weakness while watching a gymnastic contest. He was by then an old man. On his tomb is inscribed:

> His tomb is small, his fame is heaven-high:
> behold the grave of the wise and ingenious Thales.

In the first book of my *Epigrams* or *Poems in All Metres* there is an epigram on him:

> When once he was watching a gymnastic contest, O
>   Zeus of the Sun,
> you stole Thales the Sage from the stadium.
> I praise you for taking him near to you; for the old
>   man
> could no longer see the stars from the earth.

The motto 'Know Thyself' is his, though Antisthenes in his

Successions says that it was Phemonoe's and that Chilon appropriated it.

(Diogenes Laertius, *Lives of the Philosophers* I 22–28, 33–40)

3

ANAXIMANDER

Anaximander, like Thales, came from Miletus. 'Apollodorus of
Athens says in his *Chronicles* that he was sixty-four in the second
year of the fifty-eighth Olympiad [547/546 BC] and that he
died shortly afterwards' (Diogenes Laertius, *Lives of the Philosophers* II 2). *If Apollodorus is right, Anaximander was born in 610
and died in about 540 BC. Unlike Thales, he wrote a book, which was
later in circulation under the title* On Nature. *He also produced a
star-map and a map of the world:*

Anaximander of Miletus, a pupil of Thales, was the first man
bold enough to draw the inhabited world on a tablet; after
him, Hecataeus of Miletus, a great traveller, made it more
accurate so that it was greatly admired.

(Agathemerus, *Geography* I i)

The leading ideas of Anaximander's work On Nature *are summa-
rized by a late doxographer as follows:*

Anaximander was a pupil of Thales — Anaximander, son of
Praxiades, a Milesian. He said that a certain infinite nature is
first principle of the things that exist. From it come the heavens
and the worlds in them. It is eternal and ageless, and it contains
all the worlds. He speaks of time, since generation and existence and destruction are determinate.

Anaximander said that the infinite is principle and element
of the things that exist, being the first to call it by the name of
principle. In addition, there is an eternal motion in which the
heavens come into being.

The earth is aloft, not supported by anything but resting where it is because of its equal distance from everything. Its shape is rounded, circular, like a stone pillar. Of its surfaces, we stand on one while the other is opposite. The heavenly bodies come into being as a circle of fire, separated off from the fire in the world and enclosed by air. There are certain tubular channels or breathing-holes through which the heavenly bodies appear; hence eclipses occur when the breathing-holes are blocked, and the moon appears sometimes waxing and sometimes waning according to whether the channels are blocked or open. The circle of the sun is twenty-seven times greater <than the earth and the circle> of the moon <eighteen times greater>. The sun is highest, the circles of the fixed stars lowest.

Animals come into being <from moisture> evaporated by the sun. Humans originally resembled another type of animal, namely fish.

Winds come into being when the finest vapours of air are separated off, collect together and move. Rain comes from vapour sent up by the things beneath the sun. Lightning occurs when wind breaks out and parts the clouds.

He was born in the third year of the forty-second Olympiad [610/609 BC].

(Hippolytus, *Refutation of All Heresies* I vi 1–7)

A second doxographical report contains some supplementary material:

Anaximander, an associate of Thales, says that the infinite is the universal cause of the generation and destruction of the universe. From it, he says, the heavens were separated off and in general all the worlds, infinite in number. He asserted that destruction and, much earlier, generation occur from time immemorial, all the same things being renewed.

He says that the earth is cylindrical in shape and is a third as deep as it is broad.

He says that at the generation of this world that which is productive from the eternal of hot and cold separated off and from it a ball of flame grew round the air about the earth, like bark on a tree. When the ball burst and was enclosed in certain circles, the sun and the moon and the stars came into being.

Further, he says that originally humans were born from animals of a different kind, because the other animals can soon look after themselves while humans alone require a long period of nursing; that is why if they had been like this originally they would not have survived.

([Plutarch], *Miscellanies* fragment 179.2, in Eusebius, *Preparation for the Gospel* I vii 16)

Anaximander's most striking thoughts concern biology, astronomy and the conception of 'the infinite'. In biology, the remarks of Hippolytus and pseudo-Plutarch can be eked out by three further texts:

Anaximander says that the first animals were born in moisture, surrounded by prickly barks. As they grew older they emerged on to drier parts, the bark burst, and for a short time they lived a different kind of life.

([Plutarch], *On the Scientific Beliefs of the Philosophers* 908D)

Anaximander of Miletus says he thinks that from hot water and earth there arose fish, or animals very like fish, that humans grew in them, and that the embryos were retained inside up to puberty whereupon the fish-like animals burst and men and women emerged already able to look after themselves.

(Censorinus, *On Birthdays* IV 7)

The descendants of old Hellen actually sacrifice to Poseidon the Ancestor, believing that men grew from the moist substance – as do the Syrians. That is why they revere fish, as being of the same species and the same nurture as themselves. Here their philosophy is better than that of Anaximander. For he says, not that fish and men were born in the same surroundings, but that at first men came into being inside fish and were nourished there – like sharks – only emerging and taking to the land when they were able to look after themselves. So just

73

as fire consumes the matter from which it was kindled (its own mother and father, as the poet who inserted the marriage of Ceyx into Hesiod's poems said), so Anaximander, having declared that fish are at once fathers and mothers of men, urges us not to eat them.

(Plutarch, *Table Talk* 730DF)

The astronomical theory described by Hippolytus can be given a little more colour:

Anaximander holds that there is a circle twenty-eight times as great as the earth. It is like the wheel of a cart, with a hollow rim full of fire, which at a certain point reveals the fire through a mouthpiece, as through the tube of a bellows. This is the sun.

([Plutarch], *On the Scientific Beliefs of the Philosophers* 889F)

The heavenly bodies are concentric hollow wheel-rims, filled with fire and perforated. They circle a stationary earth. Aristotle adds to Hippolytus' account of the stability of the earth:

Some say that [the earth] rests where it is because of the similarity (so, among the ancients, Anaximander). For there is no reason why what is situated in the middle and is similarly related to the edges should move upwards rather than downwards or sideways. But it cannot move in opposite directions at the same time. So it necessarily rests where it is.

(Aristotle, *On the Heavens* 295b11–16)

As for the infinite principle or element of all things, we have a few words from Anaximander's book preserved in a passage of Simplicius. These are the earliest surviving words of western philosophy. Unfortunately, it is uncertain – and a matter of vigorous scholarly controversy – exactly how extensive Simplicius' citation is.

Of those who hold that the first principle is one, moving, and infinite, Anaximander, son of Praxiades, a Milesian, who was a successor and pupil of Thales, said that the infinite is principle and element of the things that exist. He was the first to introduce this word '*principle*'. He says that it is neither water nor any other of the so-called elements but some different infinite nature, from which all the heavens and the worlds in them come into being. And the things from which existing things come into being are also the things into which they are destroyed, in accordance with what must be. For *they give justice and reparation to one another for their injustice in accordance with the arrangement of time* [12 B 1] (he speaks of them in this way in somewhat poetical words). It is clear that he observed the change of the four elements into one another and was unwilling to make any one of them the underlying stuff but rather chose something else apart from them. He accounts for coming into being not by the alteration of the element but by the separating off of the opposites by the eternal motion.

(Simplicius, *Commentary on the Physics* 24.13–25)

Simplicius explains why Anaximander's 'element' was different from the four traditional elemental stuffs (earth, air, fire, water). He does not explain why it was unlimited or infinite. A passage in Aristotle's Physics *alludes to Anaximander and lists some reasons for belief in infinitude: it is possible that one or more of those reasons originally came from Anaximander.*

It is with reason that they all make [the infinite] a principle; for it can neither exist to no purpose nor have any power except that of a principle. For everything is either a principle or derived from a principle. But the infinite has no principle – for then it would have a limit. Again, it is ungenerated and indestructible and so is a principle. For what comes into being must have an end, and there is an end to every destruction. Hence, as I say, it has no principle but itself is thought to be a principle for everything else and to govern everything . . . And it is also the divine; for it is deathless and unperishing, as Anaximander and most of the natural scientists say.

Belief in the existence of something infinite comes mainly from five considerations: from time (since this is infinite), from the division of magnitudes (mathematicians actually *use* the infinite); again, because generation and destruction will give out unless there is something infinite from which what comes into being is subtracted; again, because what is finite is always limited *by* something, so that there cannot be an [ultimate] limit if one thing must always be limited by another; last and most importantly, there is something which raises a puzzle for everyone alike: because they do not give out in *thought*, numbers seem to be infinite, and so do mathematical magnitudes and the region outside the heavens. But if the region outside is infinite, then body and worlds also seem to be infinite – for why should they be here rather than there in the void? Hence if body is anywhere, it is everywhere. Again, if void and space are infinite, body too must be infinite – for with eternal things there is no difference between being possible and being actual.

(Aristotle, *Physics* 203b6–11, 13–30)

4
ANAXIMENES

Anaximenes was a younger contemporary of Anaximander, and like him a Milesian. Our sources offer some precise dates, but their interpretation is controversial: we may be satisfied with the thought that Anaximenes was active in the middle of the sixth century BC. He is said to have been a pupil of Anaximander. Whether or not that is literally true, his work certainly followed the same general pattern as that of Anaximander. According to Diogenes Laertius, he wrote in 'a simple and economical Ionian style' – *in contrast, perhaps, to* Anaximander's 'somewhat poetical words'.

Of the various doxographical accounts of his views, the fullest is the one given by Hippolytus:

Anaximenes, son of Eurystratus, was also a Milesian. He said that the first principle is infinite air, from which what is coming into being and what has come into being and what will exist and gods and divinities come into being, while everything else comes into being from its offspring. The form of the air is this: when it is most uniform it is invisible, but it is made apparent by the hot and the cold and the moist and the moving. It is always in motion; for the things that change would not change if it were not in motion. For as it is condensed and rarefied it appears different: when it dissolves into a more rarefied condition it becomes fire; and winds, again, are condensed air, and cloud is produced from air by compression. Again, when it is more condensed it is water, when still further condensed it is earth, and when it is as dense as possible it is stones. Thus the most important factors in coming into being are opposites – hot and cold.

The earth is flat and rides on air; in the same way the sun and the moon and the other heavenly bodies, which are all fiery, ride the air because of their flatness. The heavenly bodies have come into being from earth, because mist rose from the earth and was rarefied and produced fire, and the heavenly bodies are composed of this fire when it is aloft. There are also some earthy substances in the region of the heavenly bodies which orbit with them. He says that the heavenly bodies move not under the earth, as others have supposed, but round the earth – just as a felt cap turns on the head. And the sun is hidden not because it goes under the earth but because it is screened by the higher parts of the earth and because of its greater distance from us. The heavenly bodies do not heat us because of their great distance.

Winds are generated when the air is condensed and driven along. As it collects together and is further thickened, clouds are generated and in this way it changes into water. Hail comes about when the water falling from the clouds solidifies, and snow when these same things solidify in a more watery form. Lightning occurs when the clouds are parted by the force of winds; for when they part a bright and fiery flash occurs. Rainbows are generated when the sun's rays fall on compacted air; earthquakes when the earth is considerably altered by heating and cooling.

These are the views of Anaximenes. He flourished in the first year of the fifty-eighth Olympiad [548/547 BC].

(Hippolytus, *Refutation of All Heresies* I vii 1–9)

The curious reference to felt caps may go back to Anaximenes himself, as may the notion of the stars 'riding' on air. Anaximenes seems to have liked such similes: he also held that the sun is 'flat like a leaf' and (perhaps) that the stars are 'fixed into the crystalline like nails' ([Plutarch], On the Scientific Beliefs of the Philosophers 890D, 889A).

Hippolytus' account of the earth's flatness can be supplemented by a passage from Aristotle:

Anaximenes and Anaxagoras and Democritus say that the

flatness [of the earth] causes it to rest where it is. For it does not cut the air beneath but covers it like a lid. Flat bodies are observed to do this – for they are not easily moved even by the winds because of their resistance. They say that because of its flatness the earth does the same thing in relation to the air underneath it (which, not having enough room to move away, stays motionless in a mass below), like the water in a clepsydra.

(Aristotle, *On the Heavens* 294b13–21)

Three texts have been supposed to contain a few of Anaximenes' own words.

Or should we, as old Anaximenes thought, treat the hot and the cold not as substances but rather as common properties of matter which supervene upon changes? For he says that matter which is concentrated and condensed is cold, while that which is rare and *slack* (that is the word he uses) is hot. [13 B 1] Hence it is not unreasonably said that men release both hot and cold from their mouths; for the breath is cooled when it is compressed and condensed by the lips, but when the mouth is relaxed and it is exhaled it becomes hot by reason of its rareness.

(Plutarch, *The Primary Cold* 947F)

Anaximenes, son of Eurystratus, a Milesian, asserted that air is the first principle of the things that exist; for everything comes into being from air and is resolved again into it. For example, *our souls*, he says, *being air, hold us together, and breath and air contain the whole world* ('air' and 'breath' are used synonymously). [B 2]

([Plutarch], *On the Scientific Beliefs of the Philosophers* 876AB)

Anaximenes believes that there is a single, moving, infinite first principle of all existing things, namely air. For he says this:

Air is close to the incorporeal; and because we come into being by an outflowing of air, it is necessary for it to be both infinite and rich because it never gives out. [B 3]

([Olympiodorus], *On the Divine and Sacred Art of the Philosopher's Stone* 25)

In the Plutarch passage the only word that can be ascribed to Anaxi-menes is 'slack', but the content of the text may be Anaximenean. The parenthetical comment at the end of pseudo-Plutarch shows that he purports to quote Anaximenes; but the citation can hardly be literal (and its sense is obscure). The 'fragment' quoted by pseudo-Olympio-dorus is regarded as spurious by most scholars.

5
PYTHAGORAS

We are told more about Pythagoras — his life, his character, his beliefs —
than about any other Presocratic philosopher. For the school of thought
to which he gave his name lasted for more than a millennium, and
several works by later Pythagoreans have survived. Yet in many ways
Pythagoras is the most obscure and perplexing of all the early thinkers.

Pythagoras himself did not set down his notions in writing, nor did
his early followers. (This is the orthodox modern view; but, as we shall
see, there was disagreement among the ancients on the point.) In the
fifth century there occurred a division among the Pythagoreans, each
group claiming to be the genuine heirs of the Master. Later, in the
fourth century, the histories of Pythagoreanism and of Platonism
became closely connected, and as a result accounts of Pythagorean
philosophy became contaminated with Platonic material. Later still,
various Pythagorean documents were produced and circulated, pro-
jecting back on to Pythagoras himself philosophical ideas of a more
recent age. It is difficult to cut through this jungle and discover the
original Pythagoras.

Legends rapidly collected about his name. If we attempt to disen-
tangle the few threads of historical truth, we shall conclude that
Pythagoras was born on the island of Samos, in about 570 BC. Some
thirty years later he left the island, which was then ruled by the culti-
vated autocrat Polycrates, and emigrated to Croton in south Italy. He
appears to have become a figure of consequence in the political life of
Croton, and to have aroused some hostility among the citizens. At all
events, he was eventually obliged to leave town: he settled in the nearby
city of Metapontum, where he died.

This chapter sets out the most important of the early texts which refer to Pythagoras, and reports the few doctrines which can be ascribed to him with any confidence. Later chapters will deal with fifth-century Pythagoreanism, and with Hippasus and Philolaus, the only Presocratic Pythagoreans about whom we have any substantial evidence.

Pythagoras is mentioned by Xenophanes, Heraclitus, Ion and (perhaps) Empedocles:

As to [Pythagoras'] having become different people at different times, Xenophanes bears witness in an elegy which begins with the line:

Now I will attempt another theme and show the path . . .
What he says about him goes like this:
And once when he passed a puppy that was being whipped
they say he took pity on it and made this remark:
'Stop, do not beat it; for it is the soul of a dear friend –
I recognized it when I heard the voice'. [21 B 7]
(Diogenes Laertius, *Lives of the Philosophers* VIII 36)

[Heraclitus] was uncommonly arrogant and contemptuous, as indeed is clear from his treatise itself, in which he says:

Much learning does not teach sense – otherwise it would have
taught Hesiod and Pythagoras, and again Xenophanes and
Hecataeus. [22 B 40]

(*ibid* IX 1)

Some say that Pythagoras did not leave a single written work behind him. They are in error; at any rate, Heraclitus the natural scientist pretty well shouts it out when he says:

Pythagoras, son of Mnesarchus, practised inquiry more than any
other man, and selecting from these writings he manufactured a
wisdom for himself – much learning, artful knavery. [22 B 126]
(*ibid* VIII 6)

Ion of Chios in his *Triads* says that Pythagoras wrote some things and attributed them to Orpheus.

(*ibid* VIII 8)

Ion of Chios says about [Pherecydes]:

> *Thus he, excelling in courage and also in honour,*
> *even after death possesses in his soul a pleasant life —*
> *if indeed Pythagoras is truly wise, who above all*
> *men learned and gained knowledge.* [36 B 4]

(ibid I 120)

Empedocles bears witness to this when he says of [Pythagoras]:

> *Among them was a man of immense knowledge*
> *who had obtained the greatest wealth of mind,*
> *an exceptional master of every kind of wise work.*
> *For when he stretched out with all his mind*
> *he easily saw each and every thing*
> *in ten or twenty human generations.* [31 B 129]

(Porphyry, Life of Pythagoras 30)

Pythagoras is referred to by the fifth-century historian Herodotus:

As I learn from the Greeks who live on the Hellespont and the Black Sea, this Salmoxis was human and lived as a slave in Samos – he was a slave to Pythagoras, the son of Mnesarchus. Then he gained his freedom and accumulated a large sum of money, and having done so returned to his own country. But since the Thracians led miserable lives and were rather stupid, Salmoxis, who was acquainted with the Ionian way of life and with manners more civilized than those of the Thracians (he had, after all, associated with Greeks – and with Pythagoras who was by no means the feeblest of the Greek sages), prepared a banqueting-hall where he entertained and feasted the leading citizens. And he taught them that neither he nor his fellow-drinkers nor any of their descendants would die but would come to a country where they would live for ever in possession of all good things. In the place where he had done and said what I have reported he built an underground chamber. When the chamber was completed he vanished from among the Thracians, descending into the underground chamber and staying there for three years. They missed him and mourned for him as though he were dead. But in the fourth year he appeared to the Thracians – and in this way what Salmoxis had said appeared plausible to them. That is what they say he did. As for the man and his underground chamber, I neither disbelieve the story nor place too much credit in it – and I think that Salmoxis lived many years earlier than Pythagoras.

(Herodotus, *Histories* IV 95–96)

Plato mentions Pythagoras once:

Well, then, if Homer did no public service, is he said to have become during his lifetime an educational leader in private, with pupils who loved him for his company and who handed down a Homeric way of life to their successors – like Pythagoras, who was himself particularly loved on this account and whose successors even now talk of a Pythagorean mode of life and are thought to stand out from other men?

(Plato, *Republic* 600 A B)

Isocrates the orator, who was a contemporary of Plato, has the following account:

I am not the only man or the first to have observed [the piety of the Egyptians]: many, both now and in the past, have done so, including Pythagoras of Samos, who went to Egypt and studied with the Egyptians. He was the first to bring philosophy to Greece, and in particular he was concerned, more conspicuously than anyone else, with matters to do with sacrifices and temple purifications, thinking that even if this would gain him no advantage from the gods it would at least bring him high repute among men. And that is what happened. For he so exceeded others in reputation that all the young men desired to be his pupils, while the older men were more pleased to see their children associating with him than looking after their own affairs. Nor can we distrust their judgement; for even now those who claim to be his pupils receive for their silence more admiration than those who have the greatest reputation for speaking.

(Isocrates, *Busiris* 28–29)

Some of the legends about Pythagoras were collected by Aristotle in his lost work On the Pythagoreans. *Here is a representative sample:*

Pythagoras, the son of Mnesarchus, first studied mathematics and numbers but later also indulged in the miracle-mongering of Pherecydes. When at Metapontum a cargo ship was entering harbour and the onlookers were praying that it would dock safely because of its cargo, he stood up and said: 'You will see that this ship is carrying a corpse.' Again, in Caulonia, as Aristotle says, <he foretold the appearance of the white she-bear; and Aristotle> in his writings about him tells many stories including the one about the poisonous snake in Tuscany which bit him and which he bit back and killed. And he foretold to the Pythagoreans the coming strife – which is why he left Metapontum without being observed by anybody. And while he was crossing the river Casas in company with others he heard a superhuman voice saying 'Hail, Pythagoras' – and those who were there were terrified. And once he appeared both in Croton and in Metapontum on the same day and at the same hour. Once, when he was sitting in the theatre, he stood up, so Aristotle says, and revealed to the audience his own thigh, which was made of gold. Several other paradoxical stories are told of him; but since I do not want to be a mere transcriber, enough of Pythagoras.

(Apollonius, *Marvellous Stories* 6)

A large body of teachings came to be ascribed to Pythagoras. They divide roughly into two categories, the mathematico-metaphysical and the moral – as the poet Callimachus put it, Pythagoras

> was the first to draw triangles and polygons
> and *to bisect* the circle – and to teach men to abstain
> from living things.

(*Iambi* fragment 191.60–62 Pfeiffer)

Most modern scholars are properly sceptical of these ascriptions, and their scepticism is nothing new. The best ancient commentary on Pythagoras' doctrines is to be found in a passage of Porphyry:

Pythagoras acquired a great reputation: he won many followers in the city of Croton itself (both men and women, one of whom, Theano, achieved some fame), and many from the nearby foreign territory, both kings and noblemen. What he said to his associates no-one can say with any certainty; for they preserved no ordinary silence. But it became very well known to everyone that he said, first, that the soul is immortal; then, that it changes into other kinds of animals; and further, that at certain periods whatever has happened happens again, there being nothing absolutely new; and that all living things should be considered as belonging to the same kind. Pythagoras seems to have been the first to introduce these doctrines into Greece.

(Porphyry, *Life of Pythagoras* 19)

The theory of metempsychosis, or the transmigration of the soul, is implicitly ascribed to Pythagoras by Xenophanes in the text quoted above. Herodotus also mentions it:

The Egyptians were the first to advance the idea that the soul is immortal and that when the body dies it enters into another animal which is then being born; when it has gone round all the creatures of the land, the sea and the air, it again enters into the body of a man which is then being born; and this cycle takes it three thousand years. Some of the Greeks – some earlier, some later – put forward this idea as though it were their own: I know their names but I do not transcribe them.

(Herodotus, *Histories* II 123)

The names Herodotus coyly refrains from transcribing will have included that of Pythagoras. Two later passages are worth quoting even though they belong to the legendary material.

Heraclides of Pontus reports that [Pythagoras] tells the following story of himself: he was once born as Aethalides and was considered to be the son of Hermes. Hermes invited him to choose whatever he wanted, except immortality; so he asked that, alive and dead, he should remember what happened to him. Thus in his life he remembered everything, and when he died he retained the same memories. Some time later he became Euphorbus and was wounded by Menelaus. Euphorbus used to say that he had once been Aethalides and had acquired the gift from Hermes and learned of the circulation of his soul – how it had circulated, into what plants and animals it had passed, what his soul had suffered in Hades and what other souls experienced. When Euphorbus died, his soul passed into Hermotimus, who himself wanted to give a proof and so went to Branchidae, entered the temple of Apollo and pointed to the shield which Menelaus had dedicated (he said that he had dedicated the shield to Apollo when he sailed back from Troy); it had by then decayed and all that was left was the ivory boss. When Hermotimus died, he became Pyrrhus, the Delian fisherman; and again he remembered everything – how he had been first Aethalides, then Euphorbus, then Hermotimus, then Pyrrhus. When Pyrrhus died, he became Pythagoras and remembered everything I have related.

(Diogenes Laertius, *Lives of the Philosophers* VIII 4–5)

Pythagoras believed in metempsychosis and thought that eating meat was an abominable thing, saying that the souls of all animals enter different animals after death. He himself used to say that he remembered being, in Trojan times, Euphorbus, Panthus' son, who was killed by Menelaus. They say that once when he was staying at Argos he saw a shield from the spoils of Troy nailed up, and burst into tears. When the Argives asked him the reason for his emotion, he said that he himself had borne that shield at Troy when he was Euphorbus. They did not believe him and judged him to be mad, but he said he would provide a true sign that it was indeed the case: on the inside of the shield there had been inscribed in archaic lettering EUPHORBUS. Because of the extraordinary nature of his claim they all urged that the shield be taken down – and it turned out that on the inside the inscription was found.

(Diodorus, *Universal History* X vi 1–3)

The theory of transmigration was later adopted by Empedocles: further texts will be found in the chapter under his name.

The idea of eternal recurrence had a wide currency in later Greek thought. It is ascribed to 'the Pythagoreans' *in a passage from Simplicius:*

The Pythagoreans too used to say that *numerically* the same things occur again and again. It is worth setting down a passage from the third book of Eudemus' *Physics* in which he paraphrases their views:

> One might wonder whether or not the same time recurs as some say it does. Now we call things 'the same' in different ways: things the same in kind plainly recur – e.g. summer and winter and the other seasons and periods; again, motions recur the same in kind – for the sun completes the solstices and the equinoxes and the other movements. But if we are to believe the Pythagoreans and hold that things the same in number recur – that you will be sitting here and I shall talk to you, holding this stick, and so on for everything else – then it is plausible that the same time too recurs.

(Simplicius, *Commentary on the Physics* 732.23–33)

Eternal recurrence, like metempsychosis, will be found again in connection with Empedocles.

6
ALCMAEON

Alcmaeon came from Croton. The township was famous for its doctors and Alcmaeon himself was a medical man, the first of a distinguished line of Greek philosopher-physicians. No dates are recorded for his life; but he is said to have been a younger contemporary of Pythagoras, and he was probably active in the early part of the fifth century BC.

The short notice on Alcmaeon by Diogenes Laertius is worth quoting in full:

Alcmaeon of Croton: he too heard Pythagoras. Most of what he says concerns medicine; nevertheless he sometimes engages in natural science too – when he says:
Most human things come in pairs.
He is thought to have been the first to compose a treatise on natural science (as Favorinus says in his *Universal History*), and to have held that the moon and everything above it possess an eternal nature.

He was the son of Peirithous, as he himself says at the beginning of his treatise:
Alcmaeon of Croton, son of Peirithous, said this to Brontinus and Leo and Bathyllus: About matters invisible the gods possess clarity, but as far as humans may judge etc. [24 B 1]
He said that the soul is immortal and that it moves continuously like the sun.

(Diogenes Laertius, *Lives of the Philosophers* VIII 83)

Brontinus, Leo, and Bathyllus are elsewhere said to have been Pythagoreans – Brontinus being a relation by marriage of Pythagoras himself.

Diogenes' first 'quotation', about things coming in pairs, is in fact taken from a report in Aristotle:

Alcmaeon held similar views to [the Pythagoreans]. For he says that most human things come in pairs, speaking not, like them, of a determinate set of oppositions but rather of a haphazard collection – such as black and white, sweet and bitter, good and bad, great and small.

(Aristotle, *Metaphysics* 986a30–34)

These oppositions had a medical application:

Alcmaeon says that health is conserved by egalitarianism among the powers – wet and dry, cold and hot, bitter and sweet and the rest – and that autocracy among them produces illness; for the autocracy of either partner is destructive. And illness comes about *by* an excess of heat or cold, *from* a surfeit or deficiency of nourishment, and *in* the blood or the marrow or the brain. It sometimes occurs in them from external causes too – water of a particular kind, or locale, or fatigue, or constraint, or something else of that sort. Health is the proportionate blending of the qualities.

([Plutarch], *On the Scientific Beliefs of the Philosophers* 911A)

Alcmaeon's ideas about the immortality of the soul, mentioned in Diogenes, are reported at slightly greater length by Aristotle:

Alcmaeon seems to have held a similar view about the soul. For he says that it is immortal because it is like the immortals – and that it is like them insofar as it is always in motion. For the divinities too are always in continuous motion – the moon, the sun, the stars and the whole heaven.

(Aristotle, *On the Soul* 405a29–b1)

At the same time, he held that men, unlike their souls, perish:

Alcmaeon says that men die because they cannot attach the

beginning to the end – a clever saying if you take it to have been meant loosely and do not try to make it precise.

([Aristotle], *Problems* 916a33–37)

Theophrastus' essay on the senses contains a summary of Alcmaeon's views on perception:

Of those who do not explain perception by similarity, Alcmaeon first defines the differences among animals. For he says that humans differ from the other animals because they alone understand, whereas the others perceive but do not understand. (He supposes that thinking and perceiving are distinct, not – as Empedocles holds – the same thing.)

Then he discusses each of the senses. He says that we hear with our ears because there is an empty space inside them which echoes: the cavity sounds and the air echoes in return. We smell with our noses at the same time as we breathe in, drawing the breath towards the brain. We discriminate flavours with our tongues; for, being soft and warm, they dissolve things with their heat, and they accept and transmit them because they are loose-textured and delicate. The eyes see through the water surrounding them. It is clear that they contain fire; for when they are struck it flashes out. They see by the gleaming and transparent part, when it reflects – and the purer it is, the better they see.

All the senses are somehow connected to the brain. That is why they are incapacitated if it is moved or displaced; for it obstructs the passages through which the senses work.

As for touch, he said neither how nor by what means it works.

So much for Alcmaeon's views.

(Theophrastus, *On the Senses* 25–26)

In this connection the following report deserves mention (although scholars have doubted its veracity):

We must now give an account of the nature of the eye. On this subject many scientists, including Alcmaeon of Croton (who busied himself with natural science and who was the first to undertake dissections) . . . published much of value.

(Calcidius, *Commentary on the Timaeus* ccxlvi 279)

Finally, there is an isolated moral maxim:

Alcmaeon of Croton says that it is easier to be on your guard against an enemy than against a friend.

(Clement, *Miscellanies* VI ii 16.1)

7
XENOPHANES

Xenophanes, who came from Colophon in Ionia, was a man of many parts. He was a peripatetic poet, who travelled about Greece reciting his own and other men's verses. He wrote on traditional poetical subjects — drink, love, war, games — and also on historical themes. A number of his verses are philosophical in content. The later tradition regarded him as a serious philosopher, the teacher of Parmenides and the founder of the Eleatic school of thought. Many modern scholars have doubted whether he was a systematic thinker, and some have denied that he ever wrote a properly philosophical poem. However that may be, there are enough surviving fragments to warrant our calling him a philosopher — and indeed to justify our regarding him as one of the early philosophical geniuses of Greece.

According to Diogenes Laertius,

he wrote in verse, both elegiac and iambic, against Hesiod and Homer, censuring them for their remarks about the gods. He also recited his own poems. He is said to have disagreed with Thales and with Pythagoras, and to have attacked Epimenides. He lived to an advanced age, as he himself says:

> *By now have seven and sixty years*
> *been tossing my thought about the land of Greece;*
> *and from my birth there were twenty five to add to them*
> *if I know how to speak truly about these things.* [21 B 8]

(Diogenes Laertius, *Lives of the Philosophers* IX 18)

Xenophanes, by his own reckoning, was ninety-three when he wrote these lines. He is said to have lived to be over a hundred, and the rest of our evidence suggests that his life spanned the century from 580 to 480 BC.

Not all his surviving verses deserve a place here, but I shall translate all the extant fragments which have philosophical content. (The fragment on Pythagoras has already been cited in Chapter Five.) They divide roughly into three groups: on knowledge, on the gods, on nature.

In the later tradition, Xenophanes acquired a reputation for scepticism. It rested primarily on the first of the following three fragments.

According to some, Xenophanes takes this sceptical position, saying that everything is inapprehensible when he writes:

And the clear truth no man has seen nor will anyone
know concerning the gods and about all the things of which I speak;
for even if he should actually manage to say what was indeed the case,
nevertheless he himself does not know it; but belief is found over all.
[B 34]

(Sextus Empiricus, *Against the Mathematicians* VII 49)

Ammonius prefaced his remarks, as he usually does, with the line of Xenophanes:

Let these things be believed as similar to the truth, [B 35]
and invited us to state and say what we believed.

(Plutarch, *Table Talk* 746B)

No comparatives ending in -*on* have a penultimate upsilon; hence Xenophanes' *glusson* ['sweeter'] is remarkable:

If god had not made yellow honey, they would say
that the fig was far sweeter. [B 38]

(Herodian, *On Singularities of Language* 946.22–24)

But Xenophanes also spoke in a modestly optimistic way about the progress of human knowledge:

Xenophanes:

Not from the start did the gods reveal all things to mortals,
but in time, by inquiring, they make better discoveries. [B 18]

(Stobaeus, *Anthology* I viii 2)

In verbs ending in -*si* the penultimate syllable is naturally
long . . . But the poets often make it short, as in Xenophanes:

Since all at first have learned from Homer . . . [B 10]

and again:

As many things as are clear for mortals to see . . . [B 36]

(Herodian, *On Double Quantities* 16. 17–22)

*Among the theological fragments there are several which are sharply
critical of traditional religious notions:*

[The myths of the theologians and poets] are full of impiety;
hence Xenophanes in his criticism of Homer and Hesiod says:

*Homer and Hesiod attributed to the gods all the things
which among men are shameful and blameworthy —
theft and adultery and mutual deception.* [B 11]

(Sextus Empiricus, *Against the Mathematicians* IX 193)

Homer and Hesiod, according to Xenophanes of Colophon,
*told many lawless deeds of the gods —
theft and adultery and mutual deception.* [B 12]

(*ibid* I 289)

Xenophanes of Colophon, claiming that god is one and incorporeal, says:

*There is one god, greatest among gods and men,
similar to mortals neither in shape nor in thought.* [B 23]

And again:

*But mortals think that the gods are born,
and have clothes and speech and shape like their own.* [B 14]

And again:

*But if cows and horses or lions had hands
or could draw with their hands and make the things men can
    make,
then horses would draw the forms of gods like horses,
cows like cows, and they would make their bodies
similar in shape to those which each had themselves.* [B 15]

(Clement, *Miscellanies* V xiv 109.1–3)

The Greeks suppose that the gods have not only human shapes but also human feelings: just as each race depicts their shapes as similar to their own, as Xenophanes of Colophon says (the Ethiopians making them dark and snub-nosed, the Thracians red-haired and blue-eyed), so too they invent souls for them similar to their own.

(Clement, *Miscellanies* VII iv 22.1: cf B 16)

Further fragments reveal a positive side to Xenophanes' thought about the gods, and the doxography suggests (perhaps anachronistically) that his views were elaborated with some sophistication and detail.

If the divine exists, it is a living thing; if it is a living thing, it sees – for

he sees as a whole, he thinks as a whole, he hears as a whole.
[B 24]

If it sees, it sees both white things and black.

(Sextus Empiricus, *Against the Mathematicians* IX 144)

Theophrastus says that Xenophanes of Colophon, the teacher of Parmenides, supposed that the first principle, or the existing universe, was one and neither finite nor infinite, neither changing nor changeless. Theophrastus allows that the account of his views belongs to a different inquiry from the study of nature; for Xenophanes said that this one universe was god. He shows that god is one from the fact that he is most powerful of all things; for if there were more than one, he says, they would all have to possess equal power, but what is most powerful and best of all things is god. He showed that it was ungenerated from the fact that what comes into being must do so either from what is similar or from what is dissimilar; but similar things, he says, cannot be affected by one another (for it is no more fitting that what is similar should generate than that it should be generated by what is similar to it), and if it comes into being from what is dissimilar, then what is will come from what is not. In this way he showed it to be ungenerated and eternal. It is neither infinite nor finite because it is what does not exist which is infinite (having no beginning, no middle and no end), while it is several things which are finite, being limited by one another. He does away with change and changelessness in a similar fashion: it is what does not exist which is changeless (for nothing else passes into it and it does not pass into anything else), while it is several things which change (for one thing changes into another). Hence when he says that it remains in the same state and does not change –

> Always he remains in the same state, changing not at all,
> nor is it fitting for him to move now here now there [B 26]

– he means not that it rests in virtue of the stationariness which is opposed to change but in virtue of the rest which is distinct from change and from stationariness. According to Nicolaus of Damascus in his work *On Gods*, he says that the first principle is infinite and changeless, and according to Alexander he says that it is finite and spherical. But it is clear from what I have said that he shows it to be neither infinite nor finite. ([Alexander supposes that] it is finite and spherical because [Xenophanes] says that it is similar from all directions.) And he says that it thinks of all things, when he writes:

> But far from toil he governs everything with his mind. [B 25]
> (Simplicius, *Commentary on the Physics* 22.26–23.20)

The fragments dealing with natural science are sparse, and require no comment.

Porphyry says that Xenophanes held the dry and the moist – i.e. earth and water – to be first principles, and he quotes an example which indicates this:

> Earth and water are all things which grow and come into being. [B 29]
> (Philoponus, *Commentary on the Physics* 125.27–30)

Xenophanes, according to some, holds that everything has come into being from earth:

> For all things are from earth and in earth all things end. [B 27]

. . . the poet Homer holds that everything has come into being

97

from two things, earth and water, . . . and according to some Xenophanes of Colophon agrees with him. For he says:

> *For we all come into being from earth and water.* [B 33]
> (Sextus Empiricus, *Against the Mathematicians* x 313–314)

Xenophanes in *On Nature*:

> *Sea is source of water and source of wind;*
> *for neither in the clouds <would the force of the wind come about,*
> *breathing out> from inside, without the great ocean,*
> *nor would the streams of the rivers nor the rain-water of the air;*
> *but the great ocean is generator of clouds and winds*
>   *and rivers.* [B 30]
> (Geneva scholium on Homer, *Iliad* XXI 196)

Xenophanes thinks that the earth is not aloft but reaches downwards *ad infinitum*; for he says:

> *Of the earth this, the upper limit, is seen at our feet*
> *next to the air; but below, it proceeds to infinity.* [B 28]
> (Achilles, *Introduction to Aratus* 4)

One should understand the sun to be 'going above' inasmuch as it always passes above the earth – as I think Xenophanes of Colophon also says:

> *And the sun, passing above and warming the earth, . . .* [B 31]
> (Heraclitus, *Homeric Questions* 44.5)

Xenophanes says:

> *And in certain caves* [speatessi] *the water drips down . . .*
> [B 37]

But the form *speas* does not occur.

> (Herodian, *On Singularities of Language* 936.18–20)

Remember that Xenophanes describes the rainbow in his hexameters thus:

> *What men call Rainbow, that too is a cloud,*
> *purple and scarlet and yellow to see.* [B 32]
> (Eustathius, *Commentary on the Iliad* XI 24)

It is worth appending the brief doxographical account which Hippolytus transmits:

He says that nothing comes into being or is destroyed or changes, and that the universe is one and changeless. He also says that god is eternal and unique and homogeneous in every way and limited and spherical and capable of perception in all his parts.

The sun comes into existence each day from small sparks which congregate. The earth is infinite and surrounded neither by air nor by the heavens. There are infinitely many suns and moons. Everything is made from earth.

He said that the sea is salty because many mixtures flow together in it. (Metrodorus holds that it is salty because it is filtered in the earth, but Xenophanes thinks that the earth mixes with the sea.) He holds that the earth in time is dissolved by the moisture, urging as proof the fact that shells are found in the middle of the land and on mountains; and he says that in the quarries in Syracuse there were found impressions of fish and of seaweed, on Paros the impression of a bay-leaf deep in the rock, and on Malta shapes of all sea-creatures. He says that these were formed long ago when everything was covered in mud – the impressions dried in the mud. All men are destroyed when the earth is carried down into the sea and becomes mud; then they begin to be born again – and this is the foundation of all the worlds.

(Hippolytus, *Refutation of All Heresies* I xiv 2–6)

8
HERACLITUS

*Heraclitus came from Ephesus in Asia Minor; he belonged to an emi-
nent family; he flourished about 500 BC. His thought and his
writings were notorious for their difficulty: he was nicknamed 'The
Obscure' and 'The Riddler'. One anecdote, no doubt apocryphal, is
worth repeating:*

They say that Euripides gave [Socrates] a copy of Heraclitus'
book and asked him what he thought of it. He replied: 'What
I understand is splendid; and I think that what I don't understand is so too – but it would take a Delian diver to get to the
bottom of it'.

(Diogenes Laertius, *Lives of the Philosophers* II 22)

*Socrates' attitude of puzzled admiration has been shared by many later
students of Heraclitus.*
  *It is hard to know how best to present the surviving fragments of
Heraclitus' work. The Greek texts are uncertain in more cases than
usual; and since Heraclitus wrote in prose it is frequently difficult to
tell which words – if any – in a given passage purport to be his.
But the chief problem concerns the arrangement of the texts; for any
arrangement will insinuate some general interpretation of Heraclitus'
thought, and every such interpretation is controversial. (A random
ordering is no solution; for that will suggest that Heraclitus was not a
systematic thinker at all, a suggestion which has itself had several
scholarly advocates.)*
  *It will be uncontroversial to begin with the opening words of Hera-
clitus' book. After that, it may prove most helpful to quote two long and
complementary doxographical texts, which incidentally have a number*

of important fragments embedded in them. Then the remaining fragments will be collected under various thematic headings.

First, then, the opening passage of Heraclitus' book. It is referred to by Aristotle:

It is difficult to punctuate Heraclitus' writings because it is unclear whether a word goes with what follows or with what precedes it. E.g. at the very beginning of his treatise, where he says:

> Of this account which holds forever men prove uncomprehending,
> [cf 22 B 1]

it is unclear which 'forever' goes with.

(Aristotle, *Rhetoric* 1407b14–18)

A longer quotation is preserved by Hippolytus (see below) and by Sextus Empiricus. I cite the passage from Sextus because it is fuller (but I have tacitly altered his text once or twice in the light of Hippolytus' readings).

At the beginning of his writings on nature, and pointing in some way at the environment, [Heraclitus] says:

> Of this account which holds forever men prove uncomprehending, both before hearing it and when first they have heard it. For although all things come about in accordance with this account, they are like tiros as they try the words and the deeds which I expound as I divide up each thing according to its nature and say how it is. Other men fail to notice what they do when they are awake, just as they forget what they do when asleep. [B 1]

Having thus explicitly established that everything we do or think depends upon participation in the divine account, he continues and a little later on adds:

> For that reason you must follow what is common (i.e. what is universal – for 'common' means 'universal'). But although the account is common, most men live as though they had an understanding of their own. [B 2]

(Sextus Empiricus, *Against the Mathematicians* VII 132–133)

The first doxographical passage comes from the Refutation of All

Heresies. *In it Hippolytus presents what is supposed to be a rounded summary of Heraclitus' main ideas.*

Heraclitus says that the universe is divisible and indivisible, generated and ungenerated, mortal and immortal, Word and Eternity, Father and Son, God and Justice.

> *Listening not to me but to the account, it is wise to agree that all things are one,* [B 50]

says Heraclitus. That everyone is ignorant of this and does not agree he states as follows:

> *They do not comprehend how, in differing, it agrees with itself — a backward-turning connection, like that of a bow and a lyre.* [B 51]

That an account exists always, being the universe and eternal, he says in this way:

> *Of this account which holds forever men prove uncomprehending, both before hearing it and when first they have heard it. For although all things come about in accordance with this account, they are like tiros as they try the words and the deeds which I expound as I divide up each thing according to its nature and say how it is.* [B 1]

That the universe is a child and an eternal king of all things for all eternity he states as follows:

> *Eternity is a child at play, playing draughts: the kingdom is a child's.* [B 52]

That the father of everything that has come about is generated and ungenerated, creature and creator, we hear him saying:

> *War is father of all, king of all: some it shows as gods, some as men; some it makes slaves, some free.* [B 53]

That < . . .

> . . . > *connection, like that of a bow and a lyre.* [cf B 51]

That God is unapparent, unseen, unknown to men, he says in these words:

> *Unapparent connection is better than apparent* [B 54]

— he praises and admires the unknown and unseen part of his power above the known part. That he is visible to men and not undiscoverable he says in the following words:

I honour more those things which are learned by sight and hear-ing, [B 55]

he says – i.e. the visible more than the invisible. <The same> is easily learned from such words of his as these:

Men have been deceived, he says, *as to their knowledge of what is apparent in the same way that Homer was – and he was the wisest of all the Greeks. For some children who were killing lice deceived him by saying: 'What we saw and caught we leave behind, what we neither saw nor caught we take with us'.* [B 56]

Thus Heraclitus gives equal rank and honour to the apparent and unapparent, as though the apparent and the unapparent were confessedly one. For, he says,

unapparent connection is better than apparent; [B 54]

and:

I honour more those things which are learned by sight and hearing [B 55]

(i.e. the organs) – and he does not honour the unapparent more.

Hence Heraclitus says that dark and light, bad and good, are not different but one and the same. For example, he re-proaches Hesiod for not knowing day and night – for day and night, he says, are one, expressing it thus:

A teacher of most is Hesiod: they are sure he knows most who did not recognize day and night – for they are one. [B 57]

And so are good and bad. For example, doctors, Heraclitus says,*who cut and cauterize and wretchedly torment the sick in every way are praised – they deserve no fee from the sick, for they have the same effects as the diseases* [B 58]. And straight and twisted, he says, are the same:

The path of the carding-combs, he says, *is straight and crooked* [B 59]

(the movement of the instrument called the screw-press in a fuller's shop is straight and crooked, for it travels upwards and in a circle at the same time) – he says it is one and the same. And up and down are one and the same:

The path up and down is one and the same. [B 60]

And he says that the polluted and the pure are one and the

same, and that the drinkable and the undrinkable are one and the same:

> *The sea*, he says, *is most pure and most polluted water: for fish, drinkable and life-preserving; for men, undrinkable and death-dealing.* [B 61]

And he explicitly says that the immortal is mortal and the mortal immortal in the following words:

> *Immortals are mortals, mortals immortals: living their death, dying their life.* [B 62]

He also speaks of a resurrection of this visible flesh in which we are born, and he is aware that god is the cause of this resurrection – he says:

> *There they are said to rise up and to become wakeful guardians of the living and the dead.* [B 63]

And he says that a judgement of the world and of everything in it comes about through fire; for

> *fire*, he says, *will come and judge and convict all things.* [B 66]

He says that this fire is intelligent and the cause of the management of the universe, expressing it thus:

> *The thunderbolt steers all things* [B 64]

(i.e. directs everything) – by 'the thunderbolt' he means the eternal fire, and he calls it need and satiety [B 65] (the establishment of the world according to him being need and the conflagration satiety).

In the following passage he has set down all of his own thought – and at the same time that of the sect of Noetus, whom I have briefly shown to be a disciple not of Christ but of Heraclitus. For he says that the created universe is itself the maker and creator of itself:

> *God is day and night, winter and summer, war and peace, satiety and famine* (all the opposites – that is his meaning); *but he changes like olive oil which, when it is mixed with perfumes, gets its name from the scent of each.* [B 67]

It is clear to everyone that the mindless followers of Noetus and the champions of his sect, even if they deny they are disciples of Heraclitus, yet in subscribing to the opinions of Noetus evidently confess the same beliefs.

(Hippolytus, *Refutation of All Heresies* IX ix 1–x 9)

*Diogenes Laertius' Life also offers a summary account, with sup-
porting quotations and paraphrases, of Heraclitus' thought:*

Heraclitus, son of Bloson (or, as some say, of Heracon), from
Ephesus. He flourished in the sixty-ninth Olympiad [504/501
BC]. He was uncommonly arrogant and contemptuous, as
indeed is clear from his treatise itself, in which he says:

> *Much learning does not teach sense — otherwise it would have
> taught Hesiod and Pythagoras, and again Xenophanes and
> Hecataeus. [B 40]*

For he says that the wise is one, grasping the knowledge how all
things are steered through all [B 41]. And he said that Homer
deserved to be thrown out of the games and flogged — and
Archilochus too. [B 42] He also said:

> *You should quench violence more quickly than arson. [B 43]*

And:

> *The people should fight for the law as for the city wall. [B 44]*

He also assails the Ephesians for expelling his friend Hermo-
dorus. He says:

> *The Ephesians deserve to be hanged to the last man, every one of
> them: they should leave the city to the young. For they expelled
> Hermodorus, the best man among them, saying: 'Let no one of us
> be best: if there is such a man, let him be elsewhere and with
> others.' [B 121]*

When they asked him to write laws for them, he refused on the
grounds that the city had already been mastered by a wicked
constitution. He retired into the temple of Artemis and played
dice with the children. When the Ephesians stood round him,
he said: 'Why are you staring? Isn't it better to do this than to
play politics with you?'

In the end he became a misanthrope, leaving the city and
living in the mountains where he fed on plants and herbs.
Because of this he contracted dropsy and returned to the town.
He asked the doctors in his riddling fashion if they could
change a rainstorm into a drought. When they failed to understand him, he buried himself in a byre, hoping that the dropsy
would be vaporized by the heat of the dung. But he met with
no success even by this means and died at the age of sixty . . .

He was remarkable from an early age: as a young man, he used to say that he knew nothing, and when he had become adult that he had learned everything. He was no-one's pupil, but said that he had inquired into himself [cf B 101] and learned everything from himself. Sotion reports that some say that he was a pupil of Xenophanes, and that Aristo, in his book *On Heraclitus*, says that he was actually cured of the dropsy and died of another disease. Hippobotus too says this.

The book of his which is in circulation is, as far as its general tenor goes, on nature; but it is divided into three accounts — one on the universe, one political, one theological. He deposited it in the temple of Artemis (having, as some say, written somewhat unclearly) in order that the powerful should have access to it and it should not easily be despised by the people. Timon gives a sketch of him as follows:

> Among them Heraclitus the mocker, the reviler of the mob,
> the riddler, rose up.

Theophrastus says that because of his impulsive temperament he wrote some things in a half-finished style and others in different ways at different times. As a sign of his arrogance Antisthenes says in his *Successions* that he resigned from the kingship in favour of his brother. His treatise gained such a high reputation that it actually produced disciples, the so-called Heracliteans.

His views, in general, were the following. All things are constituted from fire and resolve into fire. All things come about in accordance with fate, and the things that exist are fitted together by the transformation of opposites. All things are full of souls and spirits. He spoke also about all the events that occur in the world, and he said that the sun is the size it appears [cf B 3]. He also said:

> *If you travel every path you will not find the limits of the soul, so deep is its account.* [B 45]

He said that conceit is a sort of epilepsy, and that sight is fallacious [B 46]. Sometimes in his treatise he expresses himself brilliantly and clearly, so that even the most stupid easily understand him and gain an enlargement of soul; and the brevity and weight of his style are incomparable.

In detail, his doctrines are these. Fire is an element, and all things are an exchange for fire [cf B 90], coming about by rarefaction and condensation. (But he expresses nothing clearly.) All things come about through opposition, and the universe flows like a river [cf B 12]. The universe is finite, and there is one world [cf B 30]. It is generated from fire and it is consumed in fire again, alternating in fixed periods throughout the whole of time. And this happens by fate.

Of the opposites, that which leads to generation is called war and strife [cf B 80], and that which leads to conflagration is called agreement and peace. The change is a path up and down [cf B 60], and the world is generated in accordance with it. For fire as it is condensed becomes moist, and as it coheres becomes water; water as it solidifies turns into earth – this is the path downwards. Then again the earth dissolves, and water comes into being from it, and everything else from water (he refers pretty well everything to the exhalation given off by the sea) – this is the path upwards.

Exhalations are given off by the earth and by the sea, some of them bright and pure, others dark. Fire is increased by the bright exhalations, moisture by the others. He does not indicate what the surrounding heaven is like. But there are bowls in it, their hollow side turned towards us. The bright exhalations gather in them and produce flames, and these are the heavenly bodies. The flame of the sun is the brightest and hottest. For the other heavenly bodies are further away from the earth and for that reason give less light and heat, while the moon, though it is nearer the earth, does not travel through a pure region. The sun, however, lies in a translucent and uncontaminated region, and it preserves a proportionate distance from us; that is why it gives more heat and light. The sun and the moon are eclipsed when the bowls turn upwards. The moon's monthly changes of shape come about as its bowl gradually turns. Day and night, the months and seasons and years, rains and winds and the like, come about in virtue of the different exhalations. For the bright exhalation, when it bursts into flame in the circle of the sun, makes day, and the opposite exhalation, when it has gained power, produces night. As the heat from the brightness increases it makes summer, and as the moisture from the darkness mounts up it effects winter.

He gives explanations of the other phenomena in the same way, but he does not say anything about what the earth is like, nor even about the bowls. Those were his views.

The story about Socrates and what he said when he looked at the treatise (having got it from Euripides, according to Aristo), I have recounted in the *Life* of Socrates. Seleucus the grammarian, however, says that Croton relates in his *Diver* that a certain Crates first brought the book to Greece and that it was he who said that it would take a Delian diver not to get drowned in it. Some entitle it *Muses*, others *On Nature*; Diodotus calls it

A certain steerage to the goal of life;

others *Judgement, Manners, Turnings, One World for All* . . .

Demetrius in his *Homonyms* says that he despised even the Athenians, though he had the highest reputation <among them>, and that though he was scorned by the Ephesians he preferred what was familiar to him. Demetrius of Phaleron mentions him too in his *Apology of Socrates*. Very many people have offered interpretations of his treatise: Antisthenes, Heraclides of Pontus, Cleanthes, Sphaerus the Stoic, Pausanias (who was called the Heraclitean), Nicomedes, Dionysius – and of the grammarians, Diodotus, who says that the treatise is not about nature but about politics and that the remarks on nature are there by way of illustrations. Hieronymus says that Scythinus the iambic poet attempted to put his account into verse.

(Diogenes Laertius, *Lives of the Philosophers* IX 1–3, 5–12, 15)

The rest of the chapter assembles the remaining fragments, together with some paraphrastic texts. Let me stress again that the distinction between quotation and paraphrase is often hard to make out, and that the reliability of purported paraphrases and quotations is often uncertain. After two short passages from Stobaeus, the texts are grouped roughly by subject matter, the main themes of which have been indicated in the passages already cited. But assignment to these groups is fairly arbitrary; in addition, when two texts are quoted together in an ancient source I have kept them together even if they deal with different issues.

First, there are two short sequences of quotations, or purported quotations, in the Anthology of John Stobaeus.

Heraclitus:

> Of those whose accounts I have heard, no-one has come so far as to recognize that the wise is set apart from all things. [B 108]
> It is better to hide folly than to make it public. [B 109]
> It is not good for men to get all they want. [B 110]
> Sickness makes health sweet and good, hunger plenty, weariness rest. [B 111]
> To be temperate is the greatest excellence. And wisdom is speaking the truth and acting with knowledge in accordance with nature. [B 112]
> Thinking is common to all. [B 113]
> Speaking with sense one should rely on what is common to all, as a city on its law – and with yet greater reliance. For all human laws are nourished by the one divine; for it is as powerful as it wishes, and it suffices for all, and it prevails. [B 114]

Socrates:

> Soul has a self-increasing account. [B 115]

(Stobaeus, Anthology III i 174–180)

Heraclitus:

> All men can know themselves and be temperate. [B 116]
> A man when he is drunk is led by a boy, stumbling, not knowing where he goes, his soul moist. [B 117]
> A dry soul is wisest and best. [B 118]

(ibid III v 6–8)

[Despite Stobaeus' heading, B 115 is universally ascribed by scholars to Heraclitus rather than to Socrates. On the other hand, the authenticity of B 109, B 112, B 113 and B 116 has frequently been doubted.]

The first group of texts documents Heraclitus' attitude to ordinary mortals and to other thinkers.

'Let thy fountains be dispersed abroad, and rivers of waters in the streets' [Proverbs 5:16]. For

> most people do not understand the things they meet with, nor do they know when they have learned; but they seem to themselves to do so, [B 17]

according to the good Heraclitus. So you see that he too finds fault with unbelievers.

(Clement, *Miscellanies* II ii 8.1)

The Ionian Muses [i.e. Heraclitus] say explicitly that most men who think themselves wise follow the popular singers and *obey the laws*, not knowing that most men are bad and few good [cf B 104], but that the best pursue reputation. For

> the best, he says, *choose one thing in return for all: ever-flowing fame from mortals; but most men satisfy themselves like beasts,* [B 29]

measuring happiness by the belly and the genitals and the most shameful parts in us.

(*ibid* V ix 59.4–5)

Heraclitus caustically remarks that some people are without faith,

> not knowing how to hear or even to speak [B 19]

– he was aided here, no doubt, by Solomon: 'If thou desire to hear, thou shalt receive; and if thou incline thine ear, thou shalt be wise' [Ecclesiasticus 6:33].

(*ibid* II v 24.5)

The excellent Heraclitus rightly excoriates the mob as unintelligent and irrational. For

> *what sense or thought,* he says, *do they have? They follow the popular singers and they take the crowd as their teacher, not knowing that most men are bad and few good.* [B 104]

Thus Heraclitus – which is why Timon called him 'the reviler of the mob'.

(Proclus, *Commentary on the First Alcibiades* 256.1–6)

The contemptuous and the brash get little benefit from what

they hear, while those who are credulous and guileless are harmed – they confirm Heraclitus' saying:

A foolish man is put in a flutter by every word. [B 87]

(Plutarch, *On Listening to Lectures* 40F)

Iamblichus, *On the Soul*: How much better, then, is Heraclitus, who regards human opinions as children's toys. [B 70]

(Stobaeus, *Anthology* II i 16)

Some say that Pythagoras did not leave a single written work behind him. They are in error; at any rate, Heraclitus the natural scientist pretty well shouts it out when he says:

Pythagoras, son of Mnesarchus, practised inquiry more than any other man, and selecting from these writings he manufactured a wisdom for himself – much learning, artful knavery. [B 129]

(Diogenes Laertius, *Lives of the Philosophers* VIII 6)

Bias is also mentioned by Hipponax, as I said before, and the fastidious Heraclitus gave particular praise to him when he wrote:

In Priene lived Bias, son of Teutames, who is of more account than the others. [B 39]

(*ibid* I 88)

Heraclitus says that Homer is an astronomer on the basis of this line [namely *Iliad* XVIII 251] and [*Iliad* VI 488]. [B 105]

(Scholiasts A and T to Homer, *Iliad* XVIII 251)

The orators' *Introduction* bends all its theorems to this end [sc. deception] and is, according to Heraclitus, the leader of cheats. [B 81]

(Philodemus, *Rhetoric* I 351S)

The second group of passages, closely connected with the first, indicates Heraclitus' attitude to the scope and nature of human knowledge.

Nevertheless, [Celsus] wanted to show that this too was a

fiction we [Christians] had taken from the Greek philosophers who said that human wisdom is one thing, divine wisdom another. And he quotes remarks of Heraclitus, in one of which he says:

> For human nature has no insights, divine nature has; [B 78]

and in another:

> A man is called foolish by a god as a child is by a man. [B 79]
>
> (Origen, *Against Celsus* VI xii)

In all respects superior to us, [god] is especially unlike and different from us in his acts; but of divine acts, the majority, according to Heraclitus,

> escape our knowledge through lack of faith. [B 86]
>
> (Plutarch, *Coriolanus* 232D)

> *Those who search for gold*, says Heraclitus, *dig over much earth and find little.* [B 22]
>
> (Clement, *Miscellanies* IV ii 4.2)

Perhaps god is not willing that such harmony should ever be found among men. For

> nature, according to Heraclitus, *likes to hide itself* [B 123]

– and still more so the creator of nature, whom we especially revere and admire because knowledge of him is not readily gained.

> (Themistius, *Speeches* V 69B)

According to the Pyrrhonian sceptics, Xenophanes and Zeno of Elea and Democritus were sceptics ... Also Heraclitus, who said:

> Let us not make aimless conjectures about the most important things. [B 47]
>
> (Diogenes Laertius, *Lives of the Philosophers* IX 73)

Thus the prophet's remark, 'If ye will not believe, surely ye shall not be established' [Isaiah 7:9], is proved abundantly true. And Heraclitus of Ephesus was paraphrasing it when he observed:

If you do not expect the unexpected you will not discover it;
for it cannot be tracked down and offers no passage. [B 18]
(Clement, *Miscellanies* II iv 17.8)

Heraclitus says, as though he had achieved something great
and noble,
I inquired into myself, [B 101]
and of the proverbs at Delphi 'Know thyself' is thought the
most divine.

(Plutarch, *Against Colotes* 1118c)

Knowledge and ignorance are the boundaries of happiness
and unhappiness. For
philosophical men must be versed in very many things, [B 35]
according to Heraclitus, and it is indeed necessary to make
many journeys in the search to be good.

(Clement, *Miscellanies* V xiv 140.5–6)

Heraclitus rejects perception when he says, in these very
words:
Bad witnesses for men are the eyes and ears of those who have
foreign souls [B 107]
– i.e. it is the mark of a foreign soul to trust in non-rational
perceptions.

(Sextus Empiricus, *Against the Mathematicians* VII 126)

We have two natural instruments, as it were, by which we
learn everything and conduct our business, namely hearing
and sight; and sight, according to Heraclitus, is not a little
truer – for
eyes are more accurate witnesses than ears. [B 101a]
(Polybius, *Histories* XII xxvii 1)

Hence the apostle exhorts us that 'your faith should not
stand in the wisdom of men' who promise to persuade you,
'but in the power of God' [I Corinthians 2:5] which in itself
and without proofs has the power to save by faith alone.

> For the most esteemed of men knows and guards what he
> believes, [B 28a]

and moreover

> justice will convict the fashioners and witnesses of falsehoods,
> [B 28b]

as the Ephesian says. For he too learned from foreign philosophy about the purification through fire of those who have
lived evil lives.

(Clement, *Miscellanies* V i 9.2–3)

*The third group of texts can be given the vague label 'metaphysics':
these fragments begin with some general reflections on the nature of
things and then illustrate three more specific aspects of Heraclitus'
thought – his notion of the unity of opposites, his concept of relativity,
his ideas about instability or flux.*

[Celsus] says that the ancients refer riddlingly to a war among
the gods, as when Heraclitus says:

> One should know that war is common, that justice is strife, that
> all things come about in accordance with strife and with what
> must be. [B 80]

(Origen, *Against Celsus* VI xlii)

Surely nature longs for the opposites and effects her harmony from them . . . That was also said by Heraclitus the
Obscure:

> Combinations – wholes and not wholes, concurring differing,
> concordant discordant, from all things one and from one all
> things. [B 10]

In this way the structure of the universe – I mean, of the
heavens and the earth and the whole world – was arranged
by one harmony through the blending of the most opposite
principles.

([Aristotle], *On the World* 396b7–8, 20–25)

On this topic [i.e. friendship] some seek a deeper and more
scientific account. Euripides says that the earth when dried
up longs for rain, and the majestic heaven when filled with

rain longs to fall to the earth. Heraclitus says that opposition concurs and the fairest connection comes from things that differ [B 8] and everything comes about in accordance with strife [cf. B 80].

(Aristotle, *Nicomachean Ethics* 1155b2–6)

Old Heraclitus of Ephesus was called clever because of the obscurity of his remarks:

Cold things grow hot, the hot cools, the wet dries, the parched moistens. [B 126]

(Tzetzes, *Notes on the Iliad* p.126H)

It seems that the ancients used the word *bios* ambiguously to mean 'bow' and 'life'. For example, Heraclitus the Obscure:

The name of the bow is bios, *its function death.* [B 48]

(*Etymologicum Magnum*, s.v. *bios*)

But the circumference of a circle as a whole no longer has a direction; for whatever point on it you think of is both a beginning and an end – for

beginning and end are common

on the circumference of a circle [B 103], according to Heraclitus.

(Porphyry, *Notes on Homer*, on *Iliad* XIV 200)

They say it is indecent if the sight of warfare pleases the gods. But it is not indecent; for the noble deeds please the gods. Again, wars and battles seem terrible to us, but to god not even they are terrible. For god makes all things contribute to the harmony of the universe, managing it commodiously – so Heraclitus says that to god all things are fair and just but men have supposed some things unjust others just [B 102].

(Porphyry, *Notes on Homer*, on *Iliad* IV 4)

Don't you realize the truth of Heraclitus' remark that the most beautiful ape is ugly when compared with another species . . .? [B 82] Doesn't Heraclitus say the same thing, that the wisest of men, when compared to a god, will seem an ape in wisdom and beauty and everything else? [B 83]

(Plato, *Hippias Major* 289AB)

It seems that each animal has its own pleasure ... The pleasures of horses, dogs, and men are different – so Heraclitus says that donkeys would prefer rubbish to gold [B 9] (for food is more pleasing to donkeys than gold).

(Aristotle, *Nicomachean Ethics* 1176a3, 5–8)

Dry dust and ash ... should be put in the poultry-run so that the birds can sprinkle themselves with it; for this is how they wash their feathers and wings, if we are to believe Heraclitus of Ephesus who says that pigs wash in mud and farmyard birds in dust or ashes [B 37].

(Columella, *On Agriculture* VIII iv 4)

[Vetch] is the cow's favourite pasture, and the cow eats it with pleasure. Hence Heraclitus said that if happiness resided in bodily pleasures, we should call cows happy when they discover some vetch to eat [B 4].

(Albert the Great, *On Vegetables* VI ii 14)

On the subject of the soul, Cleanthes sets out the doctrines of Zeno [the Stoic] in order to compare them to those of the other natural scientists. He says that Zeno, like Heraclitus, holds the soul to be a percipient exhalation. For, wanting to show that souls as they are exhaled always become new, he likened them to rivers, saying:

> On those who enter the same rivers, ever different waters flow – and souls are exhaled from the moist things. [B 12]

Now Zeno, like Heraclitus, says that the soul is an exhalation; but he holds that it is percipient, for the following reasons.

(Arius Didymus, fragment 39 Diels, quoted by Eusebius, *Preparation for the Gospel* XV xx 2)

Heraclitus the Obscure theologizes the natural world as

something unclear and to be conjectured about through symbols. He says:

> Gods are mortal, humans immortal, living their death, dying their life. [cf B 62]

And again:

> We step and do not step into the same rivers, we are and we are not. [B 49a]

Everything he says about nature is enigmatic and allegorized.

(Heraclitus, *Homeric Questions* 24.3–5)

For it is not possible to step twice into the same river, according to Heraclitus, nor to touch mortal substance twice in any condition: by the swiftness and speed of its change, it scatters and collects itself again – or rather, it is not again and later but simultaneously that it comes together and departs, approaches and retires [B 91].

(Plutarch, *On the E at Delphi* 392B)

Things which have a natural circular motion are preserved and stay together because of it – if indeed, as Heraclitus says, the barley-drink separates if it is not moving [B 125].

(Theophrastus, *On Vertigo* 9)

Heraclitus, who urges us to inquire into [how the soul comes to be within the body], posits necessary exchanges from the opposites and talks of a path up and down [cf B 60], and

> changing, it rests, [B 84a]

and

> it is weariness for the same to labour and be ruled [B 84b]

– he leaves us to conjecture and omits to make his argument clear to us, no doubt because we should inquire for ourselves as he himself inquired and found [cf B 101].

(Plotinus, *Enneads* IV viii 1)

The fourth group collects further fragments of a religious or theological significance.

Heraclitus of Ephesus, finding fault with those who sacrifice
to the spirits, says:

> *They vainly purify themselves with blood when they are defiled: as
> though one were to step in the mud and try to wash it off with mud.
> Any man who saw him doing that would think he was mad. And
> they pray to these statues as though one were to gossip to the houses,
> not knowing who the gods and who the heroes are.* [B 5]

The same man said to the Egyptians:

> *If they are gods, why do you grieve? If you grieve, no longer think
> them gods.* [B 127]

(anonymous *Theosophia* 68–69)

As a mystical reminder of that affair, phalluses are set up
throughout the cities to Dionysus. For

> *if they did not make a procession for Dionysus and sing a
> paean to the penis, they would act most shamelessly,* Heraclitus
> says, *and Hades is the same as Dionysus for whom they rave
> and celebrate their rites* [B 15]

– not, I think, from drunkenness of the body so much as
from their disgraceful doctrines of licentiousness.

(Clement, *Protreptic* II 34 5)

Hence Heraclitus reasonably called [phallic ceremonies] rem-
edies, since they will cure our troubles and drain our souls
of the misfortunes of mortal life [B 68].

(Iamblichus, *On the Mysteries* I 119)

> *The Sibyl's raving mouth,* according to Heraclitus, *speaks
> without mirth* [B 92]

or adornment or perfume: with the help of the god her
voice continues for a thousand years.

(Plutarch, *Why the Pythia No Longer Prophesies in Verse*
397 A B)

I think that you too know Heraclitus' remark that the king
whose is the oracle at Delphi neither speaks nor conceals but
indicates [B 93] – attend to these wise words and suppose

that the god here uses the priestess with regard to hearing in the same way as the sun uses the moon with regard to sight.

(ibid 404 DE)

All animals are born, flourish, and die in obedience to the ordinances of god; for

> *every beast is pastured by blows,* [B 11]

as Heraclitus says.

([Aristotle], On the World 401a8–11)

A man may perhaps escape the attention of the visible fire, but the invisible he cannot – for, as Heraclitus says,

> *how could anyone escape the attention of that which never sets?*
> [B 16]

Then let us not wrap ourselves in darkness; for the light is within us.

(Clement, Pedagogue II x 99.5)

I know that Plato, too, supports Heraclitus when he writes:

> *One alone is the wise, unwilling and willing to be called by the name of Zeus.* [B 32]

And again:

> *It is law also to follow the counsel of one.* [B 33]

And if you want to bring in the saying 'He that hath ears to hear, let him hear' [Luke 14: 35], you will find it expressed somewhat as follows by the Ephesian:

> *The uncomprehending, when they hear, are like the deaf: the saying applies to them – though present they are absent.* [B 34]

(Clement, Miscellanies V xiv 115.1–3)

In the fifth group come passages bearing upon psychology: most of them deal with the linked topics of sleep and death.

Does not Heraclitus, like Pythagoras and Socrates in the *Gorgias*, call birth death when he says:

> *Death is what we see awake, sleep what we see abed?* [B 21]

(ibid V xiv 115.1–3)

Heraclitus says that awake we have a common world, asleep each enters a private world [B 89] – but the superstitious have no common and no private world.

(Plutarch, *On Superstition* 166C)

We are all fellow-workers to one end, some knowingly and consciously, others unknowingly – just as Heraclitus, I think, says that even those asleep are workers and fellow-workers in what happens in the world [B 75].

(Marcus Aurelius, *Meditations* VI 42)

And when is death not present in our very selves? As Heraclitus says,

> the same thing is present living and dead, awake and asleep, young and old; for the latter change and are the former, and again the former change and are the latter. [B 88]

([Plutarch], *Consolation to Apollonius* 106E)

What is said of sleep should be understood also of death. For each of them – one more, the other less – shows the absence of the soul, as we can also learn from Heraclitus:

> A man in the night kindles a light for himself, his sight being quenched: living, he kindles the dead; awake, he kindles the sleeping. [B 26]

(Clement, *Miscellanies* IV xxii 141.1–2)

Heraclitus seems to agree with [Socrates in the *Phaedo*] when, speaking of men, he says:

> There await men when they die things they neither expect nor even think of. [B 27]

(*ibid* IV xxii 144.3)

For whom does Heraclitus prophesy? For night-prowlers, magicians, bacchants, revellers, initiates. For them he threatens judgement after death, for them he prophesies fire. For the mystery rites practised among men have impious initiations [B 14].

(Clement, *Protreptic* II xxii 1–2)

Heraclitus is clearly berating birth when he says:
> *Being born, they wish to live and to meet their fates* (or rather,
> to rest) *and they leave behind children, born for their fates.*
> [B 20]

(Clement, *Miscellanies* III iii 14.1)

[Food without salt] is heavy and nauseous to the taste; for
> *corpses should be thrown out more readily than dung,* [B 96]
according to Heraclitus, and meat is corpse or part of a
corpse.

(Plutarch, *Table Talk* 669A)

Orpheus wrote:

> Water is death for souls, . . .
> But from water comes earth, from earth again water,
> and thence soul, rushing to all the ether.

Heraclitus put together the words from these lines and wrote
somewhat as follows:
> *For souls it is death to become water, for water death to become
> earth; but from earth water comes into being, from water soul.*
> [B 36]

(Clement, *Miscellanies* VI ii 17.1–2)

Heraclitus says that for souls it is pleasure or death to become
moist, and that for them the fall into mortal life is pleasure
[B 77]; and elsewhere that we live their death and they live
our death [cf B 62].

(Numenius, fragment 30 des Places, in Porphyry, *The
Cave of the Nymphs* 10)

[Souls on the moon] are nourished by various exhalations,
and Heraclitus was right in saying that souls smell things in
Hades [B 98].

(Plutarch, *On the Face in the Moon* 943E)

Heraclitus well compares the soul to a spider and the body
to a spider's web. Just as a spider, he says, standing in the

middle of its web, is aware as soon as a fly has broken one of its threads and runs there quickly as though grieving over the cutting of the thread, so a man's soul, when some part of his body is hurt, hurries quickly there as if unable to bear the hurt to the body to which it is firmly and proportionately joined [B 67a].

(Hisdosus, *On Plato's World-Soul* 17v)

The sixth group of fragments and reports consists of a few texts which bear upon the issues of natural science — issues which are sketched more fully in the doxographical report in Diogenes Laertius' Life.

Heraclitus of Ephesus is most clearly of this opinion [i.e. that everything will change into fire]. He holds that there is a world which is eternal and a world which is perishing, and he is aware that the created world is the former in a certain state. Now that he recognized that the world which is uniquely characterized by the totality of substance is eternal, is evident when he says:

> *The world, the same for all, neither any god nor any man made; but it was always and is and will be, fire ever-living, kindling in measures and being extinguished in measures.* [B 30]

And that he believed it to be generated and destructible is indicated by the following words:

> *Turnings of fire: first, sea; of sea, half is earth, half lightning-flash.* [B 31a]

— He says in effect that, by reason and god which rule everything, fire is turned by way of air into moisture, the seed, as it were, of creation, which he calls sea; and from this, again, come earth and heaven and what they contain. He shows clearly in the following words that they are restored again and become fire:

> *Sea is dissolved and measured into the same proportion that existed at first.* [B 31b]

And the same holds for the other elements.

(Clement, *Miscellanies* V xiv 104.1–5)

The first principle alternately creates the world from itself and again itself from the world, and

> *all things,* Heraclitus says, *are an exchange for fire and fire for all things, as goods are for gold and gold for goods.* [B 90]
> (Plutarch, *On the E at Delphi* 388DE)

They would think it unreasonable if, while the whole heaven and each of its parts all have order and reason in their shapes and powers and periods, there is no such thing in the first principles but the most beautiful world, as Heraclitus says, is like a heap of rubbish aimlessly piled up. [B 124]

> (Theophrastus, *Metaphysics* 7a10–15)

Each of the planets revolves in a single sphere, as though on an island, and preserves its station. For

> *the sun will not overstep its measures,* Heraclitus says, *otherwise the Furies, ministers of justice, will find it out.* [B 94]
> (Plutarch, *On Exile* 604A)

The sun is overseer and guardian of these periods, defining and arbitrating and revealing and illuminating the changes and the seasons which bring all things, according to Heraclitus. [B 100]

> (Plutarch, *Platonic Questions* 1007D)

If, as they say, [the sun] were nourished in the same way [as flames are], then it is clear that the sun is not only, as Heraclitus says, new each day [B 6], but always and continuously new.

> (Aristotle, *Meteorology* 355a13–15)

Heraclitus . . . [says that the sun] as to its size has the breadth of a human foot. [B 3]

> (Stobaeus, *Anthology* I xxv 1g)

Water makes for collaboration and friendship. Heraclitus indeed says that if the sun did not exist it would be night

[B 99]; but we may say that if the sea did not exist man would be the most wild and destitute of animals.

([Plutarch], *Is Fire or Water the More Useful?* 957A)

I have discussed elsewhere whether one should suppose that certain days are unlucky, or whether Heraclitus rightly rebuked Hesiod, who makes some good and others bad, for not recognizing that the nature of every day is the same [B 106].

(Plutarch, *Camillus* 138A)

Heraclitus is better and more Homeric (and like Homer he calls the arctic circle the bear):

Limits of morning and evening are the bear and, opposite the bear, the boundary of bright Zeus [B 120]

– for the arctic circle, not the bear, is the boundary of the sun's rising and setting.

(Strabo, *Geography* I i 6)

Some think that the smoky exhalation is smell, since it is composed of earth and air. That is why Heraclitus said that if all the things that exist were to become smoke the nose would distinguish them [B 7].

(Aristotle, *On the Senses and their Objects* 443a22–25)

Finally, there are some items which could be reckoned as belonging to moral and political philosophy:

For 'The law is not made for a righteous man', say the Scriptures [I Timothy 1:9]. Thus Heraclitus rightly says:

They would not know the name of justice if these things did not exist, [B 23]

and Socrates says that law would not have come into being for the sake of the good.

(Clement, *Miscellanies* IV iii 10.1)

Heraclitus said that a man's character is his fate. [B 119]

(Stobaeus, *Anthology* IV xl 23)

Worse men have conquered better, but to set up in your soul a victory monument over anger – with which Heraclitus says it is hard to fight, for

whatever it wants, it buys with soul [B 85]

– that is a mark of great and victorious power.

(Plutarch, *The Control of Anger* 457D)

Next, Heraclitus says:

Gods and men honour those slain in battle. [B 24]

(Clement, *Miscellanies* IV iv 16.1)

For

greater fates win greater shares, [B 25]

according to Heraclitus.

(*ibid* IV vii 49.3)

Envy, the greatest of political ills, scarcely attacks old age; for

dogs bark at those they do not know, [B 97]

according to Heraclitus, and envy attacks the beginner at the door of office.

(Plutarch, *Should Old Men Take Part in Politics?* 787C)

If we hear that one swallow does not make a summer, yet you do so – for you excel all the other swallows. For if, as Heraclitus says, one man is worth ten thousand if he is the best [B 49], then surely one swallow should be reckoned as worth ten thousand if it is well chosen.

(Theodorus Prodromus, *Letters* 1 [*Patrologia Graeca* XXXIII 1240A])

Always remember Heraclitus' view that the death of earth is to become water, and the death of water to become air, and of air fire, and the reverse. Remember too the man who forgets where the road leads [B 71]; and that most are at odds with that with which they most constantly associate – the account which governs the universe – and that what they meet with every day seems foreign to them [B 72]; and that we should not act and speak like those asleep [B 73] – for then too we think we act and speak; and that we should not behave like children of our parents [B 74] – i.e., in plain prose, in the way in which we have been brought up.

(Marcus Aurelius, *Meditations* IV 46)

PART
II

9
PARMENIDES

Parmenides, son of Pyres, came from Elea, a Greek foundation in southern Italy. He was of a noble family, and it is reported that 'he organized his own country by the best laws, so that each year the citizens still get the officials to swear that they will abide by Parmenides' laws' *(Plutarch, Against Colotes 1126AB). His dates are uncertain: the Greek chroniclers put his birth in 540 BC, but a passage in Plato (which will be quoted in the chapter on Zeno) suggests that he was born in about 515.*

According to Diogenes Laertius,

He was a pupil of Xenophanes but did not follow him. He was also associated (as Sotion said) with Ameinias, son of Diochaitas, the Pythagorean, a poor man but of good character. It was rather Ameinias that he followed, and when he died he set up a shrine for him, since he came from a famous and wealthy family, and he was led to calm by Ameinias and not by Xenophanes.

(Diogenes Laertius, *Lives of the Philosophers* IX 21)

The story about Ameinias has led some scholars to look (in vain) for Pythagorean elements in Parmenides' thought.

Parmenides produced one short work written in ungainly hexameter verse. A substantial proportion of the poem survives. It opened with a fanciful prologue, after which the main body of the work divided into two parts: the first part, the Way of Truth, gives Parmenides' own views about the true nature of reality, the second part, the Way of Opinion, followed the traditional Ionian pattern of works On Nature.

The prologue and most of the Way of Truth survive; there are frag-
ments of the Way of Opinion.

  It should be said at the outset that Parmenides' poem is in many ways
a bizarre and puzzling production. He presents an account the second
half of which, the Way of Opinion, is confessedly 'deceitful' or false,
and he does not clearly explain why he has written these lies. The Way
of Truth is not intended to be deceitful, but the views it advocates are
paradoxical in the extreme. Moreover, Parmenides is never an easy
writer. His meaning is rarely plain to the first glance, and some lines
of the poem are obscure to the point of unintelligibility. There are
also textual uncertainties. Nonetheless, Parmenides had, through the
medium of Plato, an unrivalled influence on the course of western
philosophy.

  The prologue is preserved by Sextus Empiricus, who also offers an
allegorical interpretation of Parmenides' verses which I shall not tran-
scribe.

Xenophanes' friend Parmenides condemned the reason
associated with belief, which has weak opinions, and, since he
also gave up trust in the senses, supposed that the reason
associated with knowledge, or infallible reason, was the crit-
erion of truth. Thus at the beginning of his *On Nature* he writes
in this way:

> The mares that carry me as far as my heart may aspire
> were my escorts: they had guided me and set me on the celebrated
>   road
> of the god which carries the man of knowledge *. . .*
> There was I being carried; for there the wise mares were carrying
>   me,
> straining at the chariot, and maidens were leading the way.
> The axle in the axle-box roared from its socket
> as it blazed – for it was driven on by two whirling
> wheels on either side – while the maidens, daughters of the sun,
> hastened to escort it, having left the house of Night
> for the light and pushed back with their hands the veils from their
>   heads.
>   Here are the gates of the paths of Night and Day,
> and a lintel and a stone threshold enclose them.

They themselves, high in the air, are filled by great doors,
and all-avenging Justice holds their alternate keys.
Her the maidens appeased with soft words,
skilfully persuading her to push back for them the bolted bar
swiftly from the gates. They flew back
and made a yawning gap between the doors, swinging
in turn in their sockets the bronze pivots,
fitted with pegs and pins. And through them
the maidens held the chariot and mares straight on the highway.

And the goddess graciously received me, taking
my right hand in hers; and she spoke thus and addressed me:
'Young man, companion to the immortal charioteers
with the mares who carry you as you come to my house,
I greet you. For no evil fate was sending you to travel
this road (for indeed it is far from the tread of men)
but Right and Justice. You must learn all things,
both the unwavering heart of persuasive truth
and the opinions of mortals in which there is no true trust.'
[28 B 1.1–30]

(Sextus Empiricus, *Against the Mathematicians* VII 111)

Simplicius adds two further lines:

Parmenides says:

You must learn all things,
both the unwavering heart of well-rounded truth
and the opinions of mortals in which there is no true trust.
But nevertheless you will learn these things too — how what seems
had reliably to be, forever traversing everything. [B 1.28–32]

(Simplicius, *Commentary on On the Heavens* 557.24–558.2)

A couplet from the prologue is quoted by Proclus, who then cites a
further eight lines:

Plato explicitly distinguishes different types of reason and
knowledge, corresponding to the different objects of knowledge. Parmenides too, though his poetry makes him obscure,
nevertheless points in this direction himself when he says:

> Both the unwavering heart of well-lit truth
> and the opinions of mortals in which there is no true trust;
> [B 1.29–30]

and again:

> But come, I will tell you – preserve the account when you hear
>   it –
> the only roads of enquiry there are to be thought of:
> one, that it is and cannot not be,
> is the path of persuasion (for truth accompanies it);
> another, that it is not and must not be –
> this I say to you is a trail devoid of all knowledge. [B 2.1–6]

And:

> For you could not recognize that which is not (for it is not to be
>   done),
> nor could you mention it. [B 2.7–8]
>
> >   (Proclus, *Commentary on the Timaeus* I 345.11–27)

*[Note that in B 1.29 Sextus, Simplicius and Proclus attach different
adjectives to the noun 'truth'.]*
   *The half-line at the end of fragment B 2 can be completed, both metri-
cally and philosophically, by a half-line preserved elsewhere:*

At an earlier date, Parmenides too touched on this doctrine
inasmuch as he identified being and thought and did not locate
being in sensible objects. He said:

> For the same things can be thought of and can be. [B 3]
>
> >   (Plotinus, *Enneads* V i 8)

   *The next surviving lines of the poem can be patched together from
two separate passages in Simplicius. One of them, which assembles a
few short quotations from Parmenides, includes these sentences:*

That there is one and the same account of everything, the
account of what is, Parmenides states in the following words:

> What is for being and for thinking must be; for it can be,
> and nothing can not. [B 6.1–2]

Now if whatever anyone says or thinks is being, then there will
be one account of everything, the account of what is.

>   (Simplicius, *Commentary on the Physics* 86.25–30)

The second passage begins by quoting B 2 (except for the first line) and continues thus:

That contradictories are not true together he shows in the verses in which he finds fault with those who identify opposites. For having said:

> *for it can be,*
> *and nothing can not. This I bid you say.*
> *For from this first road of inquiry <I restrain> you,* [B 6.1–3]

<he adds:>

> *and then from the road along which mortals who know nothing*
> *wander, two-headed; for impotence in their*
> *breasts guides their erring mind. And they are borne along*
> *alike deaf and blind, amazed, undiscerning crowds,*
> *for whom to be and not to be are deemed the same*
> *and not the same; and the path of all turns back on itself.*
> [B 6.4–9]

> > *(ibid* 117.2–13)

A continuous passage of some sixty-six verses, which includes perhaps the whole of the Way of Truth, can be put together from three sources. The first two lines are quoted by Simplicius, and also, much earlier, by Plato:

When we were boys, my boy, the great Parmenides would testify against this [namely the view that what is not is] from beginning to end, constantly saying both in prose and in verse that:

> *Never will this prevail, that what is not is:*
> *restrain your thought from this road of inquiry.* [B 7.1–2]

> > (Plato, *Sophist* 237A)

Plato's quotation is continued by Sextus (though Sextus himself quotes the lines as though they were continuous with B 1):

> *Restrain your thought from this road of inquiry,*
> *and do not let custom, based on much experience, force you along*
> *   this road,*
> *directing unobservant eye and echoing ear*

and tongue; but judge by reason the battle-hardened proof
which I have spoken. Only one story, one road, now
  is left. [B 7.2–6]
  (Sextus Empiricus, *Against the Mathematicians* VII 111)

Sextus' quotation in turn is continued by Simplicius:

At the risk of seeming prolix, I would like to transcribe in this commentary Parmenides' verses on the one being (they are not many), both to justify what I have said about the matter and because of the rarity of Parmenides' treatise. After he has done away with what is not, he writes:

  Only one story, one road, now
is left: that it is. And on this there are signs
in plenty that, being, it is ungenerated and indestructible,
whole, of one kind and unwavering, and complete.
Nor was it, nor will it be, since now it is, all together,
one, continuous. For what generation will you seek for it?
How, whence, did it grow? That it came from what is not I shall
    not allow
you to say or think — for it is not sayable or thinkable
that it is not. And what need would have impelled it,
later or earlier, to grow — if it began from nothing?
Thus it must either altogether be or not be.
Nor from what is will the strength of trust permit it
to come to be anything apart from itself. For that reason
Justice has not relaxed her fetters and let it come into being or
    perish,
but she holds it. Decision in these matters lies in this:
it is or it is not. But it has been decided, as is necessary,
to leave the one road unthought and unnamed (for it is not a true
road), and to take the other as being and being genuine.
How might what is then perish? How might it come into being?
For if it came into being it is not, nor is it if it is ever going to be.
Thus generation is quenched and perishing unheard of.
  Nor is it divided, since it all alike is —
neither more here (which would prevent it from cohering)
nor less; but it is all full of what is.

Hence it is all continuous; for what is approaches what is.

And unmoving in the limits of great chains it is beginningless
and ceaseless, since generation and destruction
have wandered far away, and true trust has thrust them off.
The same and remaining in the same state, it lies by itself,
and thus remains fixed there. For powerful necessity
holds it enchained in a limit which hems it around,
because it is right that what is should be not incomplete.
For it is not lacking — if it were it would lack everything.

The same thing are thinking and a thought that it is.
For without what is, in which it has been expressed,
you will not find thinking. For nothing either is or will be
other than what is, since fate has fettered it
to be whole and unmoving. Hence all things are a name
which mortals lay down and trust to be true —
coming into being and perishing, being and not being,
and changing place and altering bright colour.

And since there is a last limit, it is completed
on all sides, like the bulk of a well-rounded ball,
equal in every way from the middle. For it must not be at all
*   greater*
or smaller here or there.

For neither is there anything which is not, which might stop it
*   from reaching*
its like, nor anything which is in such a way that it might be
more here or less there than what is, since it all is, inviolate.
Therefore, equal to itself on all sides, it lies uniformly in its limits.

Here I cease for you my trustworthy argument and thought
about the truth. Henceforward learn mortal opinions,
listening to the deceitful arrangement of my words. [B 8.1–52]

These, then, are Parmenides' verses about the one. After them
he next discusses the objects of opinion, laying down for them
different first principles.

(Simplicius, *Commentary on the Physics* 144.25–146.27)

Two other short fragments have been thought to come from the Way
of Truth, though it is hard to see where they should be inserted.

Parmenides too in his poem riddles about Hope in these words:

> Look at things which, though absent, are yet present firmly to the
>   mind;
> for you will not cut off for yourself what is from holding to what
>   is,
> neither scattering everywhere in every way about the world
> nor coming together. [B 4]

For one who hopes, like one with faith, sees with his mind the objects of thought and the things to come.

(Clement, *Miscellanies* V iii 15.5)

Parmenides, as I have said before, saw being itself in that which is separated from all and the highest of all beings, in which being was primarily manifested; but he was not unaware of the plurality of intelligible objects. For it is he who says:

> For what is approaches what is, [B 8.25]

and again:

> it is indifferent to me
> whence I begin, for there again shall I return, [B 5]

and elsewhere:

> equal from the middle [B 8.43]

– in all these passages he shows that he actually supposes there to be *many* intelligible objects.

(Proclus, *Commentary on the Parmenides* 708.7–22)

The first lines of the Way of Opinion are preserved by Simplicius:

Having completed his account of the intelligible realm, Parmenides continues thus:

> Here I cease for you my trustworthy argument and thought
> about the truth. Henceforward learn mortal opinions,
> listening to the deceitful arrangement of my words.
>   For they determined in their minds to name two forms,
> of which one they should not – and that is where they have erred.
> And they distinguished them as opposite in form and set up signs
>   for them
> separately from one another, here the ethereal flame of fire,
> gentle, very light, in every direction the same as itself

*and not the same as the other; and that other in itself
is opposite – unknowing night, dense in form and heavy.
This whole fitting arrangement I tell you
so that a mortal mind may never outstrip you.* [B 8.50–61]

Now he calls this account a matter of opinion and deceitful not
because it is simply false but because he has moved from the
intelligible world of truth into the perceptible realm of
appearance and seeming. A little later, having discussed the
two elements, he continues by mentioning the active cause:

*The narrower [bands] are full of unmixed fire,
the next with night (but a portion of flame is emitted),
and in the middle of them, a goddess who governs all things.*
[B 12.1–3]

He says that she is actually the cause of the gods –

First of all the gods she devised Love [B 13]

etc. He says that she sends souls sometimes from light to darkness and sometimes in the other direction.

I am compelled to write at length on this point because
people now are generally ignorant of the ancient writings.

(Simplicius, *Commentary on the Physics* 38.29–39.21)

*Some idea of the contents of the Way of Opinion can be gained from
a passage in Plutarch:*

But Parmenides did not abolish fire or water or precipices
or – *pace* Colotes – the cities of Europe and Asia. After all, he
composed a cosmology, and by mixing the bright and the dark
as elements he produces from them and by them all the
phenomena. He has much to say about the earth and the sky
and the moon and the stars, and he has an account of the
origins of men: like an old natural philosopher, who is compos-
ing a book of his own and not criticizing a book of someone
else, he has left nothing of any importance unsaid.

(Plutarch, *Against Colotes* 1114 BC)

*Simplicius had earlier quoted a slightly longer version of fragment
B 12:*

The next with night (but a portion of flame is emitted),

and in the middle of them, a goddess who gòverns all things.
For she rules the hateful birth and copulation of all things,
sending female to mingle with male and again conversely
male to female. [B 12]

        (Simplicius, *Commentary on the Physics* 31.13–17)

The 'bands' of B 12 are described in more detail in a doxographical
passage:

Parmenides says that there is a sequence of bands embracing
one another, one from the rare, one from the dense, and
others between them mixed from light and darkness. What
surrounds them all, like a wall, is solid, and beneath it is a fiery
band. So too what is in the middle of them all, around which
is a fiery band. Of the mixed bands the middlemost is cause of
all motion and coming into being for all of them: this he calls
the governing goddess and the keyholder, Justice and Necessity. The air is a secretion of the earth, vaporized by its more
violent compression. The sun and the circle of the Milky Way
are exhalations of fire. The moon is a mixture of both – air
and fire. The ether surrounds them, above everything; under
it is arranged the fiery part we call the sky, and under that the
regions around the earth.

        (Stobaeus, *Anthology* I xxii 1a)

There are a few further fragments from the Way of Opinion. Sim-
plicius reports a curiosity:

In the middle of the verses a short passage in prose is inserted
which purports to come from Parmenides himself. It goes like
this:

> *Next to this are the rare and the hot and brightness and the soft*
> *and the light; next to the dense are named the cold and darkness*
> *and hard and heavy; for these have been separated off, each group*
> *in its own way.*

        (Simplicius, *Commentary on the Physics* 31.3–7)

No doubt Simplicius is right to be sceptical about the authenticity of
this prose fragment.

Simplicius quotes the beginning of the Way in another passage; there he adds:

And again a little later:
> *And since all things have been named light and night*
> *and things corresponding to their powers [have been named] for*
>   *each,*
> *everything is full alike of light and invisible night,*
> *both equal since nothing has a share in neither.* [B 9]
>
> *(ibid* 180.8–12)

But they both [sc. Parmenides and Melissus] clearly refer to the generation of perceptible objects – Melissus when he says that the cold becomes hot etc . . .; and Parmenides, beginning his remarks about perceptible objects, says he will tell
> *how earth and sun and moon*
> *and the common ether and the Milky Way and outermost Olympus*
> *and the hot force of the stars were impelled*
> *to come into being.* [B 11]

And they have described the generation of things that are born and die, right down to the parts of animals.
>   (Simplicius, *Commentary on On the Heavens* 559.18–27)

Once he has attained to the true teaching [sc. of Christ] let who will listen to the promises of Parmenides of Elea:
> *You will know the nature of the ether and all the signs*
> *in the ether and the bright sun's pure*
> *torch and its destructive works and whence they came into being,*
> *and you will learn the circling works of the round-faced moon*
> *and its nature, and you will know too the sky which encloses it –*
> *whence it grew and how necessity led and fettered it*
> *to hold the limits of the stars.* [B 10]
>   (Clement, *Miscellanies* V xiv 138.1)

Someone who denies that red-hot iron is fire or that the moon is a sun – thinking it rather, with Parmenides,
> *another's light, night-shining, wandering about the earth*
> [B 14] –

139

does not abolish the use of iron or the reality of the moon.
(Plutarch, *Against Colotes* 1116A)

Of the things in the heavens, numerous though they are, only
[the moon] goes about in need of another's light, as Parmenides says,
always gazing at the rays of the sun. [B 15]
(Plutarch, *On the Face in the Moon* 929AB)

Two short passages from the doxography are worth quoting here.

[Parmenides] was the first to say that the earth is spherical and
lies in the middle [of the universe].
(Diogenes Laertius, *Lives of the Philosophers* IX 21)

Parmenides places the Morning Star first in order in the ether
(he thinks that it is the same as the Evening Star). After it comes
the sun, beneath which are the stars in the fiery part which he
calls the sky.
(Stobaeus, *Anthology* I xxiv 2e)

*Next, two fragments on biology, the second of which survives only
in a Latin translation.*

Others of the oldest generation have also said that the male is
conceived in the right part of the womb. Parmenides put it like
this:
In the right boys, in the left girls. [B 17]
(Galen, *Commentary on Hippocrates' Epidemics* XVIIA 1002K)

In the books he wrote *On Nature* Parmenides says that as the
result of conception men are sometimes born soft or smooth.
Since his Greek is in verse, I too shall put the point in verses –
for I have composed some Latin verses, as close to his as I
could, so as to avoid a mixture of languages:
When a man and a woman together mix the seeds of Love,
a power which forms in the veins from the different bloods
produces well-built bodies by preserving the blending.
For if, when the seed is mixed, the powers fight

*and do not combine into one power in the mixed body, then cruelly
will they trouble .he sex that is being born from a twin seed.* [B 18]
(Caelius Aurelianus, *Chronic Diseases* IV 9)

Theophrastus gives an account of Parmenides' ideas about thought.

Parmenides really said nothing at all about [the senses] – only
that there are two elements and that knowledge depends on
which is excessive. For as the hot or the cold exceeds, so
thought becomes different – better and purer when it depends
on the hot, though this too requires a certain proportion-
ality:

> *For as on each occasion,* he says, *is the blending of the wandering
>   limbs,*
> *so stands the mind for men; for it is the same thing*
> *which thinks – the nature of the limbs –*
> *for each and every man; for what exceeds is thought.* [B 16]

For he speaks of perceiving and thinking as the same thing –
that is why he thinks that memory and forgetfulness derive
from these things through their blending. (But he said nothing
further about what happens if they are equal in the mixture –
whether or not it will be possible to think, and what the disposition will be.) That he makes perception too occur by
opposites in their own right is clear from the passage where
he says that corpses do not perceive light, heat and sound
because of the deficiency of fire, but that they *do* perceive their
opposites – cold and silence and so on. And in general, everything which exists has some knowledge.

(Theophrastus, *On the Senses* 3–4)

*Finally, Simplicius preserves three lines from the end of Parmenides'
poem:*

Having described the world of perception, he adds:
> *Thus, according to opinion, these things grew and now are,*

and then, after this, having matured they will cease to be:
and for each of them men laid down a distinctive name. [B 19]
(Simplicius, *Commentary on On the Heavens* 558.8–11)

10
MELISSUS

Melissus came from the island of Samos. In 441 BC Athens made war upon Samos and despatched a fleet to the island. At some point during the protracted operations, Pericles, the Athenian commander, led some of his ships away on an expedition.

When he had sailed off, Melissus, son of Ithagenes, a philosopher who was then in command at Samos, despising the small number of their ships or the inexperience of their commanders, persuaded his fellow-citizens to attack the Athenians. In the battle that followed the Samians were victorious. They captured many men and destroyed many ships, thereby gaining control of the sea and acquiring many supplies for the prosecution of the war which they had not previously possessed. Aristotle says that Pericles himself had earlier been defeated by Melissus in a sea-battle.

(Plutarch, Pericles 166CD)

The Samians were eventually defeated. But Melissus had made a mark on history unusual in a philosopher.

The year of the battle gives us the only known date in Melissus' life: we may suppose that he flourished in the third quarter of the fifth century. In philosophy, he was a follower of Parmenides. His book indeed is in effect a modified version, in clear prose, of Parmenides' poem. Substantial fragments of Melissus' work have survived, all of them preserved by Simplicius. In addition, there are two paraphrases of his whole argument, one in the essay On Melissus, Xenophanes and Gorgias, *falsely ascribed to Aristotle, the other in Simplicius' commentary on Aristotle's* Physics. *It is worth transcribing the latter as a convenient introduction to the fragments.*

Melissus uses the axioms of the natural philosophers and begins his treatise on generation and destruction as follows:

If it is nothing, what could be said about it as though it were something? If it is something, either it came into being or it has always existed. But if it came into being, it did so either from the existent or from the non-existent. But it is not possible for anything to come into being either from the non-existent (not even something else which is nothing, let alone something actually existent) or from the existent (for in that case it would have existed all along and would not have come into being). What exists, therefore, has not come into being. Therefore it has always existed. Nor will what exists be destroyed. For what exists can change neither into the non-existent (the natural scientists agree on this) nor into the existent (for in that case it would still remain and not be destroyed). Therefore it always has existed and will exist.

Since what comes into existence has a beginning, what does not come into existence has not got a beginning. But what exists has not come into being. Therefore it has not got a beginning. Again, what is destroyed has an end, and if something is indestructible it has not got an end. Therefore what exists, being indestructible, has not got an end. But what has neither beginning nor end is in fact infinite. Therefore what exists is infinite.

If something is infinite, it is unique. For if there were two things they could not be infinite but would have limits against one another. But what exists is infinite. Therefore there is not a plurality of existents. Therefore what exists is unique.

If it is unique, it is also changeless. For what is unique is always homogeneous with itself, and what is homogeneous can neither perish nor grow nor change its arrangement nor suffer pain nor suffer anguish. For if it underwent any of these things it would not be homogeneous. For anything that undergoes any change of whatever sort moves from one state into a different one. But nothing is different from what exists. Therefore it will not change. Again, nothing that exists is empty; for what is empty is nothing, and what is nothing cannot exist. So what exists does not move – for it has nowhere to move to if nothing is empty. Nor can it contract into itself. For in that case it would be both rarer and denser than itself, and that is impossible. Rather, what is rare is thereby emptier than what is dense – but what is empty does not exist. One should judge whether what exists is full or not by seeing whether or not it accommodates anything else: if it does not, it is full; if it does, it is not full. Now if it is not empty it is necessarily full; and if so it cannot move – not because it is not possible to move through what is full, as we say in the case of bodies, but because the whole of what exists can move neither into the existent (for there exists nothing apart from it) nor into the non-existent (for the non-existent does not exist).

(Simplicius, *Commentary on the Physics* 103.13–104.15)

All the surviving fragments of Melissus' deduction are preserved by Simplicius.

Melissus showed the ungenerability of what exists, using this common axiom [i.e. the axiom that nothing comes into being from nothing]. He writes as follows:

> Whatever existed always existed and always will exist. For if it had come into being, then necessarily before coming into being it would have been nothing. Now if it had been nothing it would in no way have come to be anything from being nothing. [30 B 1]

(*ibid.* 162.23–26)

Melissus puts the point as follows:

> Now since it did not come into being but exists, it always existed and always will exist, and it has no beginning and no end but is infinite. For if it came into being it would have a beginning (for it would at some time have begun coming into being) and an end (for it would at some time have ceased coming into being). And if if neither began nor ended and always existed and always will

exist, it has no beginning and no end. For what does not exist wholly cannot exist always. [B 2]

. . . Just as he asserts that what has come into being is finite in its being, so he says that what always exists is infinite in its being. He has made this clear when he writes:

But just as it exists always, so in magnitude too it must always be infinite. [B 3]

By magnitude he does not mean extension; for he himself shows that what exists is indivisible:

If what exists has been divided, he says, *it is moving; but if it is moving it does not exist.* [B 10]

Rather, by magnitude he means the eminence of its reality. For he has indicated that he means what exists to be incorporeal in saying:

Now if it exists, it must be one; but being one it must fail to possess a body. [cf B 9]

And he co-ordinates infinity in being with eternity when he says:

Nothing which has a beginning and an end is either eternal or infinite, [B 4]

so that what does not have them is infinite.

From infinity he inferred uniqueness, by way of the notion that if it were not one it would be limited against something else. [B 5]

(Simplicius, *Commentary on the Physics* 109.19–110.6)

Elsewhere, Simplicius reports the inference to uniqueness in Melissus' own words:

And if Melissus entitled his work *On Nature or on What Exists*, it is clear that he thought nature to be what exists and natural objects, i.e. perceptible objects, to be the things that exist. Perhaps that is why Aristotle said that, in declaring what exists to be one, he supposed that there was nothing else apart from perceptible substances. For given that what is perceptible plainly seems to exist, then if what exists is unique there will not exist anything else apart from what is perceptible. Melissus says:

For if it is infinite it will be one. For if it is two, they cannot be infinite, but they will have limits against one another. [B 6]

(Simplicius, *Commentary on On the Heavens* 557.10–17)

But since Melissus wrote in an archaic style but not unclearly, let us set down those archaic sentences themselves so that those who read them may more accurately judge among the more appropriate interpretations. Now, concluding his earlier remarks and introducing his treatment of change, Melissus says:

> *In this way, then, it is eternal and infinite and one and wholly homogeneous. And it will neither perish nor grow larger nor change its arrangement nor suffer pain nor suffer anguish. For if it underwent any of these things it would no longer be one.*

> *For if it alters, necessarily what exists will not be homogeneous but what previously existed will perish and what did not exist will come into being. Now if it were to become altered by a single hair in ten thousand years, it would perish wholly in the whole of time.*

> *Nor can it change in arrangement. For the arrangement which previously existed is not destroyed nor does that which did not exist come into being. And since nothing is added or perishes or alters, how could anything which exists change its arrangement? For if it altered in any way it would thereby also change its arrangement.*

> *Nor does it suffer pain. For if it were in pain it would not exist wholly; for a thing that is in pain cannot exist always, nor does it have equal power with what is healthy. Nor would it be homogeneous were it to suffer pain; for it would suffer pain by the loss or the addition of something, and it would no longer be homogeneous. Nor could what is healthy suffer pain; for the health that existed would perish and that which did not exist would come into being.*

> *As for suffering anguish, the same argument holds as for being in pain.*

> *Nor is it empty in any respect. For what is empty is nothing; and so, being nothing, it would not exist.*

> *Nor does it move. For it has no way to retreat but is full. For if it were empty it would retreat into the empty part, but since it is not empty it has nowhere to retreat. And it will not be dense and*

*rare. For what is rare cannot be as full as what is dense, but what
is* rare *thereby becomes emptier than what is dense. You should
distinguish between what is full and what is not full in this way:
if it yields at all or receives, it is not full; if it neither yields nor
receives, it is full. Now necessarily it is full if it is not empty. So
if it is full it does not move.* [B 7]

That is what Melissus says.

(Simplicius, *Commentary on the Physics* 111.15–112.15)

Their unique existent, being indivisible, will not be finite or
infinite in the way bodies are. For Parmenides places bodies
among the objects of opinion, and Melissus says:

*Being one, it must fail to possess a body. But if it had bulk it would
have parts and would no longer be one.* [cf B 9]

(*ibid* 87.4–7)

*The final fragment shows that Melissus' book contained a critical as
well as a constructive section.*

Melissus, inasmuch as he wrote in prose, gave a clearer account
[than Parmenides] of his own views on [perceptible objects],
both implicitly throughout his argument and explicitly in the
following passage. Having said about what exists that it is one
and ungenerated and motionless and interrupted by no empti-
ness but is wholly full of itself, he continues:

*Now this argument is the greatest sign that there exists just one
thing; but there are also the following signs. If there existed many
things, they would have to be such as I say the one thing is. For
if there exist earth and water and air and fire and iron and gold
and living things and dead and black and white and the other
things that men say are true – if these things exist and we see and
hear correctly, then each of them must be such as it seemed to us
at first, and they cannot change or come to be different, but each
must always be just what it is. But now we are saying that we see
and hear and understand correctly. But what is hot seems to us to
become cold, and what is cold hot, and what is hard soft, and what
is soft hard, and living things seem to die and to come into being
from what is not alive, and all these things seem to change, and*

whatever was and is now seems to be in no way homogeneous, but iron, which is hard, is rubbed away by contact with the fingers, and so are gold and stones and anything else that seems to be strong; and earth and stones seem to come into being from water. [[So that it results that we neither see nor know the things that exist.]]*

Now these things do not agree with one another. For we said that there are many eternal things with forms and strength of their own, but they all seem to us to alter and to change from what they were each time they were seen. So it is clear that we do not see correctly, and that those many things do not correctly seem to exist. For they would not change if they were true, but each would be as it seemed to be; for nothing is stronger than what is true. And if they changed, what exists would have perished and what does not exist would have come into being. In this way, then, if there exist many things, they must be such as the one thing is. [B 8]

Melissus thus clearly explains why they [i.e. Parmenides and Melissus] say that perceptible objects do not exist but seem to exist.

(Simplicius, *Commentary on On the Heavens* 558.17–559.13)

---

* The sentence enclosed in double square brackets appears here in our manuscripts of Simplicius; but it is clearly out of place and should probably be deleted.

11
ZENO

Zeno came from Elea. He was a friend, and in some sense a disciple, of Parmenides. We know nothing about his life and a precise chronology escapes us. Plato tells a story of an encounter between Zeno and Socrates: although the reliability of the narrative is a matter of dispute, the passage is worth quoting at length.

According to Antiphon, Pythodorus said that Zeno and Parmenides once came [to Athens] for the festival of the Great Panathenaea. Parmenides was already a very old man, white-haired but of distinguished appearance – he was about sixty-five years old. Zeno was then nearly forty, tall and pleasing to look at – he was said to have been Parmenides' lover. They were staying with Pythodorus, outside the city wall in the Ceramicus. There Socrates and a few others visited them, eager to hear Zeno's writings – for this was the first time they had been brought by them to Athens. Socrates was then very young.

Zeno himself read to them, while Parmenides happened to be out. There was only very little of the argument still left to be read, Pythodorus said, when he himself came back and with him Parmenides and Aristotle (who became one of the thirty tyrants); so they heard just a little of the writings – although Pythodorus himself had actually heard Zeno before.

When Socrates had heard him out, he asked Zeno to read again the first hypothesis of the first argument. When it had been read he said: 'Zeno, what do you mean? Are you saying that if more things than one exist, then they must be both similar and dissimilar, but that is impossible – for dissimilar things cannot be similar or similar things dissimilar?'

'Yes,' said Zeno.

'So that if it is impossible for dissimilar things to be similar and similar things dissimilar, it cannot be that more things than one exist. For if several things did exist, they would have impossible properties. Is this what your arguments are aiming at – at contesting, against everything that people say, that there do not exist more things than one? And do you take each of your arguments to be evidence for that very conclusion, so that you suppose yourself to provide as many pieces of evidence as you have composed arguments to show that there do not exist several things? Is that what you mean, or have I misunderstood you?'

'No,' said Zeno, 'you have grasped perfectly the overall aim of the book.'

'I see, Parmenides,' said Socrates, 'that Zeno here wants to be associated with you not only by his love for you but also by his treatise. For he has in a way written the same thing as you, although by changing it he is trying to mislead us into thinking that he is saying something different. *You* say in your poems that the universe is one, and you produce excellent evidence for that view. *He* says that there do not exist several things, and he too produces many impressive pieces of evidence. One of you says that one thing exists, the other that there do not exist several things, and each of you expresses himself in such a way that you seem not to be saying the same things at all even though you *are* saying pretty well the same things – something which seems to be above the heads of the rest of us.'

'Yes, Socrates,' said Zeno; 'but you haven't altogether grasped the truth about my book. Like a Spartan hound, you are good at chasing and tracking down what I have said. But, first, you haven't seen that my book isn't really so very conceited – I did not write with the intention you describe only to hide the fact from people, as though that were a great achievement. You have mentioned an accidental feature of the book: in truth it is a sort of defence of Parmenides' arguments against those who try to ridicule him on the grounds that if there exists only one thing then the argument leads to many absurd and contradictory conclusions. My book attacks those who say that several things exist, aiming to show that their hypothesis, that several things exist, leads to even more ridiculous results, if you examine it properly, than the hypothesis that only one thing exists. It was with that sort of ambition that I wrote it when I was young. After it was written someone stole it, so that I could not even consider whether it should be brought out into the light or not.'

(Plato, *Parmenides* 127A–128D)

Zeno's treatise consisted of a series of arguments designed to show that the common sense 'hypothesis' that there are several things in existence leads to absurdity. Later sources say that there were forty arguments in all. There are substantial fragments of two of those arguments; Aristotle provides a critical paraphrase of four more of them; and we possess accounts of a further two.

The fragments are all preserved in Simplicius' commentary on the Physics. *Simplicius is discussing a passage where Aristotle refers to two arguments, the argument that 'everything is one' and the argument 'from dichotomy'. The passage was understood in different ways by Aristotle's commentators, and Simplicius' citations of Zeno occur in his survey of their dispute.*

Alexander says that the second argument, from the dichotomy, is Zeno's and that he claims that if what exists has magnitude and is divided, then it will be many and no longer one, thus proving that the one does not exist . . . Alexander seems to have taken his opinion that Zeno does away with the one from Eudemus' writings. For in his *Physics* Eudemus says:

Then does this not exist although some one thing does exist? That was the puzzle. They report that Zeno said that he would be able to talk about what exists if only someone would explain to him what on earth the one was. He was puzzled, it seems, because each perceptible item is called many things both by way of predication and by being divisible into parts, whereas points are nothing at all (for he thought that what neither increases when added nor decreases when subtracted was not an existent thing). Now it is indeed likely that Zeno argued on both sides by way of intellectual exercise (that is why he is called 'two-tongued') and that he actually published arguments of this sort to raise puzzles about the one. But in his treatise, which contains many arguments, he shows in each case that anyone who says that several things exist falls into inconsistencies.

There is one argument in which he shows that if several things exist they are both large and small – so large as to be infinite in magnitude, so small as to have no magnitude at all. Here he shows that what has no magnitude, no mass, and no bulk, does not even exist. For, he says,

> if it were added to anything else, it would not make it larger. For if it is of no magnitude but is added, [the other thing] cannot increase at all in magnitude. Thus what is added will therefore be nothing. And if when it is subtracted the other thing is no smaller – and will not increase when it is added again – then clearly what was added and subtracted was nothing. [29 B 2]

Zeno says this not to do away with the one but in order to show that the several things each possess a magnitude – a magnitude which is actually infinite by virtue of the fact that, because of infinite divisibility, there is always something in front of whatever is taken. And he shows this having first shown that they possess *no* magnitude from the fact that each of the several things is the same as itself and one. (Themistius actually says that Zeno's argument establishes that what exists is one from the fact that it is continuous and indivisible; 'for if it were divided,' he says, 'it would not strictly speaking be one because of the infinite divisibility of bodies.' But Zeno seems rather to say that there do not exist several things.)

Porphyry holds that the argument from dichotomy belonged to Parmenides who attempted to show by it that what exists is one. He writes as follows:

> Parmenides had another argument, the one based on dichotomy, which purports to show that what exists is one thing only and, moreover, partless and indivisible. For were it divisible, he says, let it have been cut in two – and

then each of its parts in two. Since this goes on for ever, it is clear, he says, that either some final magnitudes will remain which are minimal and atomic and infinite in number, so that the whole thing will be constituted from infinitely many *minima*; or else it will disappear and be dissolved into nothing, and so be constituted from nothing. But these consequences are absurd. Therefore it will not be divided but will remain one. Again, since it is everywhere alike, if it is really divisible it will be divisible everywhere alike, and not divisible in one place and not in another. Then let it have been divided everywhere. It is clear, again, that nothing will remain but that it will disappear; and if it is constituted at all, it will again be constituted from nothing. For if anything remains, it will not yet have been divided everywhere. Thus from these considerations too it is evident, he says, that what exists will be indivisible and partless and one . . .

Porphyry is right here to refer to the argument from dichotomy as introducing the indivisible one by way of the absurdity consequent upon division; but it is worth asking whether the argument is really Parmenides' rather than Zeno's, as Alexander thinks. For nothing of the sort is stated in the Parmenidean writings, and most scholars ascribe the argument from dichotomy to Zeno – indeed it is mentioned as Zeno's in Aristotle's work *On Motion* [i.e. *Physics* 239b9]. And why say more when it is actually found in Zeno's own treatise? For, showing that if several things exist the same things are finite and infinite, Zeno writes in the following words:

> *If several things exist, it is necessary for them to be as many as they are, and neither more nor fewer. But if they are as many as they are, they will be finite. If several things exist, the things that exist are infinite. For there are always others between the things that exist, and again others between them. And in this way the things that exist are infinite.* [B 3]

And in this way he has proved infinity in quantity from the dichotomy. As for infinity in magnitude, he proved that earlier in the same argument. For having first proved that if what exists had no magnitude it would not even exist, he continues:

*But if it exists, it is necessary for each thing to have some bulk and
magnitude, and for one part of it to be at a distance from the
other. And the same argument applies to the protruding part. For
that too will have a magnitude, and a part of it will protrude.
Now it is all one to say this once and to say it for ever. For it will
have no last part of such a sort that there is no longer one part in
front of another. In this way if there exist several things it is
necessary for them to be both small and large – so small as not to
have a magnitude, so large as to be infinite.* [B 1]

Perhaps, then, the argument from dichotomy is Zeno's, as
Alexander holds, but he is not doing away with the one but
rather with the many (by showing that those who hypothesize
them are committed to inconsistencies) and is thus confirming
Parmenides' argument that what exists is one.

(Simplicius, *Commentary on the Physics* 138.3–6,
138.29–140.6, 140.18–141.11)

Aristotle discusses four of Zeno's arguments in the Physics. *The
account is concise, and the text in crucial places is uncertain.*

Zeno argues fallaciously. For if, he says, everything is always
at rest when it is in a space equal to itself, and if what is travelling is always in such a space at any instant, then the travelling
arrow is motionless. That is false; for time is not composed of
indivisible instants – nor is any other magnitude.

Zeno's arguments about motion which provide trouble for
those who try to resolve them are four in number.

The first maintains that nothing moves because what is
travelling must first reach the half-way point before it reaches
the end. We have discussed this earlier.

The second is the so-called Achilles. This maintains that the
slowest thing will never be caught when running by the fastest.
For the pursuer must first reach the point from which the
pursued set out, so that the slower must always be ahead of it.
This is the same argument as the dichotomy, but it differs in
that the additional magnitudes are not divided in *half*. Now
it follows from the argument that the slower is not caught,
and the same error is committed as in the dichotomy (in both

arguments it follows that you do not reach the end if the magnitude is divided in a certain way – but here there is the additional point that not even the fastest runner in fiction will reach his goal when he pursues the slowest); hence the solution must also be the same. And it is false to claim that the one ahead is not caught: it is not caught *while it is ahead*, but nonetheless it *is* caught (provided you grant that they can cover a finite distance).

Those, then, are two of the arguments. The third is the one we have just stated, to the effect that the travelling arrow stands still. It depends on the assumption that time is composed of instants; for if that is not granted the inference will not go through.

The fourth is the argument about the bodies moving in the stadium from opposite directions, an equal number past an equal number; the one group starts from the end of the stadium, the other from the middle; and they move at equal speed. He thinks it follows that half the time is equal to its double. The fallacy consists in claiming that equal magnitudes moving at equal speeds, the one past a moving object and the other past a stationary object, travel for an equal length of time. But this is false.

For example, let the stationary equal bodies be AA; let BB be those beginning from the middle, equal in number and in magnitude to them; and let CC be those beginning from the end, equal in number and in magnitude to them and equal in speed to the Bs. It follows that, as they move past one another, the first B and the first C are at the end at the same time. And it follows that the C has travelled past all of them but the B past half of them. Hence the time is half – for each of the two is alongside each for an equal time. At the same time it follows that the first B has travelled past all the Cs; for the first C and the first B will be at opposite ends at the same time (being, as he says, alongside each of the Bs for a time equal to that for which it is alongside each of the As) – because both are alongside the As for an equal time. That is the argument, and it rests upon the falsity we have mentioned.

(Aristotle, *Physics* 239b5–240a18)

Aristotle refers back to his earlier discussion of the first of Zeno's arguments:

Zeno's argument assumes that it is impossible to traverse an infinite number of things, or to touch an infinite number of things individually, in a finite time. But this is false. For both lengths and times – and indeed all *continua* – are said to be infinite in two ways: either by division or in respect of their extremities. Now it is not possible to touch a quantitatively infinite number of things in a finite time, but it *is* possible so to touch things infinite by division. For time itself is infinite in this way. Hence it follows that what is infinite is traversed in an infinite and not in a finite time, and that the infinite things are touched at infinitely not at finitely many instants.

(ibid 233a21–31)

Later authors add nothing to Aristotle's account of these paradoxes. Diogenes Laertius purports to quote a sentence of Zeno's, but most scholars doubt his evidence:

Zeno does away with motion by saying:
> What is moving is moving neither in the place in which it is nor in the place in which it is not. [B 4]

(Diogenes Laertius, *Lives of the Philosophers* IX 72)

Two further Zenonian arguments are referred to by Aristotle and explained in more detail by Simplicius:

It is clear that nothing can be in itself as its primary place. Zeno's puzzle – that if places exist then they will be *in* something – is not difficult to resolve. For nothing prevents the primary place of a thing from being in something else – but not in it as in a place.

(Aristotle, *Physics* 210b22–25)

Zeno's argument seemed to do away with the existence of place. It was propounded as follows: If places exist, they will be in something; for everything that exists is in something. But

157

what is in something is in a place. Therefore places are in
places – and so *ad infinitum*. Therefore places do not exist . . .
Eudemus relates Zeno's view as follows:

> Zeno's puzzle seems to lead to the same conclusion. For
> he claims that everything that exists is somewhere. But if
> places are among the things that exist, where will they be?
> Surely in another place – and that in another, and so on.

(Simplicius, *Commentary on the Physics* 562.3–6, 563.17–20)

Zeno's argument – that any part of a millet-seed makes a
sound – is false; for nothing prevents it from having no effect
at all, in any length of time, on the air which the whole bushel
sets in motion.

(Aristotle, *Physics* 250a19–22)

Having said that if the whole force moved the whole weight a
certain distance in a certain time it does not thereby follow that
half the force will in the same time move the whole weight
half – or any part – of the distance (nor will every part of the
force which moved the whole weight be capable of moving
the whole weight for a given time and over a given distance),
[Aristotle] thus solves the problem which Zeno of Elea put to
Protagoras the sophist. 'Tell me, Protagoras,' he said, 'does
one millet-seed – or the ten-thousandth part of a seed – make
a sound when it falls?' Protagoras said that it did not. 'But,' he
said, 'does a bushel of millet-seed make a sound when it falls
or not?' When he replied that a bushel does make a sound,
Zeno said: 'Well, then, isn't there a ratio between the bushel of
millet-seed and the single seed – or the ten-thousandth part of
a single seed?' He agreed. 'Well, then,' said Zeno, 'will there
not be similar ratios between the sounds? For as are the sound-
ers so are the sounds. And if that is the case, then if the bushel
of millet-seed makes a sound, the single seed – and the ten-
thousandth part of a single seed – will also make a sound.' That
was Zeno's argument.

(Simplicius, *Commentary on the Physics* 1108.14–28)

PART
III

12
EMPEDOCLES

Empedocles came from Acragas in Sicily. His family was rich and distinguished – his grandfather won a victory in the horse-racing at the Olympic Games of 496 BC. His dates are uncertain, since the various figures cited by our sources do not tally with one another. Aristotle allegedly said that he died at the age of sixty: the remainder of our evidence suggests that the period from about 495 BC to about 435 may be roughly right for his life-span.

He was apparently a person of some political importance (the tradition makes him a keen democrat), and in addition he may have worked as a doctor. He wrote several works, all of them in verse, of which the most important were later entitled On Nature *and* Purifications. *Numerous fragments of these works survive, some of them quite lengthy; but the sources rarely ascribe them to one poem rather than the other and rarely indicate the order in which they appeared within their original poem. Questions of ascription and arrangement have greatly exercised scholars, but little progress has been achieved.*

I shall translate first the passages which certainly or probably or perhaps come from On Nature, *and then the passages which certainly or probably or perhaps come from the* Purifications. *I should stress that many of the ascriptions implicit in the following pages are highly uncertain.*

On Nature

The dedication and perhaps the first line of On Nature *are preserved:*

Pausanias, according to Aristippus and Satyrus, was [Empedocles'] lover, to whom he addressed *On Nature*, thus:

Pausanias, son of wise Anchitus, listen . . . [31 B 1]
(Diogenes Laertius, *Lives of the Philosophers* VIII 60)

Empedocles promised Pausanias remarkable powers, and urged him to guard his knowledge carefully:

According to Satyrus, Gorgias says that he himself was present when Empedocles performed magical deeds, and Empedocles himself professes as much – and much else beside – in his poems where he says:

> *What drugs there are for ills and what help against old age*
> *you will learn, since for you alone shall I accomplish all this.*
> *And you will stop the power of the tireless winds which sweep over*
> *   the earth*
> *and destroy the crops with their breath,*
> *and again, if you wish, you will bring on compensating breezes.*
> *And after black rain you will produce a seasonable drought*
> *for men, and after the summer drought you will produce*
> *tree-nurturing streams which live in the ether.*
> *And you will lead from Hades the power of dead men.* [B 111]
> (*ibid* VIII 59)

. . . Such according to Empedocles is the generation and destruction of our world and its composition from good and evil. He says that there is also a third intelligible power which again can be made from these. He writes:

> *For if you press them into your throbbing mind*
> *and watch over them in kindly fashion with pure attentions,*
> *these will indeed all remain with you throughout your life,*
> *and you will gain many others from them; for they themselves will*
> *   increase*
> *each into its character as is the nature of each.*
> *But should you reach out for things of a different kind which*
> *   among men*
> *are numberless and trifling and blunt their thoughts,*
> *they will leave you at once as time revolves,*

desiring to come to their own dear kind;
for know that they all have thought and a share of mind. [B 110]
    (Hippolytus, *Refutation of All Heresies* VII xxix 25–26)

[Empedocles] advises Pausanias, in Pythagorean fashion, to *guard* his doctrines *within a silent mind* [B 5]; and in general, those men think that silence is divine.

    (Plutarch, *Table Talk* 728E)

Empedocles' superior understanding depended on a proper appreciation of the sources of human knowledge:

As for the view that the discernment of truth does not lie with the senses, [Empedocles] writes as follows:
> *For narrow are the devices dispersed over the limbs,*
> *and there are many wretched impediments which blunt the*
>   *thought.*
> *Having seen a small part of life,*
> *swift to die, men rise and fly away like smoke,*
> *persuaded only of what each has met with*
> *as they are driven in every direction. Who then claims to find the*
>   *whole?*
> *These things are not in this way to be seen by men nor to be heard*
> *nor to be grasped in their minds.* [B 2.1–8]

As for the view that truth is not completely unattainable but can be grasped insofar as human reason reaches it, he makes this clear when he continues the lines just quoted:
> *So you, since you have come here,*
> *will learn no more than mortal mind attains to.* [B 2.8–9]

In the following lines he attacks those who pretend to know more and establishes that what is grasped through each sense is trustworthy provided that reason is in charge of it (even though he had earlier run down the reliability of the senses). For he says:
> *But, O gods, turn the madness of these men from my tongue,*
> *and from holy mouths channel forth a pure spring.*
> *And you, Muse of long memory, white-armed maiden,*

I beseech: what it is right for mortals to hear,
send to me, driving the well-reined chariot of piety.
She will not compel you to accept the flowers of reputation and
honour
from mortals on condition that you say more than is holy
with temerity. And then indeed do you sit on the summit of wisdom.
　But come, observe with every device in the way in which each
　thing is clear:
neither hold sight higher in trust than hearing
or resounding hearing above the clarities of the tongue,
nor let any of the other limbs by which thought has a way
be deprived of trust, but think in the way in which each thing is
clear. [B 3]
(Sextus Empiricus, *Against the Mathematicians* VII 122–125)

For the divine, as the poet from Acragas says,
　cannot be approached by the eyes
　of men or grasped by their hands, by which the greatest
　path to persuasion leads to the minds of men. [B 133]
(Clement, *Miscellanies* V xii 81.2)

For most people require proof as a pledge of the truth, not
being satisfied with the bare security which comes from faith:
　But whereas those who are very evil when in power have no trust,
　you, as the assurances from our Muse enjoin,
　must learn, once you have sifted the argument in your breast.
　[B 4]
For evil men, says Empedocles, customarily want to have
power over the truth by distrusting it.

(*ibid* V iii 18.3–4)

　Happy,
then, it seems, according to Empedocles,
　is he who has gained the wealth of divine thoughts,
　wretched he whose beliefs about the gods are dark. [B 132]
(*ibid* V xiv 140.5)

With the invocation to the Muse in fragment B 3 compare:

The just account which strives on the side of Love is called the Muse by Empedocles, and he invokes her to strive on his side, in these lines:

If ever for the sake of some creature of a day, immortal Muse,
it pleased you that my cares should pass through your mind,
now, as I pray, stand by me again, Calliope,
as I reveal a good account about the blessed gods. [B 131]

(Hippolytus, *Refutation of All Heresies* VII xxxi 4)

On Nature described a complex, cyclical history of the universe. Everything is compounded from four elements or 'roots'. The primary moving factors are two powers, Love and Strife. The elements periodically unite into a divine and homogeneous Sphere. The Sphere then dissolves and the world is established in a series of stages. History then reverses itself, and the universe gradually returns to the state of the Sphere. The cosmic cycle rolls on repeatedly, without beginning and without end.

Empedocles' poem contained repetitions and reprises. This is clear in the surviving fragments, and Empedocles himself avows it:

But, lest, as Empedocles puts it, I shall be thought
to attach one heading to another
and not complete a single path in my tales, [B 24]
let me bring my introductory remarks to their appropriate end.

(Plutarch, *On the Decline of Oracles* 418c)

'Twice and thrice for the fine': a proverb, meaning that one should speak often about what is fine. The verse from which the proverb comes is by Empedocles. He says:

For it is fine to speak twice of what one should. [B 25]

(Scholiast to Plato, *Gorgias* 498e)

Two long extracts from Simplicius' commentary on the Physics *provide good accounts of the general structure of Empedocles' cosmic history.*

In the first book of his *Physics* Empedocles talks about the one and the finitely many and the periodic creation and generation and destruction by association and dissociation in the following way:

> I will tell a two-fold story. At one time they grew to be one alone
> from being many, and at another they grew apart again to be
>   many from being one.
> Double is the generation of mortal things, double their passing
>   away:
> one is born and destroyed by the congregation of everything,
> the other is nurtured and flies apart as they grow apart again.
> And these never cease their continual change,
> now coming together by Love all into one,
> now again all being carried apart by the hatred of Strife.
> <Thus insofar as they have learned to become one from many>
> and again become many as the one grows apart,
> to that extent they come into being and have no lasting life;
> but insofar as they never cease their continual change,
> to that extent they exist forever, unmoving in a circle.
>   But come, hear my words; for learning enlarges the mind.
> As I said before when I revealed the limits of my words,
> I will tell a two-fold story. At one time they grew to be one alone
> from being many, and at another they grew apart again to be
>   many from being one —
> fire and water and earth and the endless height of air,
> and cursed Strife apart from them, balanced in every way,
> and Love among them, equal in length and breadth.
> Her you must regard with your mind: do not sit staring with your
>   eyes.
> She is thought to be innate also in the limbs of mortals,
> by whom they think thoughts of love and perform deeds of union,
> calling her Joy by name and Aphrodite,
> whom no-one has seen whirling among them —
> no mortal man. Listen to the course of my argument, which does
>   not deceive:
> these are all equal and of the same age,
> but they hold different offices and each has its own character;
> and in turn they come to power as time revolves.
> And in addition to them nothing comes into being or ceases.

> *For if they were continually being destroyed they would no longer*
> *   exist.*
> *And what could increase this universe? and whence might it*
> *   come?*
> *And where indeed might it perish, since nothing is empty of them?*
> *But these themselves exist, and passing through one another*
> *they become different at different times — and are ever and always*
> *   the same.* [B 17]

Here he says that that which comes from many — from the four elements — is one, and he shows that it exists sometimes when Love is dominant and sometimes when Strife is. For that neither of these completely passes away, is shown by the fact that they are all equal and of the same age and that nothing comes into being in addition to them or ceases. The many from which the one derives are plural — for Love is not the one, since Strife too brings them into unity.

Having mentioned the many other things, he continues by sketching the character of each of them, calling fire Sun, air Brightness and Heaven, and water Rain and Sea. This is what he says:

> *But come, consider these witnesses to my former words,*
> *if anything I said before was incomplete in form:*
> *the sun, hot to see and radiant everywhere,*
> *the divine bodies flooded in heat and shining brightness,*
> *rain everywhere, dark and cold,*
> *and from earth flow forth things firm and solid.*
> *In Anger they have different forms and are all apart,*
> *but in Love they come together and are desired by one another.*
> *For from these comes everything which was and which is and will*
> *   be —*
> *trees spring up, and men and women*
> *and beasts and birds and fish that live in the water*
> *and even gods, long-lived and highest in honour.*
> *For these themselves exist, and passing through one another*
> *they become different; for the mixture interchanges them.* [B 21]

He gave a clear illustration of how different things come from the same elements:

> *Just as painters, when they decorate offerings —*

men well taught by skill in their art —
take the many-coloured pigments in their hands,
and, harmoniously mixing them, some more some less,
make from them shapes resembling all things,
creating trees and men and women
and beasts and birds and fish that live in the sea
and even gods, long-lived and highest in honour:
so let not deceit persuade your mind that there is any other source
for the countless mortal things we see.

But know this clearly, having heard the tale from a god. [B 23]

He considers these many things, and not just Love and Strife, to be in the generated world, as is clear when he says that trees and men and women and beasts have come into being from them. And they change into one another, as he shows when he says:

In turn they come to power as the circle revolves,
and they decline into one another and increase in their allotted
*   turn.* [B 26.1–2]

He indicates that even what comes into being and is destroyed possesses immortality by way of succession when he says:

But insofar as they never cease their continual change,
to that extent they exist forever, unmoving in a circle. [B 17.12–13]

He also hints at a double world – one intelligible and the other perceptible, one divine and the other mortal, one containing things as paradigms and the other as copies. He showed this when he said that not only generated and perishable things are composed of these but so too are the gods (unless this should be explained in terms of Empedoclean usage). In the following verses too you might think he is hinting at a double world:

For they are all in union with their own parts —
Sun and Earth and Heaven and Sea —
which have been separated from them and grown in mortal things.
In the same way, those that are more ready to blend
are made similar by Aphrodite and love one another.
But most hostile are the things which differ most from one another
in birth and blending and moulded shape,

quite unaccustomed to come together and deeply dismal
at their strife-birth because they were born in anger. [B 22]

He shows that they are harmonized even in mortal things, but in the intelligible world they are more united and

are made similar by Aphrodite and love one another. [B 22.5]

And even if this happens everywhere, nevertheless intelligible things are made similar by Love whereas perceptible things are overpowered by Strife and torn further apart and in the blending of their birth they subsist in shapes which are moulded and copied, strife-born and unaccustomed to union with one another.

He also supposed that generation takes place in virtue of some association and dissociation, as is shown by the first passage I set down:

At one time they grew to be one alone
from being many, and at another they grew apart again to be
    many from being one. [B 17.1–2]

See also his remark to the effect that generation and destruction are nothing

but there is only mixing and interchange of what is mixed [B 8.3]
and allotted congregation and flying apart.

(Simplicius, *Commentary on the Physics* 157.25–161.20)

Most think that according to Empedocles Love alone made the intelligible world and Strife alone the perceptible world. But in fact he gives both of them their appropriate functions everywhere, as we can see from his words in the *Physics*, where he says that Aphrodite or Love is a cause of the creative composition of this world too. He calls fire Hephaestus and Sun and Flame, water Rain, air Ether. He says this in many places, including the following verses:

Earth, roughly equal to them, happened together with
Hephaestus and Rain and shining Ether,
anchored in the perfect harbours of Aphrodite,
either a little more earth or less where they were more.
And from them came blood and different forms of flesh. [B 98]

Before these lines he refers in others to the activity of both [Love and Strife] in the same things, as follows:

> When Strife reached the lowest depth
> of the vortex, and Love comes to be in the middle of the whirl,
> in her all these things come together to be one thing only,
> not suddenly, but coming together at will from different directions.
> As they mingle, innumerable types of mortal things pour forth.
> But many stand unmixed among them as they blend –
> those which Strife holds, still aloft; for not completely
> does it all yet stand out at the furthest limits of the circle,
> but parts of it remain in the limbs, and parts have stepped out.
> And as it ever runs out ahead, so ever pursues
> the gentle, immortal onrush of complete Love.
> And at once become mortal those things which formerly learned
> to be immortal,
> and mixed those which formerly were unmixed, interchanging
> their paths.
> As they mingle, innumerable types of mortal things pour forth,
> fitted with every sort of shape, a wonder to see. [B 35.3–17]

Here he clearly says both that mortal things were constructed
by Love and that Strife did not yet all stand outside the areas
where Love predominated.

Again, in the lines where he gives the characteristics of each
of the four elements and of Strife and Love, he clearly refers
to the mixture of both – of Strife and of Love – in all of them.
The lines are these:

> The sun, hot to see and radiant everywhere;
> the divine bodies, flooded in heat and shining brightness;
> rain everywhere, dark and cold;
> and from earth flow forth things firm and solid.
> In Anger they have different forms and are all apart,
> but in Love they come together and are desired by one another.
> For from these comes everything which was and which is and will
> be –
> trees sprang up, and men and women
> and beasts and birds and fish that live in the water,
> and even gods, long-lived and highest in honour. [B 21.3–12]

A little further on he says:

> In turn they come to power as the circle revolves,

*and they decline into one another and increase in their allotted
    turn.
For these themselves exist, and passing through one another
they become men and the other kinds of animals,
now by Love coming together into one arrangement,
now again each carried apart by the hatred of Strife,
until, having grown together as one, they are completely subdued.
Thus insofar as they have learned to become one from many
and again become many as the one grows apart,
to that extent they come into being and have no lasting life;
but insofar as they never cease their continual change,
to that extent they exist forever, unmoving in a circle.* [B 26]

Thus both the one-from-many (which comes about because
of Love) and the many-from-one (which occurs when Strife
predominates) are located by him in this sublunary world too
in which mortal things are found, it being clear that at different times and for different periods now Strife and now Love
dominates.

(Simplicius, *Commentary on the Physics* 31.31–34.8)

*The remaining fragments can best be read as supplements to and
expansions upon the texts quoted by Simplicius in these two passages.
    Certain lines in the passages show that Empedocles was aware of the
Parmenidean objections against generation and change, and that he
hoped to have evaded them. Some further fragments have a Parmenidean background.*

Then Colotes, as though he were talking to an unlettered king,
fastens next on Empedocles:
    *Another thing I will tell you: there is no birth for any
    mortal thing, nor any cursed end in death.
    But there is only mixing and interchange of what is mixed —
    but men name these things birth.* [B 8]

(Plutarch, *Against Colotes* 1111F)

[Empedocles] was so far from upsetting what exists and
fighting against the appearances that he did not even banish
the expressions from ordinary language: rather, he removed

the harmful factual misunderstanding which they cause and
then restored them to current use, in these lines:

> When they come into the air mixed in the form of a man
> or of a kind of wild beast or of a plant
> or of a bird, then people call this coming into being;
> and when they have separated off, this they call wretched fate.
> They do not call things as they should, but I myself also subscribe
> to the convention. [B 9]

Colotes himself cites these lines but does not notice that
Empedocles did not do away with men and beasts and plants
and birds, which he says are produced as the elements mix;
and having pointed out their mistake to those who call this
association and dissociation birth and *wretched fate* and *evil death*
[B 10], he did not disallow the use of the customary expressions
for them.

   Now I do not think that Empedocles is here upsetting our
mode of expression; rather, as I said earlier, he is in substantial
disagreement over generation from the non-existent, which
some call birth. He shows this most clearly in the following
verses:

> Fools – they have no far-ranging thoughts:
> they *suppose that what did not exist before comes into being*
> or that *something may die and perish entirely.* [B 11]

These are verses of one who shouts aloud to all who have ears
that he is not doing away with coming into being but only
with coming into being from what does not exist, nor with
destruction but only with complete destruction, i.e. destruction
into what does not exist. If you wish something gentler than
that savagely simple denunciation, the following passage might
lead you to accuse him of excessive kindness. There Empedocles says:

> No man wise in these things would suppose in his mind
> that while men live – what they call life –
> for so long do they exist and experience ill and good,
> but that before they were made men and after they are dissolved
>   they are nothing. [B 15]

Those are the words not of one who denies that those who
have been born and are living exist, but rather of one who

thinks that both those who have not yet been born and those who have already died exist.

(Plutarch, *Against Colotes* 1113AD]

Again, even if it is quite impossible both for what does not exist to come into being and for what exists to perish, why should not some things nevertheless be generated and others eternal, as Empedocles says? For he too, having admitted all this – namely that

> *from what does not exist nothing can come into being,*
> *and for what exists to be destroyed is impossible and*
> *unaccomplishable –*
> *for it will always remain wherever anyone may fix it* [B 12]

– nevertheless he says that some things are eternal (fire, water, earth, air) while others come and have come into being from them.

([Aristotle], *On Melissus, Xenophanes, Gorgias* 975a36–b6)

Similarly, Empedocles says that all the things that exist are always continuously moving as they associate, and nothing is empty – he says:

> *No part of the universe is empty: whence, then, might anything*
> *come?* [B 13]

And when they have been associated together into a single form, so as to be one, he says that

> *in no respect is it empty, nor yet overfull.* [B 14]

For what prevents them from being carried into one another's places and from moving round simultaneously, one into the place of another, the other into that of another, and something else always changing into that of the first?

(*ibid* 976b23–30)

The four 'roots' or elements are described more than once.

Empedocles [derives everything] from four elements:

> *Hear first the four roots of all things:*
> *bright Zeus, life-bringing Hera, Aidoneus,*

and Nestis, who waters with her tears the mortal fountains. [B 6]
(Sextus Empiricus, *Against the Mathematicians* X 315)

There will be no such thing as growth according to Empedocles – except by way of addition; for fire increases by fire
and earth increases her own form, ether ether. [B 37]
But these are additions, and what grows is not thought to grow in this way.

(Aristotle, *On Generation and Corruption* 333a35–b3)

It is better to think of the ether as containing and binding everything, as Empedocles says:
Come and I will tell you *. . .*
from which all the things we now see came to be:
earth and the billowy sea and the damp air
and the Titan ether, binding everything in a circle. [B 38]
(Clement, *Miscellanies* V viii 48.3)

Some think that [the word *anopaia*] is used instead of 'upward'. They refer to Empedocles, who says of fire
swiftly upward [B 51].

(Eustathius, *Commentary on the Odyssey* I 321)

Love and Strife are generally presented as the twin causal powers in the universe:

The creator and maker of the generation of all generated things is deadly Strife, while the change and departure of generated things from the world and the establishment of the One is the work of Love. Empedocles says of both that they are immortal and ungenerated and never had a beginning of generation – he writes as follows:
For they are as they were before and as they will be, nor ever, I think,
will boundless eternity be emptied of these two. [B 16]
And who are these two? – Love and Strife.

(Hippolytus, *Refutation of All Heresies* VII xxix 9–10)

Perhaps even though Strife predominates in this world and Love in the Sphere, yet both are said to be produced by both. There is no reason why we should not set down some of Empedocles' verses which make this clear:

> But I shall return to the path of songs
> which I traced before, channelling this account from that:
> when Strife reached the lowest depth . . . [B 35.1–3]

. . . Here it is made clear that in the creation of the world Strife draws back and Love predominates when it

> comes to be in the middle of the whirl, [B 35.4]

i.e. of the *vortex*; hence the vortex exists even when Love predominates. It is clear too that some of the elements remain unmixed by Strife, while those that are mixing make mortal animals and plants, since what is mixing is again dissolved. And speaking about the creation of these corporeal eyes, he says:

> From which divine Aphrodite fashioned tireless eyes, [B 86]

and a little later:

> Aphrodite, fitting them with pegs of affection. [B 87]

And explaining why some see better by day and others by night, he says:

> When first they grew together at the hands of Cypris. [B 95]

– He is speaking about the things in this world, as appears from the following verses:

> If your trust was at all deficient on any of these matters –
> how when water and earth and ether and sun
> were blended, and the forms and colours of mortal things came
>   into being
> as many as there are now, fitted together by Aphrodite. [B 71]

And a little later:

> So then Cypris, when she had moistened earth with rain,
> busily making forms, gave it to swift fire to harden. [B 73]

And again:

> Those which are dense inside but loose outside,
> chancing upon such a fluidity in the hands of Cypris . . . [B 75]

I have set down these verses from the first few I hit upon.

(Simplicius, *Commentary on On the Heavens* 529.21–530.11)

For Empedocles says that here too [i.e. in the sublunary world] Love and Strife predominate by turns over men and fish and beasts and birds. He writes as follows:

> *This is plain in the bulk of mortal members:*
> *somtimes by Love they all come together into one,*
> *limbs which the body acquires when life is thriving at its peak;*
> *sometimes again, divided by evil Conflicts,*
> *each wanders apart along the shore of life.*
> *So too is it with plants and fish of the watery halls*
> *and beasts of the mountain lairs and flying gulls.* [B 20]

(Simplicius, *Commentary on the Physics* 1124.9–18)

But, as the ancient scholars noted, Empedocles sometimes ascribes causal powers to the elements themselves, he sometimes invokes the force of necessity and he sometimes appears to allow room in the universe for chance events.

In general, fire divides and separates, water is adhesive and retentive, holding and gluing by its moisture. Empedocles alluded to this every time he referred to fire as *cursed Strife* [cf B 17.19] and to water as *tenacious Love* [B 19].

(Plutarch, *The Primary Cold* 952A)

[Friendship] collects and compacts and conserves, bringing men together by conversation and good will –

> *as when rennet pegs and ties white milk,* [B 33]

as Empedocles says.

(Plutarch, *On Having Many Friends* 95A)

The moist causes the dry to be bounded, and each is a sort of glue for the other, as Empedocles said in his *Physics*,

> *gluing barley with water* [B 34]

– and for this reason the bounded body is made of both.

(Aristotle, *Meteorology* 381b31–382a3)

Eudemus takes it that the period of motionlessness occurs under the dominance of Love during the Sphere, when everything has been collected together,

> *where neither the swift limbs of the sun are discerned,* [B 27.1]

but, as he says,

> in this way it is held fast in the close covering of Harmony,
> a rounded Sphere, rejoicing in its pleasant rest. [B 27.3–4]

When Strife has again begun to predominate, then again motion occurs in the Sphere:

> For all the limbs of the god shook, one after another. [B 31]

What is the difference between saying 'because that is its nature' and saying 'by necessity', without adding any explanation? That is what Empedocles appears to say in the line:

> In turn they come to power as time revolves, [B 17.29]

and again where he makes necessity the cause of what comes into being:

> There is an oracle of necessity, an ancient seal of the gods,
> eternal, sealed by broad oaths. [B 115.1–2]

For he says that each predominates in turn because of necessity and these oaths. Empedocles says this too of the predominance of Strife:

> But when Strife had grown great in the limbs
> and rose to office as the time was completed,
> which was laid down for them in turn by the broad oath . . .
> [B 30]

Now [Aristotle] says that to say this without any explanation is simply to say that 'that was its nature'.

(Simplicius, *Commentary on the Physics* 1183.28–1184.18)

Necessity is unmusical, Persuasion musical – she loves the Muses far more, I should say, than Empedocles' Grace and

> hates intolerable necessity. [B 116]

(Plutarch, *Table Talk* 745D)

Empedocles says that air does not always separate off to the highest point, but as chance has it. At all events, he says in his cosmogony that

> Then it happened to be running in this way, but often otherwise.
> [B 53]

And he says that the parts of animals are mostly formed by chance.

(Aristotle, *Physics* 196a20–24)

Ether was carried upwards not by Strife but, as he sometimes
says, as if by chance –

> Then it happened to be running in this way, but often otherwise
> [B 53]

– and sometimes he says that fire is naturally carried upwards,
while ether, he says,

> sank with long roots into the earth. [B 54]

> (Aristotle, *On Generation and Corruption* 334a1–5)

That [the early natural scientists] had some notion of things
happening by chance is shown by the fact that they sometimes
use the word – as Empedocles says that fire does not always
separate off upwards but as chance has it. Thus he says in his
cosmogony that

> Then it happened to be running in this way, but often otherwise,
> [B 53]

and elsewhere:

> . . . as each happened. [B 59.2]

And he says that most of the parts of animals come about by
chance, as when he writes:

> Earth, roughly equal to them, happened together . . ., [B 98.1]

and again:

> Gentle flame chanced on a little earth, [B 85]

and elsewhere:

> Chancing upon such a fluidity in the hands of Cypris. [B 75.2]

You could produce many other examples of this sort from
Empedocles' *Physics*, such as:

> Thus by the will of chance all things think, [B 103]

and a little later:

> And insofar as the most fine-textured things happened to fall
>   together. [B 104]

But Empedocles, who seems to use chance only in small matters, does not merit much attention, not having explained what
chance is.

> (Simplicius, *Commentary on the Physics* 330.31–331.16)

*The divine and homogeneous Sphere is described in several frag-
ments.*

EMPEDOCLES

About the form which the world has when it is being arranged
by Love he says this:
> There are no two limbs branching from its back,
> no feet, no swift legs, no generative organs:
> it was a Sphere, equal to itself from all directions. [B 29]
>> (Hippolytus, *Refutation of All Heresies* VII xxix 13)

> But he, from all directions equal to himself and completely
>> boundless,
> a rounded Sphere, rejoicing in his pleasant rest. [B 28]
>> (Stobaeus, *Anthology* I xv 2)

That is why the wise man of Acragas, in his criticism of the
stories of anthropomorphic gods told by the poets, said –
speaking in the first instance about Apollo (with whom his
argument was primarily concerned) but also in the same way
about all the gods –
> For no human head is fitted to his limbs,
> no two branches spring from his back,
> no feet, no swift legs, no hairy genitals:
> he is merely a mind, holy and wonderful,
> rushing with rapid thought over the whole world. [B 134]
>> (Ammonius, *Commentary on On Interpretation* 249.1–10)

Beware that you do not introduce Empedocles' Strife, or
rather stir up the old Titans and the Giants against nature,
or long to see that mythical and fearful chaos and horror,
separating everything heavy and everything light,
> where neither the bright form of the sun is seen
> nor the shaggy power of the earth, nor the sea, [cf B 27.1–2]
as Empedocles says.
>> (Plutarch, *On the Face in the Moon* 926E)

*The development of the world included a bizarre phase in which
monstrosities of various sorts came into being:*

[Aristotle] asks whether there could not then have been a

179

disorderly motion which produced mixtures . . . of the sort
which Empedocles says came about in the reign of Love:

Here many neckless heads sprang up. [B 57.1]

. . . But how could a 'neckless head' and the other things
described by Empedocles in the lines:

Naked arms strayed about, devoid of shoulders,

and eyes wandered alone, begging for foreheads, [B 57.2–3]

and many other things – how could these signify *mixtures*, when
they are certainly not examples of mixtures from which natural
objects are compounded? . . . But perhaps Empedocles does
not mean that these things come about under the predominance of Love (as Alexander thought) but rather at the time
when Strife does not yet

all stand out at the furthest limits of the circle,

but parts of it remain in the limbs, and parts have stepped out.

And as it (he means Strife) *ever runs out ahead, so ever pursues*

the gentle, immortal onrush of complete Love. [B 35.10–13]

So in *this* world the limbs, still 'single-membered' from the
dissociation of Strife, wandered about and desired to mix with
one another.

But when, he says, *god mingled more with god*

– when Love achieved complete predominance over Strife –

these things came together as each happened,

and many others in addition to these were continuously born.
[B 59]

Thus Empedocles said that the former phenomena occur in
the reign of Love not in the sense that Love was already pre-
dominant but in the sense that she was about to predominate
and was still showing unmixed and single-limbed things.

(Simplicius, *Commentary on On the Heavens* 586.6–7, 10–12,
29–587.4, 12–26)

In the second book of his *Physics*, before discussing the
articulation of male and female bodies, Empedocles has these
lines:

Come now, hear how the shoots of men and pitiable women

were raised at night by fire, as it separated,

thus – for my story does not miss the mark, nor is it ill-informed.

First, whole-natured forms sprang up from the earth,
having a portion of both water and heat.
Fire sent them up, wishing to come to its like,
and they showed as yet no desirable form in their limbs,
nor any voice, nor member native to man. [B 62]
(Simplicius, *Commentary on the Physics* 381.29–382.3)

Empedocles the natural scientist, who also speaks of the peculiarities of animals, says that some hybrids were generated, different in the blending of their forms but connected by the unity of their bodies. These are his words:

Many grew double-headed, double-chested —
man-faced oxen arose, and again
ox-headed men — creatures mixed partly from male
partly from female form, fitted with dark limbs. [B 61]
(Aelian, *The Nature of Animals* XVI 29)

These things — and many others more dramatic — are like the monsters of Empedocles they laugh at — the *lumberers with countless hands* [B 60] and the *man-faced oxen.* [B 61.2]
(Plutarch, *Against Colotes* 1123B)

Within the natural world, Empedocles' 'physics' and his 'chemistry' depend on a theory of effluences and channels:

Consider the matter, then, having with Empedocles recognized that

there are effluences from all things that have come into being
[B 89]
— for not only animals and plants and earth and sea, but stones too, and bronze and iron, continuously give off numerous streams.

(Plutarch, *Scientific Explanations* 916D)

Empedocles said that in all sublunary things — water, oil, etc. — channels and solid parts are mingled. He called the channels hollow and the solid parts dense. Where the solid parts and the channels, i.e. the hollow and the dense parts, are commensurate in such a way as to pass through one another, he said that mixing and blending take place (e.g. water and wine), but where they are incommensurate, he said they do not mix (e.g. water and oil); for he says

> *water is more suited to wine, but with oil*
> *it will not.* [B 91]

And applying this to all bodies, he attempted to explain the sterility of mules.

([Philoponus], *Commentary on the Generation of Animals* 123.13–21)

A varied diet sends from itself into the mass of the body numerous qualities and gives to each part what is appropriate; so that there occurs what Empedocles described:

> *thus sweet grasped sweet and bitter set upon bitter,*
> *sharp went to sharp, and hot rode on hot.* [B 90]

(Plutarch, *Table Talk* 663A)

Different things are appropriate and fitting to different things, as beans and purple or nitre and saffron seem to make a mixed dye –

> *The gleam of bright saffron is mixed with dark purple,* [B 93]

as Empedocles said.

(Plutarch, *On the Decline of Oracles* 433B)

The remaining fragments of On Nature *describe the natural world. I group them here under seven thematic headings.*

Astronomy

Empedocles expresses their difference charmingly:

> *sharp-arrowed sun and gentle moon.* [B 40]

(Plutarch, *On the Face in the Moon* 920C)

Apollo is called Eleleus because he turns [*elittesthai*] round the earth . . . or because he orbits in a collected mass of fire, as Empedocles says:

Hence, collected together, he orbits the great heaven. [B 41]
(Macrobius, *Saturnalia* I xvii 46)

The moon herself is invisible then, and she often hides the sun and makes it disappear –
she cuts off his rays,
as Empedocles says,
as he travels above, and casts a shadow on the earth
as great as the breadth of the bright-eyed moon. [B 42]
(Plutarch, *On the Face in the Moon* 929C)

Just as sounds when reflected give an echo duller than the original voice, and the blows of ricocheting missiles strike with less violence,
so the light, having struck the broad circle of the moon, [B 43]
flows weakly and dimly to us.

(*ibid* 929E)

You Stoics laugh at Empedocles when he says that the sun, which is produced about the earth by the reflection of heavenly light, again
shines back on Olympus with fearless face. [B 44]
(Plutarch, *Why the Pythia No Longer Prophesies in Verse* 400B)

The general view holds that the moon is nearest, since they say that it is actually a fragment from the sun – so Empedocles:
In a circle round the earth she winds, another's light. [B 45]
(Achilles, *Introduction to Aratus* 16)

[The moon] pretty well touches the earth and, orbiting near her,
turns like the track of a chariot, [B 46]
as Empedocles puts it.

(Plutarch, *On the Face in the Moon* 925B)

'Holy [*ages*]': this is taken from the compound *euages* or *pan-ages*. Empedocles:
She observes the holy circle of her king opposite her. [B 47]
(*Anecdota Graeca* [ed. Bekker] I 337.13–15)

Part of the earth blocks the sun as it travels beneath it and, as Empedocles says:

> Earth makes night by standing in the way of the light. [B 48]

(Plutarch, *Platonic Questions* 1006E)

In the dark air
> *of deserted, blind-eyed night,* [B 49]

as Empedocles puts it . . .

(Plutarch, *Table Talk* 720E)

The Earth

Some say that the region below the earth is infinite (e.g. Xenophanes of Colophon), so that they need not take the trouble to look for an explanation [of why the earth is at rest]. That is why Empedocles criticized them, saying:

> *If the depths of the earth are boundless and the ether immense,*
> *as the tongues of many mouths have vainly*
> *poured forth, seeing little of the whole . . .* [B 39]

(Aristotle, *On the Heavens* 294a21–28)

There are streams of fire under the earth, as Empedocles says:

> *Many fires burn beneath the threshold.* [B 52]

(Proclus, *Commentary on the Timaeus* II 8.26–28)

Why does water look white on the surface but black in the depths? Is it because depth is the mother of blackness inasmuch as it blunts and weakens the rays of the sun before they descend, whereas the surface, because it is immediately affected by the sun, can receive the whiteness of the light? This is the view that Empedocles assents to:

> *In the bottom of the river the shadows make the colour black,*
> *and the same is seen in hollow caverns.* [B 94]

(Plutarch, *Scientific Explanations* 39)

It is equally absurd for anyone to think, like Empedocles, that when he says that sea is earth's sweat [B 55], he has said something illuminating.

(Aristotle, *Meteorology* 357a25–26)

Empedocles:
Salt was compacted, forced by the rays of the sun. [B 56]
(Hephaestion, *Handbook* I iii 4)

Poseidon is summoned by Iris who calls him either to the sea or to the gods, as Empedocles or someone else says:
Iris brings a wind or a great rainstorm from the sea. [B 50]
(Tzetzes, *Allegories in the Iliad* XV 86)

Botany

If the air continuously favoured the trees, then perhaps even what the poets say would not seem unreasonable – as Empedocles says that, evergreen and ever-fruiting [B 77], they flourish
throughout the year with abundant fruit, thanks to the air. [B 78]
(He supposes that a certain blending of the air – the spring blending – is common to all seasons.)

(Theophrastus, *Causes of Plants* I xiii 2)

[Plants] reproduce from themselves, and the so-called seeds which they produce are not semen but embryos – Empedocles puts this well when he says
Thus tall trees first lay olives. [B 79]
For what is laid is an embryo.

(Aristotle, *Generation of Animals* 731a1–6)

Empedocles says that
This is why pomegranates are late-fruiting and apples exceptionally sweet. [B 80]

(Plutarch, *Table Talk* 683D)

Concoction seems to be a sort of rotting, as Empedocles indicates when he says:

> *Wine from the bark is water that has rotted in the wood.* [B 81]
>
> (Plutarch, *Scientific Explanations* 912C)

Zoology

I am aware that Empedocles the natural scientist used the word *kamasenes* to cover all fish in general:

> *How the tall trees and fish* [kamasenes] *of the sea* . . . [B 72]
>
> (Athenaeus, *Deipnosophists* 334B)

As for animals themselves, you could not find any creature of land or air as prolific as all the creatures of the sea are. With that in mind, Empedocles wrote:

> *Leading the unmusical tribe of fertile fish* . . . [B 74]
>
> (Plutarch, *Table Talk* 685F)

You see that god, our fine craftsman as Pindar called him, did not everywhere send fire up and earth down, but he arranged them as the needs of bodies demanded.

> *This is found in shell-fish, heavy-backed sea-dwellers —*
> *yes, and in limpets and stone-skinned turtles,*

says Empedocles,

> *where you will see earth dwelling on top of flesh.* [B 76]
>
> (*ibid* 618B)

Some animals are armoured with horns and teeth and stings,

> *and as for hedgehogs,*

Empedocles says,

> *sharp-arrowed hairs bristle on their backs.* [B 83]
>
> (Plutarch, *On Fortune* 98D)

Biology

Empedocles, by placing Strife and Love among the principles
as causes of form, . . . defines form, I suppose, by the ratio in
which each is made; for he makes flesh and bone and the rest
by a certain ratio. In the first book of the *Physics* he says:
>   *Kindly earth in her well-made hollows*
>   *received of the eight parts two of bright Nestis*
>   *and four of Hephaestus. And they became white bones,*
>   *wonderfully fitted together by the glue of Harmony.* [B 96]
>   (Simplicius, *Commentary on the Physics* 300.16–24)

I am talking of bones and hair and everything else of that sort.
They have not got a name in common, but nonetheless they
are all the same by analogy, as Empedocles says:
>   *The same are hair and leaves and the thick feathers of birds*
>   *and scales on strong limbs.* [B 82]
>   (Aristotle, *Meteorology* 387b1–6)

The body of the semen cannot be separated, part in the female
and part in the male, as Empedocles says –
>   *But the nature of the members is separated, part in a man's . . .*
>   [B 63]
>   (Aristotle, *Generation of Animals* 764b15–18)

If male and female are differentiated during gestation, as
Empedocles says –
>   *poured into pure places, some grow as women,*
>   *if they meet with cold . . .* [B 65]

>   (*ibid* 723a23–25)

Others of the older generation have also said that the male is
conceived in the right part of the womb. Parmenides put it like
this:
>   *In the right boys, in the left girls,* [28 B 17]
and Empedocles says this:
>   *For in the warmer part was the male portion* [B 67]

– and for that reason men are dark and more masculine and more hairy.

> (Galen, *Commentary on Hippocrates' Epidemics* XVIIA
> 1002 K)

Empedocles the natural scientist allegorizes and speaks of
> *the divided meadows of Aphrodite* [B 66]

wherein the generation of children takes place.

> (Scholiast to Euripides, *Phoenician Women* 18)

Milk is concocted blood, not rotten blood. Empedocles either misunderstood this or else used a poor metaphor when he said that

> *On the tenth day of the eighth month comes white pus.* [B 68]

> (Aristotle, *Generation of Animals* 777a8–10)

When the sows live and feed together with the hogs it puts them in mind of sex and stimulates their desire. Empedocles says the same of humans:

> *And on him came desire, *reminding him through sight**. [B 64]

> (Plutarch, *Scientific Explanations* 917C)

[Empedocles] says that inhalation and exhalation occur because there are certain vessels which contain blood (but are not full of blood) and which have channels leading into the external air, narrower than the parts of the flesh but broader than those of the air. Hence, since the blood naturally moves up and down, when it moves down the air flows in and inhalation occurs, and when it moves up the air flows outside the body and exhalation occurs. He makes an analogy with what happens in a clepsydra:

> *Everything inhales and exhales like this: all have bloodless*
> *tubes of flesh stretched over the surface of their bodies*
> *and at their mouths close-packed holes pierce*
> *right through the outer surface of the skin, so that the blood*
> *remains inside but channels are cut to give easy exit to the ether.*
> *Whenever the gentle blood rushes from them*
> *the bubbling air rushes down with a wild swell,*

and when it runs back, it exhales again. As when a girl
plays with a clepsydra of shining bronze —
when she covers the neck of the tube with her pretty hand
and dips it into the soft body of shining water,
no moisture enters the vessel, but it is held back
by the mass of air which presses from within on the close-packed
    perforations
until she uncovers the compressed stream. And then,
as the air leaves, the water enters in proportion.
Just so, when she holds the water in the depths of the bronze,
the neck and channel being blocked by a mortal hand,
the air outside eagerly keeps the moisture within
at the gates of the harsh-sounding strainer, controlling the
    surface,
until she releases her hand. Then again, the reverse of before,
as the air enters, water runs out in proportion.
Just so with the gentle blood pulsing through the limbs —
whenever it rushes back inside,
a stream of air at once comes down swelling and surging,
and when it runs back, it exhales again in equal quantity. [B 100]
        (Aristotle, *On Respiration* 473b1–474a5)

Perception

Empedocles [says that the soul] is composed of all the elements
and that each of them actually is a soul. He says:

    For by earth we see earth, by water water,
    by ether bright ether, and by fire flaming fire,
    love by love and strife by mournful strife. [B 109]
        (Aristotle, *On the Soul* 404b11–15)

Empedocles seems to think, as I said before, that sometimes
we see when light leaves the eyes. At any rate, he says this:

    As when someone, intending a journey, prepares a light,
    a flame of flashing fire through the winter night,
    fitting a lantern as protection against all the winds,

which stops the breeze when the winds blow,
but the light passes through to the outside, inasmuch as it is
*   finer-textured,*
and illuminates the ground with its tireless rays:
so then the ancient fire, imprisoned in the membranes
and fine tissues, lies in ambush in the round pupil;
and they hold back the deep water which flows around,
but let the fire pass through inasmuch as it is finer-textured. [B 84]

Sometimes he says we see in this way, sometimes by effluences
from the objects seen.

(Aristotle, *On the Senses and their Objects* 437b23–438a5)

As Empedocles says,
from both [namely eyes] *comes a single vision.* [B 88]

(Strabo, *Geography* VIII v 3)

Do hounds, as Empedocles says,
tracking with their nostrils the fragments of animal limbs,
[B 101.1]
pick up the effluences which the beasts leave on the matter?

(Plutarch, *Scientific Explanations* 917E)

Why do hounds not smell the tracks when the hare is dead? . . .
When it is alive they perceive it because the smell is continuously given off by the animal; but when it is dead the smell
ceases to flow. For the smell is not left behind, in the way in
which Empedocles says
it leaves from its paws in the soft grass. [B 101.2]

([Alexander], *Problems* 22.7)

Breathing is a cause of smell not in itself but accidentally, as is
clear from the case of animals and from the facts just mentioned. But again at the end of his work Empedocles – as it
were setting his seal on it – speaks as though this were the
cause:
Thus are all things allotted breath and smell. [B 102]

(Theophrastus, *On the Senses* 22)

Thought

Empedocles seems to treat the blood as the organ of understanding:

> *Nourished in a sea of churning blood*
> *where what men call thought is especially found —*
> *for the blood about the heart is thought for men.* [B 105]
>
> (Porphyry, in Stobaeus, *Anthology* I xlix 53)

In general, they supposed that thought was perception and
perception an alteration . . . Thus Empedocles says that our
thoughts change as our condition changes:

> *For men's wisdom grows in relation to what is present.* [B 106]

And elsewhere he says that:

> *Insofar as they become different, to that extent always*
> *does their thought too present different objects.* [B 108]
>
> (Aristotle, *Metaphysics* 1009b12–13, 17–21)

Thought depends on similars, ignorance on dissimilars, as
though thinking were the same as or similar to perceiving. For
having enumerated the ways in which we recognize each thing
by its like, at the end he adds that from these

> *all things are fitted together and constructed,*
> *and by these they think and feel pleasure and pain.* [B 107]

That is why we think especially with our blood; for in this the
elements of the parts are best blended.

> (Theophrastus, *On the Senses* 10)

Purifications

The Purifications *were addressed to the citizens of Acragas, Empedo-*
cles' own city. His candid greeting to them survives:

Heraclides says that the woman who did not breathe was
in such a state that her body remained without breath and
without a pulse for thirty days. That is why Heraclides calls

[Empedocles] both a doctor and a seer, relying also on the following lines:

> O friends who live in the great town of yellow Acragas
> on the heights of the citadel, caring for good deeds,
> greetings: an immortal god, no longer mortal,
> I travel, honoured by all, as is fitting,
> garlanded with bands and fresh ribbons.
> Whenever I enter a thriving town
> I am revered by men and women. They follow me
> in their thousands, asking where lies the path to gain:
> some want prophecies, others for diseases
> of every sort request to hear a healing word. [B 112.1–2, 4–11]
>
> (Diogenes Laertius, *Lives of the Philosophers* VIII 61)

Empedocles says [of the Acragantines]:

> Honourable harbours for strangers, knowing no ill. [B 112.3]
>
> (Diodorus, *Universal History* XIII lxxxiii 2)

Grammarians are blind in these matters – and also with regard to the verses written about them. Empedocles says:

> Greetings: an immortal god, no longer mortal,
> I travel, honoured by all. [B 112.4–5]

And again:

> But why do I attack them as though I were achieving something
>   great
> if I prove superior to much-perishing men? [B 113]

Grammarians and ordinary readers will suppose that the philosopher said this from boastfulness and contempt for other men – something which is alien even to one moderately versed in philosophy, let alone to a man of Empedocles' stature.

> (Sextus Empiricus, *Against the Mathematicians* I 302–303)

And it comes upon me to praise highly the Acragantine poet who hymns faith in these words:

> My friends, I know that there is truth in the stories
> which I shall tell; but hard indeed

for men and unwanted is the onrush of trust to their minds.
[B 114]

(Clement, *Miscellanies* V i 9.1)

The main theme of the Purifications *was the fall of the spirits from an original state of blessedness, and their subsequent punishments. The introduction to the story is preserved by Plutarch:*

Empedocles at the beginning of his philosophy says by way of preface that:

There is an oracle of necessity, an ancient decree of the gods,
that whenever anyone errs and defiles in fear his dear limbs
— one of the spirits who have been allotted long-lasting life —
he shall wander thrice ten thousand seasons away from the blessed
ones.
Such is the road I now follow, a fugitive from the gods and a
wanderer. [B 115.1, 3, 5–6, 13]

He then shows from his own case that not just he himself but all of us are immigrants here and strangers and fugitives. For it is not blood, my friends, nor blended breath (he says) which provides the substance and principle of our souls: from these the body is compounded, earth-born and mortal; but the soul has come here from elsewhere – and he calls birth by the gentlest of terms, a journey abroad.

And what is most true, the soul flees and wanders, driven by the decrees and laws of the gods . . . When it is tied to the body, it cannot recall or remember

from what honour and from what height of bliss [B 119]

it has fallen, having exchanged not Sardis for Athens, nor Corinth for Lemnos or Scyros, but the heavens and the moon for earth and an earthly life. And then it complains and suffers like a feeble wilting plant if here it is moved a little way from one place to another.

(Plutarch, *On Exile* 607 CE)

There is a more detailed description of the same events in Hippolytus' account of Empedocles' philosophy. (The lines quoted by Plutarch are usually amalgamated with those in Hippolytus and turned into the single fragment, B 115.)

About his own birth Empedocles speaks as follows:

> *Among them am I too now, a fugitive from the gods and a*
> *wanderer,* [cf B 115.13]

i.e. he calls god the one and its unity in which he existed before being torn away by Strife and coming to be among the many things here in the world of Strife. For, he says,

> *I trusted in mad Strife* [B 115.14]

– by Strife, mad and disturbed and unstable, Empedocles means the creator of this world. For this is the sentence and the necessity imposed on souls whom Strife tears from the one and creates and produces. He says:

> *<. . .> whoever having erred swears a false oath –*
> *one of the spirits who have been allotted long-lasting life*
> [B 115.4–5]

(he call souls 'long-lasting spirits' because they are immortal and live long lives)

> *– he shall wander thrice ten thousand seasons away from the*
> *blessed ones.* [B 115.6]

(He calls blessed those who are gathered together by Love from the many into the unity of the intelligible world.) These, then, he says must wander and

> *become in time all sorts of mortals,*
> *changing the painful paths of life;* [B 115.7–8]

for the souls change from body to body, altered and punished by Strife and not allowed to remain in unity. Rather, the souls undergo every punishment at the hands of Strife as they change from body to body:

> *The ethereal power,* he says, *pursues souls to the sea,*
> *the sea spits them up onto the threshold of the earth, the earth into*
> *the rays*
> *of the bright sun, and the sun hurls them into the whirls of the*
> *ether:*
> *each receives them from another: all hate them.* [B 115.9–12]

This is the punishment which the creator visits on them, like a smith reshaping iron and taking it from the fire to plunge it in water. For ether is fire, whence the creator hurls the souls into the sea, and earth is the land; so he means: 'from water to land, from land to air'. This is what he says:

> . . . *the earth into the rays*
> *of the bright sun, and the sun hurls them into the whirls of the* *ether:*
> *each receives them from another: all hate them.* [B 115.10–12]

Thus our souls are hated and tortured and punished in this world, according to Empedocles, and then gathered together by Love, who is good and who takes pity on their lamentation and on the disorderly and vile arrangements of mad Strife; she soon hastens to lead them from the world and to fashion them appropriately for the one, labouring to ensure that everything, led by her, comes to unity.

Such being the dispositions made by fatal Strife in this divided world, Empedocles urged his followers to abstain from all living things; for he says that the bodies of the animals we eat are the dwelling-places of punished souls. And he teaches those who hear these words of his to exhibit self-control in their dealings with women so that they may not become fellow-workers and fellow-labourers in the enterprises which Strife creates, as it continuously destroys and pulls apart the work of Love. This, according to Empedocles, is the greatest law for the ordering of the universe. He says:

> *There is an oracle of necessity, an ancient decree of the gods,*
> *eternal, sealed with broad oaths* [B 115.1–2]

– by necessity he means the change from one to many by Strife and from many to one by Love; and by the gods, as I said, he means the four mortal gods (fire, water, earth, air) and the two immortals, who are ungenerated and eternally at war with one another: Strife and Love.

> (Hippolytus, *Refutation of All Heresies* VII xxix 14–23)

After the fall, the spirits thus undergo various incarnations. Empedocles here embraces the Pythagorean notion of metempsychosis.

The fate or nature which determines the metempsychosis itself is called by Empedocles a spirit which

> *wraps in an unrecognizable garment of flesh* [B 126]

and gives the souls their new clothing.

(Porphyry, in Stobaeus, *Anthology* I xlix 60)

Empedocles says that the best move for a human is to become a lion, if death changes him into an animal, and a laurel, if into a plant. This is what he says:

> *Among the beasts they become lions, mountain-laired, sleeping on
> the ground,*
> *and laurels among fair-tressed trees.* [B 127]

(Aelian, *The Nature of Animals* XII 7)

Above all, [Empedocles] assents to the idea of metempsychosis, saying:

> *For already have I once been a boy and a girl*
> *and a bush and a bird and a silent fish in the sea.* [B 117]

He said that all souls change into every sort of animal.

(Hippolytus, *Refutation of All Heresies* I iii 2)

Empedocles too says that the souls of the wise become gods. This is what he writes:

> *In the end they are seers and hymn-writers and doctors*
> *and princes among earth-dwelling men;*
> *and then they arise as gods, highest in honour.* [B 146]

(Clement, *Miscellanies* IV xxiii 150.1)

If we live in a holy and just fashion, we shall be blessed here and more blessed when we have left here, not possessing happiness for a period of time but being able to rest for eternity

> *at the same hearth and table as the other immortals,*
> *relieved of mortal pains, tireless,* [B 147]

as Empedocles' philosophical poem puts it.

(*ibid* V xiv 122.3)

The cycle of incarnations thus ends in a return to blessedness. But life in this world now is miserable:

Heraclitus evidently vilifies generation . . . and Empedocles clearly agrees with him when he says:

I wept and I lamented as I saw the unfamiliar place. [B 118]

And again:

For from living things he made corpses, changing their forms.
[B 125]

And again:

Alas, poor race of mortals, unhappy ones,
from what conflicts and what groans were you born. [B 124]

(*ibid* III iii 14.1–2)

The Pythagoreans, and after them Plato, declared that the world was a cave or cavern. For in Empedocles the powers that guide souls say:

We have come to this roofed cave. [B 120]

(Porphyry, *The Cave of the Nymphs* 8)

For man descends and leaves the place of happiness, as Empedocles the Pythagorean says:

a fugitive from the gods and a wanderer,
I trusted in mad Strife. [B 115.13–14]

But he ascends and resumes his old condition, if he escapes earthly things and the *pleasureless country* [B 121.1], as the same man says,

where are Slaughter and Rage and the tribes of other Plagues.
[B 121.2]

Those who fall into this place

wander in the darkness on the meadows of Ruin. [B 121.4]

(Hierocles, *Commentary on the Golden Verses* XXIV 2)

It is not true, as Menander says, that

By every man a spirit stands,

as soon as he is born. A good guide for his life. But it is rather as Empedocles says: two fates or spirits take over and govern each of us when we are born –

there were Earth and far-seeing Sun,
bloody Discord and soft-faced Harmony,
Beauty and Ugliness, Speed and Slowness,
desirable Truth and black-eyed Obscurity. [B 122]

(Plutarch, *On Tranquillity of Mind* 474BC)

197

After that comes the birth of the so-called Titans. They must represent the differences among things. For Empedocles enumerates them in scientific terms –

    Birth and Death, Sleep and Wakefulness,
    Motion and Rest, much-garlanded Greatness
    **and Lowliness, Silence and Speech*, [B 123]

and many others – he is clearly hinting at the variety of things.

(Cornutus, Theology 17)

Your own poet, Empedocles of Acragas, says the same:

    For that reason, troubled by cruel evils,
    you will never relieve your heart from wretched pains. [B 145]

(Clement, Protreptic II xxvii 3)

The Purifications *appears also to have contained a description of a Utopia or a Golden Age:*

Empedocles, when he tells of the birth of the gods, also indicates his views on sacrifices when he says:

    Among them was no god Ares, nor Tumult,
    nor was Zeus king, nor Cronus, nor Poseidon,
    but Cypris was queen –

i.e. Love –

    whom they worshipped with holy statues
    and painted animals and subtly perfumed oils,
    with offerings of unmixed myrrh and of pungent frankincense,
    pouring libations of yellow honey on to the threshold
    [B 128.1–7]

– customs which even now are still preserved among some people, being as it were traces of the truth.

    But with the foul slaughter of bulls their altars were not washed.
    [B 128.8]

(Porphyry, On Abstinence II 21)

By such [i.e. vegetarian] offerings nature and every sense of the human soul was pleased –

But with the foul slaughter of bulls their altars were not washed,
but this was the greatest defilement among men:
to bereave of life and eat the noble limbs. [B 128.8–10]
(*ibid* II 27)

Empedocles bears witness to this when he says of [Pythagoras]:
Among them was a man of immense knowledge
who had obtained the greatest wealth of mind,
an exceptional master of every kind of wise work.
For when he stretched out with all his mind
he easily saw each and every thing
in ten or twenty human generations. [B 129]
(Porphyry, *Life of Pythagoras* 30)

For reason, which leads to virtue by way of philosophy, always
makes a man consistent with himself and unblamed by himself
and full of peace and good will towards himself –
there is no faction and no fateful conflict in his members. [B 27a]
(Plutarch, *Philosophers and Princes* 777C)

Empedocles uses the word [*ktilos*] of tame and gentle things:
All were gentle and amenable to men,
both beasts and birds; and kindness glowed. [B 130]
(Scholiast to Nicander, *Theriaca* 452)

In the second book of Empedocles' *Purifications* one can find
the alpha long, as is clear from a critical comparison – for he
uses *manoteros* as though it were *tranoteros*:
Of those which, with closer set roots beneath
and fewer [manoterois] branches, thrive . . .
(Herodian, *On Accentuation in General* fragment)

*The story of the fall and the doctrine of metempsychosis had impli-
cations for practical ethics.*

As everyone somehow surmises, there is by nature a common
justice and injustice, even in the absence of community and
compacts . . . This is what Empedocles says about not killing

animate creatures: it is not the case that this is just for some and not just for others,

> *but, a law for all, through the broad*
> *air it endlessly extends and through the boundless light.* [B 135]
>> (Aristotle, *Rhetoric* 1373b6–9, 14–17)

Pythagoras and Empedocles and the rest of the Italians say that we have a fellowship not only with one another and with the gods but also with the irrational animals. For there is a single spirit which pervades the whole world as a sort of soul and which unites us with them. That is why, if we kill them and eat their flesh, we commit injustice and impiety, inasmuch as we are killing our kin. Hence these philosophers urged us to abstain from meat . . . Empedocles somewhere says:

> *Will you not cease from ill-sounding slaughter? Do you not see*
> *that you tear at one another in the carelessness of your thought?*
> [B 136]

And:

> *A father lifts his son who has changed his shape*
> *and slaughters him as he prays, the fool, while he cries pitifully,*
> *beseeching his sacrificer. But he, deaf to his cries,*
> *slaughters him in the halls and prepares a foul feast.*
> *In the same way a son takes his father, children their mother:*
> *they bereave them of life and eat their dear flesh.* [B 137]
>> (Sextus Empiricus, *Against the Mathematicians* IX 127–129)

Since no-one is without sin, we can only atone for our earlier sins about food by later purifications. That will happen if we keep the horror before our eyes and cry aloud with Empedocles:

> *Alas that the pitiless day did not first destroy me*
> *before I contrived with my lips the terrible deed of eating flesh.*
> [B 139]

>> (Porphyry, *On Abstinence* II 31)

It seems that one should not only, with Empedocles,

> *keep altogether from the leaves of the laurel,* [B 140]

but also spare all other trees.

>> (Plutarch, *Table Talk* 646D)

The mistake about not eating beans seems to have arisen because in a poem of Empedocles, who followed the teachings of Pythagoras, the following verse is found:

Wretches, utter wretches, keep your hands from beans. [B 141]

(Aulus Gellius, *Attic Nights* IV xi 9)

[Gellius' discussion of the prohibition on bean-eating is quoted in full in Chapter 13.]

The last four short fragments are of uncertain location and import.

The teaching of Plato's doctrines requires, first, a sort of purification, i.e. training from childhood in the appropriate subjects. For according to Empedocles, we should

cut with long-bladed bronze from five springs, [B 143]

and wash ourselves; and Plato says that the purification comes from five branches of study.

(Theo of Smyrna, *Mathematics* 15.7–12)

[Metaphor may involve a transference] from species to species: e.g.

drawing off life with bronze [B 138]

or

cutting with long-bladed bronze [cf B 143],

where 'draw' is used to mean 'cut' and 'cut' to mean 'draw', both being forms of taking away.

(Aristotle, *Poetics* 1457b13–16)

The same [grammatical construction] is also found in Empedocles when he says:

Him neither the roofed halls of sceptre-bearing Zeus . . . [B 142]

(Herculaneum papyrus 1012, column XVIII)

In all things I have thought Empedocles' phrase,

to abstain from evil [B 144],

important and divine.

(Plutarch, *The Control of Anger* 464B)

13
FIFTH-CENTURY
PYTHAGOREANISM

*Pythagoras' followers in south Italy appear to have organized them-
selves into secret societies – a sort of freemasonry. They practised some
communal way of life; for*

[Pythagoras], according to Timaeus, was the first to say that
friends' possessions are held in common and that friendship is
equality. And his pupils contributed their goods to a common
store.

(Diogenes Laertius, *Lives of the Philosophers* VIII 10)

*Pythagoras was revered, and all things were attributed to him: the
Pythagorean phrase 'He said it himself' became a proverb. The
Pythagoreans practised no ordinary silence and their esoteric views
were not divulged to ordinary men.*

*The society is said to have had some political ambitions and interests.
In the middle of the fifth century disaster struck.*

At that time, in the regions of Italy which were then called
Great Greece, the Pythagorean meeting places were burned
down and general constitutional unrest ensued – a not unlikely
event, given that the leading men in each state had been thus
unexpectedly killed. The Greek cities in these regions were
filled with bloodshed and revolution and turmoil of every
kind.

(Polybius, *Histories* II xxxix 1–3)

The Pythagoreans who survived dispersed, some of them eventually settling in mainland Greece.

At an early stage, Pythagoras' followers divided into two groups, the acusmatici *or Aphorists and the* mathematici *or Scientists.*

There were two forms of his philosophy; for there were two kinds of people who practised it, the Aphorists and the Scientists. The Aphorists were allowed by the others to be Pythagorean, but they did not allow that the Scientists were Pythagoreans, saying that their work derived not from Pythagoras but from Hippasus. (Some say that Hippasus came from Croton, others that he came from Metapontum.)

The philosophy of the Aphorists consists of unproven and unargued aphorisms that one should act in such and such a way, and they attempt to preserve the other things [Pythagoras] said as though they were divine doctrines. They do not claim to say anything on their own behalf, nor do they think that they ought to say anything, but they hold that those of their number are best fitted for wisdom who possess the most aphorisms.

All these so-called aphorisms are divided into three kinds: some of them indicate what so and so is, others what is most such and such, others what one must or must not do.

Those which indicate what so and so is are of the following sort. What are the Isles of the Blessed? – The sun and the moon. – What is the oracle at Delphi? – The *tetractys*, which is the harmony in which the Sirens sing.

What is most such and such: What is most just? – Sacrificing. – What is most wise? – Number (and secondly, what assigned names to things). – What is most wise of the things among us? – Medicine. – What is most fine? – Harmony. – What is most powerful? – Wisdom. – What is most good? – Happiness. – What is most truly said? – That men are wretched . . .

The aphorisms indicating what should or should not be done are of the following sort. One must have children (for one must leave servants of the gods in one's place); one must put on one's right shoe first; one must not walk along the highways or dip things in the fonts or wash in the bath-house (for in all these cases it is unclear whether one's fellows are pure). And others such as: Do not help anyone to put down a burden (for one must not become a cause of idleness), but help him to take it up. Do not have intercourse for the purpose of siring children with a woman who wears gold. Do not speak in the dark. Pour libations to the gods from near the handle of the cup – for the sake of the omen and so that no-one will drink from the same place. Do not have an image of a god as a seal on your ring lest it be polluted; for it is a likeness which one should set up in one's house. Do not prosecute your own wife; for she is a suppliant (that is why at weddings women are led from the hearth and are grasped by the right hand). Do not sacrifice a white cockerel; for it is a suppliant, sacred to the Month (which is why it signifies the hour). Give no advice which is not for the good of the receiver; for advice is sacred. Labour is good: pleasures of every sort are bad; for those who have come for punishment must be punished. One should sacrifice and approach the temples without shoes. One must not turn aside into a temple; for one must not treat the gods as digressions. It is good to stand fast, receive wounds in the front, and so die: the opposite is bad. Human souls enter all animals except those which it is right to sacrifice; that is why one must only eat those sacrificial animals which it is proper to eat and no other animal.

Some of the aphorisms are of this sort. But the most expansive of them are concerned with sacrifices on various occasions and how they should be performed, with the other ways of honouring the gods, with our removal from this life, and with burials and how we must be buried. In some cases a reason is added – for example, that you must have children in order to leave behind another servant of the gods in your place. But others have no reason annexed to them. Of the additions, some will be thought to have been naturally attached, others to be far-fetched – for example, not to break bread because it is disadvantageous with regard to the judgement in Hades. The conjectural explanations added to such aphorisms are not Pythagorean but come from certain outsiders who make sophisticated attempts to attach conjectural reasons to them. For example, in the case just mentioned (why you must not break bread), some say that you should not divide what brings people together (in the old days, after the foreign fashion, all friends came together over a single loaf of bread), others that one must not make such an omen at the beginning by breaking and crumbling it.

Now all the aphorisms which deal with what to do and what not to do focus on the divine, and that is their source. The whole of their way of life is ordered with a view to following god. This is the rationale of their philosophy. For they think it absurd for men to look for the good from any source other than the gods: it is as if you were living in a monarchy and paid service to some subordinate among the citizens, ignoring the ruler of all – that, they think, is just what men actually do. For since god exists and is sovereign over everything, it is clear that one must ask for the good from the sovereign; for everyone gives good things to those whom they love and in whom they delight, and the opposite to those to whom they are disposed in the opposite way.

(Iamblichus, *On the Pythagorean Way of Life* 81–87)

There are numerous other accounts of the Pythagorean aphorisms, and of the modes of behaviour which they accompanied. One of the earliest is in Herodotus:

[The Egyptians] do not take woollen things into their temples or bury them with them: that is not holy. In this they are in agreement with those who are called Orphics and Pythagoreans. For it is not holy for one who partakes in these rites to be buried in woollen clothes. There is a sacred story told about this.

(Herodotus, *Histories* II 81)

Iamblichus' main source is likely to have been Aristotle. We know that Aristotle also wrote on Pythagorean dietary practices. There was an ancient controversy over this issue. Here is one text on the subject:

A false opinion of long standing has gained ground and

increased in strength – the opinion that Pythagoras the philosopher did not eat meat and also abstained from beans (for
which the Greek is *kuamoi*). Following this opinion the poet
Callimachus wrote:

> Keep your hands from beans, a painful food:
> so as Pythagoras enjoined I too urge.

Following the same opinion Cicero said the following in the
first book of his *On Divination*:

> So Plato bids us go to bed with our bodies so composed
> that there is nothing which may make the mind stray or
> be disturbed. That is why it is thought that the Pythagor-
> eans are forbidden to eat beans which cause considerable
> flatulence and are thus inimical to those who seek peace
> of mind.

Thus Cicero. But the musical scholar Aristoxenus, an exceed-
ingly industrious reader of old texts and a pupil of Aristotle
the philosopher, says in his book about Pythagoras that
Pythagoras ate no vegetable more frequently than beans,
because they soothe and gently relieve the bowels. These are
his very words:

> Pythagoras esteemed the bean above all other vegetables;
> for he said that it was both soothing and laxative – that is
> why he made particular use of it.

The same Aristoxenus also reports that [Pythagoras] used to
eat sucking pigs and tender young kids. He seems to have
acquired his information from the Pythagorean Xenophilus,
who was his friend, and from certain other older men who
were closer in time to Pythagoras. Alexis the poet, in his com-
edy *The Pythagorean Woman*, also makes the remark about
animals.

The mistake about not eating beans seems to have arisen
because in a poem of Empedocles, who followed the teachings
of Pythagoras, the following verse is found:

> *Wretches, utter wretches, keep your hands from beans.* [31 B 141]

For most people have supposed that the word 'beans' is being
used, as it normally is, to refer to the vegetable. But those who
have considered Empedocles' poems more closely and in a more
scholarly way assert that in this passage the word 'beans' signifies

the testicles: they were called beans, covertly and symbolically in the Pythagorean style, because they are the cause of pregnancy [the Greek *kuein*, 'to be pregnant', is fancifully connected with *kuamos*] and provide the impetus to human reproduction. Hence in this verse Empedocles wanted to restrain people not from eating beans but from sexual indulgence.

Plutarch, too, who has considerable authority in scholarly matters, says in the first book of his *On Homer* that Aristotle wrote the very same about the Pythagoreans – namely, that they did not abstain from eating animals (except for a few sorts of flesh). Since the point is surprising I have written out Plutarch's own words:

> Aristotle says that the Pythagoreans abstain from womb, heart, sea-nettle, and certain other things of that sort, but eat the rest.

(The sea-nettle is a sea creature which we call a sea-urchin.) But in his *Table Talk* Plutarch says that the Pythagoreans also abstain from mullet.

(Aulus Gellius, Attic Nights IV xi 1–13)

Such practices were easily mocked. Several fourth-century comedies – like Alexis' The Pythagorean Woman – ridiculed the Pythagorean way of life. Here are two samples.

Alexis in *The Men from Tarentum*:
> – The Pythagoreans, or so we hear,
> eat no fish nor anything else
> alive; *and* they're the only ones who don't drink wine.
> – But Epicharides eats dogs,
> and he's a Pythagorean. – Ah, but he kills them first
> and then they're no longer alive.

A little further on he says:
> – Pythagorisms and fine
> arguments and close-chopped thoughts
> feed them. Their daily bread is this:
> one plain loaf each, and a cup
> of water. That's all. – A prison
> diet! Do all the wise men

live like this and suffer such pains?
— No: these are luxurious compared to others. Don't you
    know
that Melanippides is one of them, and Phaon
and Phyromachus and Phanos: *they* dine
every four days on a single cup of bran.

(Athenaeus, *Deipnosophists* 161 BC)

In *The Pythagorean* [Aristophon] says:
    As for going hungry and not eating anything,
    imagine you can see Tithymallus or Philippides.
    For drinking water they're frogs; for enjoying thyme
    and vegetables, caterpillars; for not being washed,
        chamber-pots;
    for staying out of doors all winter, blackbirds;
    for withstanding the heat and chattering at noon,
    cicadas; for not using or seeing olive oil,
    dust-clouds; for walking about at dawn without any shoes,
    cranes; for not sleeping at all, bats.

(*ibid* 238CD)

Among the Scientists or mathematici *are Hippasus and Philolaus,
who have chapters of their own. Here I shall cite a few texts of a more
general nature about the mathematical side of Pythagorean philosophy.
The most important passage comes from Aristotle.*

At the same time as [Leucippus and Democritus] and earlier
than them, the so-called Pythagoreans touched on mathematics: they were the first to bring it forward and, having been
brought up in it, to think that its principles were the principles
of all the things that exist. Since numbers are by nature the first
of these, and since they thought they observed in numbers
many similarities to the things that exist and come into being
(more so than in fire and earth and water) — for example, that
justice is such and such a modification of numbers, soul and
mind such and such, opportunity something else, and so on
for pretty well everything else (and they also saw that the modifications and ratios of harmonies depend on numbers): since,

then, all other things appeared to have been modelled on numbers in their nature, while numbers seemed to be the first things in the whole of nature, they supposed that the elements of numbers were the elements of all the things that exist, and that the whole heaven was harmony and number. Everything in numbers and harmonies that cohered with the properties and parts of the heavens and with the whole of the created world, they collected and fitted together; and if there was anything missing anywhere they eagerly made additions so that the whole of their theory should be connected. For example, since the number ten is thought to be perfect and to include the whole nature of numbers, they say that the bodies moving in the heavens are ten in number; and since only nine are apparent, for that reason they invent the counter-earth as the tenth.

I have given a more detailed account of these things elsewhere: here my aim is to grasp in the case of the Pythagoreans too what first principles they posit and how they fit into the causes I have described. Now they, too, evidently believe that number is a first principle both as matter for existing things and as their properties and states; they hold that the elements of number are the even and the odd, one of these being finite and the other infinite; that the number one derives from both elements (it is both even and odd) and numbers derive from the number one; and that the whole heaven, as I have said, is numbers.

Other members of the same school say that the principles are ten in number, and come in co-ordinate pairs: limit – infinite, odd – even, one – quantity, right – left, male – female, resting – moving, straight – crooked, light – darkness, good – bad, square – oblong . . . How [these principles] should be collected under the types of cause I have described they do not clearly articulate. But they seem to range the elements under the head of matter; for they say that they are inherent in the substances which are composed and fashioned from them.

(Aristotle, *Metaphysics* 985b23–986a26, 986b4–8)

Aristotle says that the Pythagoreans 'touched on' mathematics. Later authors ascribe considerable mathematical achievements to them. For example:

Eudemus the Peripatetic ascribes to the Pythagoreans the discovery of this theorem (that every triangle has internal angles equal to two right angles), and he says that they prove the proposition in this way: Let ABC be a triangle, and let DE be drawn through A parallel to BC. Then since BC and DE are parallel, the alternate angles are equal; so DAB is equal to ABC and EAC to ACB. Let BAC be added in common. Then angles DAB, BAC, CAE, i.e. angles DAB, BAE, i.e. two right angles, are equal to the three angles of the triangles ABC. Hence the three angles of the triangle are equal to two right angles.

(Proclus, *Commentary on Euclid* 379.1–16)

The most celebrated piece of Pythagorean mathematics is the theorem still known as Pythagoras' theorem:

'In a right-angled triangle, the square on the hypotenuse is equal to the squares on the other two sides': if we listen to those who like to record the ancient history of the subject we shall find them ascribing this theorem to Pythagoras and saying that he sacrificed an ox on its discovery.

(*ibid* 426.1–9)

The story is not generally believed; and indeed most scholars are now inclined to think that the Pythagoreans contributed little to the technical side of mathematics.

According to Aristotle, they applied numbers to astronomy. In the chapter on Philolaus we shall rediscover the 'counter-earth'. Here, in another extract from Aristotle, is the theory of the Music of the Spheres:

It is clear from this that to say that [the heavenly bodies] produce a harmony as they move, their sounds being concordant, is a clever and ingenious theory but is nevertheless untrue. Some think that when bodies of such a size move they must produce a sound since this happens with bodies here even though they are not of the same magnitude and do not move with such speed. When the sun and the moon, and the stars of such number and such size, move at speed, it is impossible that they should not produce a sound of immense magnitude. Positing this, and supposing that their speeds, judging by their distances, have the ratios of the concords, they say that as the heavenly bodies move in a circle they produce a concordant sound. Since it seems unreasonable that we do not hear this sound, they say that the cause lies in the fact that the noise is with us from the moment of our birth so that it cannot be distinguished by reference to a contrary silence (for sound and silence are discriminated by reference to one another). Thus men are in the same case as blacksmiths whom habit makes impervious to the sound.

(Aristotle, *On the Heavens* 290b12–29)

It is worth adding four further passages from Aristotle here, three on cosmogony and one on the soul.

All those who are thought to have made a significant contribution to [natural philosophy] have given some account of the infinite, and all posit it as a sort of first principle of the things that exist. Some, like the Pythagoreans and Plato, make it a principle in its own right, supposing that the infinite exists in itself as a substance and not as an attribute of something else. The Pythagoreans locate it among perceptible objects (for they do not make numbers separate), and say that the space outside the heavens is infinite.

(Aristotle, *Physics* 203a1–8)

The Pythagoreans too said that void exists, and that it enters the heavens from the infinite breath, as though the heavens actually inhale the void which distinguishes natural things and is a sort of separation and distinction of contiguous things. They hold that this occurs first among numbers; for the void separates their natures.

(*ibid* 213b22–27)

Aristotle in the fourth book of the *Physics* writes:

The Pythagoreans too said that void exists, and that it enters the heavens from the infinite breath, as though the heavens inhale.

And in the first book of *On the Philosophy of Pythagoras* he writes that the heavens are one and that from the infinite they take in time and breath and void which distinguishes the places of each thing for ever.

(Stobaeus, *Anthology* I xviii 1c)

What the Pythagoreans say seems to have the same meaning. For some of them said that the motes in the air are soul, others that what moves them is soul. We have said how they can be seen to move continuously even if there is a complete calm.

(Aristotle, *On the Soul* 404a16–20)

The Aphorists and the Scientists seem to approach one another in the field of number mysticism. Some Pythagoreans played the numbers game in an extravagantly detailed form:

They did not even determine in what way numbers are causes of substances and of their being. Are they boundaries (as points are of magnitudes)? – This is how Eurytus determined what was the number of what (this the number of man, that the number of horse) – he modelled the shapes of plants with pebbles, just as people arrange numbers into squares and oblongs.

(Aristotle, *Metaphysics* 1092b8–13)

At the centre of the numerology was the tetractys *or 'group of four', consisting of the first four numbers, which together add up to ten. Ten is the perfect number: it contains the important musical ratios, and it can be arranged to form a perfect triangle:*

The Pythagoreans allegedly swore

By him who handed to our generation the *tetractys*,
source of the roots of ever-flowing nature.
(Iamblichus, *On the Pythagorean Way of Life* 162)

14
HIPPASUS

Hippasus was a Pythagorean. His birthplace is variously reported, and our sources record no dates for him. It seems likely that he was active in the middle of the fifth century. He was an unorthodox Pythagorean, perhaps a rebel, and he is said to have been the first of the Pythagorean mathematici or Scientists. Simplicius treats him as a conventional Presocratic cosmogonist:

Hippasus of Metapontum and Heraclitus of Ephesus also said that [the universe] is unique, in motion, and finite; but they made the first principle fire, and they produce the things that exist from fire by condensation and rarefaction, and resolve them into fire again, this being the single underlying nature.
(Simplicius, *Commentary on the Physics* 23.33–24.4)

We are ill-informed about the more distinctively Pythagorean aspects of Hippasus' thought. Two stories are worth setting down, though neither of them deserves full credence. First, Hippasus' name is associated with musical theory:

A certain Hippasus constructed four bronze discs in such a way that they all had equal diameters but the thickness of the first was one and a third times that of the second, one and a half times that of the third, and twice that of the fourth; and when they were struck they made a concord.
(Scholium to Plato, *Phaedo* 108D)

The story plainly means to ascribe to Hippasus the discovery of the fundamental musical ratios, 4:3, 3:2, and 2:1.

The second story concerns the alleged mathematical achievements of the Pythagoreans. I quote two short passages:

About Hippasus they say that he was one of the Pythagoreans but that because he was the first to publish and construct the sphere of the twelve pentagons he died at sea as an impious man. He acquired the reputation for discovering it, although everything belongs to That Man (that is how they refer to Pythagoras, never calling him by his name).

(Iamblichus, *On the Pythagorean Way of Life* 88)

Some say that the divinity punished those who made Pythagoras' views public. For the man who revealed the construction of the vigintangle perished at sea as an impious man. (The vigintangle is the dodecahedron, one of the so-called five solid figures, when it extends into a sphere.) Others said that it was the man who spoke about irrationality and incommensurability who suffered this fate.

(*ibid* 247)

The dodecahedron is the fifth of the five regular solids; it has twelve faces, each of which is a regular pentagon. The reference to irrationality and incommensurability is again geometrical: the diameter of a square is irrational, or incommensurable with its sides; that is to say, if each side is one unit long, then there is no fraction of the form n/m which gives the length of the diameter. Some scholars have supposed that these two geometrical discoveries were indeed made by the Pythagoreans and had some philosophical importance for them; other scholars are sceptical.

15
PHILOLAUS

Philolaus was probably born in Croton in the 470s. He was a Pythagorean. When the Pythagorean school in Croton was destroyed and its members dispersed, he retired to mainland Greece, spending some time in Thebes. These events cannot be dated with any precision, but it is clear that Philolaus flourished in the latter part of the fifth century BC.

We possess several passages purporting to come from Philolaus' writings. Many scholars have regarded all of them as spurious: numerous Pythagorean forgeries were put together in the ancient world, of which many survive. Recently, however, there has been a swing in scholarly opinion, and some at least of the passages are widely thought to be genuine. In this chapter I shall omit the texts which are uncontroversially spurious and include only those which the new consensus is inclined to accept.

One of Philolaus' works was later called On Nature. *The opening sentence is preserved:*

Demetrius in his *Homonyms* says that Philolaus was the first of the Pythagoreans to publish an *On Nature*. It begins as follows:
   Nature in the world was connected from things unlimited and
   things limiting, both the whole world and everything in it. [44
   B 1]
         (Diogenes Laertius, *Lives of the Philosophers* VIII 85)

[The Greek word here translated by 'unlimited' is elsewhere given as 'infinite'. The contrast with 'limiters' makes the variant translation preferable.]

216

Stobaeus transcribes a sequence of passages which, despite the different title, probably come from On Nature.

From Philolaus, *On the World*:

It is necessary that the things that exist should all be either limiting or unlimited or both limiting and unlimited. But they cannot be only unlimited. Now since it is evident that existing things come neither from limiting things only nor from unlimited things only, it is thus clear that the world and the things in it were connected together from both limiting and unlimited things. The facts too make this clear: some of them, coming from limiting things, limit; some, coming from both limiting and unlimited things, both limit and do not limit; some, coming from unlimited things, are evidently unlimited. [B 2]

And all the things that are known have a number — for without this nothing could be thought of or known. [B 4]

Now number has two proper forms, odd and even (and a third, even-odd, mixed from both); and of each form there are many shapes which each thing in itself signifies. [B 5]

On nature and connection, matters stand thus: the essence of things, being eternal, and nature itself admit of divine and not of human knowledge — except that it was not possible that any of the things which exist and are known by us should have come into being unless there subsisted the essence of the things from which the universe was constituted, both the limiting things and the unlimited things. And since the subsisting principles were neither similar nor homogeneous, it would therefore have been impossible for them to have been arranged had not a connection supervened (in whatever way it may have done so). Now similar and homogeneous things had no need at all of a connection; but things dissimilar and neither homogeneous nor equally matched must necessarily be linked by a connection if they are to be held together in the world. [B 6a]

The magnitude of a scale is a fourth and a fifth. A fifth is greater than a fourth by a tone; for from the top to the middle is a fourth, from the middle to the bottom a fifth, from the bottom to the third a fourth, from the third to the top a fifth; and between middle and third there is a tone. A fourth is 3:4, a fifth 2:3, an

*octave 1:2. Thus the scale is five tones and two semi-tones, a fifth
is three tones and a semi-tone, a fourth is two tones and a semi-
tone.* [B 6b]

*The first thing to have been connected, the one, in the middle
of the sphere is called the hearth.* [B 7]

(Stobaeus, *Anthology* I xxi 7–8)

*The arithmetical remarks in B 4 and B 5 find echoes in the following
reports:*

Plato teaches us many remarkable doctrines about the gods
by means of mathematical forms, and the philosophy of the
Pythagoreans uses these hangings to conceal the mysteries of
its divine doctrines. For that is the case throughout the *Sacred
Discourse*, in Philolaus' *Bacchae*, and in the whole of Pythagoras'
teaching about the gods.

(Proclus, *Commentary on Euclid* 22.9–16)

All the so-called mathematical sciences are like smooth flat
mirrors in which traces and images of intelligible truth are
reflected. But it is above all geometry which, according to
Philolaus, being the origin and native city of the others, turns
and elevates the mind which is purified and gently released
from perception.

(Plutarch, *Table Talk* 718E)

The Pythagoreans say that reason [is the standard of truth] –
not reason in general, but mathematical reason, as Philolaus
too used to say, which, inasmuch as it considers the nature of
the universe, has a certain affinity to it (for like is naturally
apprehended by like).

(Sextus Empiricus, *Against the Mathematicians* VII 92)

Elsewhere there will be occasion to inquire further how, when
numbers are serially squared, no less plausible results follow –
by nature and not by convention, as Philolaus says.

(Iamblichus, *Commentary on Nicomachus' Introduction to
Arithmetic* 19.21–25)

Among the Pythagoreans we shall find different angles
assigned to different gods. Thus Philolaus made the angle of
a triangle sacred to some, that of a square to others, and so on,
assigning the same angle to different gods and different angles
to the same gods according to their different powers.

(Proclus, *Commentary on Euclid* 130.8–14)

Philolaus, too, plausibly assigned the angle of a triangle to four
gods – Cronus, Hades, Ares and Dionysus, since he includes
in their scope the entire fourfold ordering of the elements
above, whether they derive from the heavens or from the four
segments of the zodiac. For Cronus provides all the moist cold
substances, Ares all the fiery natures, while Hades conserves
the whole of earthy life and Dionysus supervises moist warm
creation (of which wine, being moist and warm, is a symbol).
All these are distinct with regard to their secondary actions,
but they are united with one another. That is why Philolaus
brings them to unity under a single angle.

(*ibid* 167.1–14)

There are a few further fragments:

Magnitude is divisible to infinity but only finitely extendible;
plurality, on the other hand, is extendible to infinity but only
finitely divisible – though by nature, as far as their concepts
are concerned, both are infinite and therefore not capable of
being scientifically apprehended. For

> *there will be nothing that can have any knowledge at all if all
> things are unlimited,* [B 3]

as Philolaus says.

(Iamblichus, *Commentary on Nicomachus' Introduction to
Arithmetic* 7.18–25)

Philolaus' *Bacchae*:
> *The world is one. It began to come into being from the middle,
> and from the middle upwards and downwards in the same way;
> and what is above the middle is the opposite way about from what*

*is below. For to those below the lowest part is like the highest, and
so on; for each has the same relation to the middle, except that
they are reversed.* [B 17]

(Stobaeus, Anthology I xv 7)

*Compare here the notion of the 'counter-earth', which has already
appeared in Chapter 13:*

Philolaus the Pythagorean says that fire is central (for this is
the hearth of the universe), the counter-earth second, and
third the earth we inhabit, which is located and orbits opposite
the counter-earth (that is why the people on that earth are not
seen by those on this one).

([Plutarch], On the Scientific Beliefs of the Philosophers 895E)

*Philolaus also had something to say on biological matters. In
addition to a short fragment it is worth offering two paraphrastic
reports.*

There are four first principles of rational animals, as Philolaus
says in his *On Nature* – brain, heart, navel, genitals:
> *Head of thought, heart of soul and perception, navel of rooting
> and first growth, genitals of depositing of seed and generation.
> Brain signifies the first principle of man, heart that of animal,
> navel that of plant, genitals that of all together (for all shoot and
> sprout from seed).* [B 13]

([Iamblichus], Theological Arithmetic 25.17–26.3)

In general [the Pythagoreans] think that well-being and joy
depend on health, and they deny that health depends either
on well-being or on joy. Some of them – Philolaus included –
actually called the *tetractys*, their most solemn oath, which they
think completes the perfect number, the first principle of
health.

(Lucian, On Falling Down While Addressing People 9)

Philolaus of Croton says that our bodies are compounded from heat. For they have no share in coldness, as he argues from such considerations as these. Semen is hot, and it is what constitutes <animals>; the place into which semen is deposited, i.e. <the womb>, is hotter and similar to it; <what is similar to something has the same power as what it is similar to>; but since what constitutes animals has no share in coldness and the place in which <it is deposited> has no share in coldness, clearly the animal that is being constituted will also be of the same sort. To establish this he uses the following argument: immediately after birth the animal draws in the external air, which is cold, and then expels it as though paying off a debt. Now it desires the external air in order that, by drawing in breath from outside, its body, which is hotter, should be cooled by it. The constitution of our bodies, he says, depends on these things.

He says that diseases occur because of bile and blood and phlegm, and that these are the first principle of diseases. He says that blood is turned thick when the flesh is compressed internally, and that it becomes thin when the vessels in the flesh are enlarged. He says that phlegm is compounded from urine. He says that bile is a discharge from the flesh. <The same> man makes a paradoxical remark on this subject: he says that bile is not found near the liver and yet that it is a discharge of the flesh. And again, while most say that phlegm <is cold>, he supposes that it is by nature hot. For it is called phlegm from the verb *phlegein* [to burn], and hence inflaming agents inflame by sharing in phlegm. These he supposes are the first principles of diseases; contributory causes are excesses of heat or food or cooling and deficiencies <of these or> of things like them.

(Anonymus Londinensis, *Medical Writings* XVIII 8–XIX 1)

Finally there are two passages, of different purpose, which bear on ethics.

It is worth recording Philolaus' words; for the Pythagorean says this:

The old theologians and prophets testify that the soul has been yoked to the body as a punishment and that it is buried in it as though in a tomb. [B 14]

(Clement, *Miscellanies* III iii 17.1)

Certain thoughts and feelings – or else the actions based on such thoughts and feelings – are not in our power, but, as Philolaus said, some reasons are too strong for us.

(Aristotle, *Eudemian Ethics* 1225a30–33)

16
ION OF CHIOS

Ion, son of Orchomenes, came from the Aegean island of Chios, but he spent much of his life in Athens where he was a friend of many leading political and literary figures. He was born in about 485 BC and died in about 425. In his lifetime he was celebrated as a poet and a dramatist, his first tragedy being produced at Athens in about 450.

Ion has already been quoted in connection with Pythagoras, but he deserves a brief chapter of his own.

He composed many poems and tragedies and also a philosophical treatise entitled *Triad*. Callimachus says that its authorship is disputed, and in some copies it is entitled *Triads*, in the plural (according to Demetrius of Scepsis and Apollonides of Nicaea). In it he writes thus:

> This is the beginning of my account: all things are three, and there is nothing more or less than these three things. Of each one thing the excellence is threefold: intelligence and power and fortune. [36 B 1]

(Harpocration, *Lexicon* s.v. Ion)

We have at most one other piece of information about Ion's philosophical thought. Plutarch may well be referring to the Triad *when he reports that*

Ion the poet, in the work he wrote without metre and in prose, says that fortune, although a thing most dissimilar to wisdom, produces very similar results.

(Plutarch, *On the Fortune of the Romans* 316D)

17
HIPPO

Hippo's dates are unknown; but he was lampooned by the comic poet Cratinus in the 420s and was therefore presumably active in the latter part of the fifth century. Cratinus attacked him for impiety, and at some point he won the epithet 'atheist'. Aristotle regarded him as a tawdry thinker: 'One would not propose to place Hippo among these men because of the poverty of his thought' (*Metaphysics* 984a3). *But a fragment of his work survives, and he deserves a page or two.*

Simplicius gives a brief report of Hippo's view on the under-lying nature of things:

Of those who say that the first principle is one and in motion ([Aristotle] calls them natural scientists in the narrow sense), some assert that it is finite. Thus Thales, son of Examyes, a Milesian, and Hippo, who is actually thought to have been an atheist, said that the first principle is water. They were led to this view by the evidence of perception. For heat lives by moisture, dying things dry up, the seeds of all things are moist, and all food is juicy (each thing is naturally nourished by that from which it is constituted). But water is the first principle of natural moisture and conserves all moist things. That is why they supposed that water was the first principle of everything and declared that the earth rests on water.

(Simplicius, *Commentary on the Physics* 23.21–29)

Hippo seems to have written at some length on biological matters, and his biological speculations had some connection with his view of the first principle of things. Here is one extract:

Hippo of Croton thinks that there is an appropriate moisture in us in virtue of which we perceive and by which we live. When this moisture is in an appropriate condition, the animal is healthy; when it dries up, the animal ceases to perceive and dies. That is why old men are dry and have weak perception – because they lack moisture. In the same way the soles of the feet do not have any perception because they have no share of moisture. That is as far as he goes on these points.

In another book the same man says that what he calls moisture changes through excess of heat and excess of cold and in this way introduces diseases. He says that it changes either to being more moist or to being drier or to being thicker textured or to being thinner textured or in other directions. This is how he explains diseases – but he does not name the diseases which come about.

(Anonymus Londinensis, *Medical Writings* XI 22–42)

The surviving fragment is preserved in a scholium or note in the Geneva manuscript of Homer's Iliad. *Homer refers to 'Ocean, from which flow all rivers and all seas and all springs and the deep wells'. The scholium quotes the opinion of the scholar Crates on these lines:*

Then in the third book [of his *Homeric Studies*, Crates] says that the later natural scientists also agreed that the water which surrounds the earth for most of its extent is Ocean, and that fresh water comes from this. Hippo:

> *All drinking waters come from the sea. For the wells from which we drink are surely not deeper than the sea is. If they were, the water would come not from the sea but from somewhere else. But in fact the sea is deeper than the waters. Now all waters that are higher than the sea come from the sea.* [38 B 1]

Homer said the same as this.

(Geneva scholium on Homer, *Iliad* XXI 195)

18
ANAXAGORAS

Anaxagoras was born in Clazomenae on the coast of Asia Minor in about 500 BC. He spent much of his life in Athens, where he was associated with Pericles, the leading statesman of the age, and with Euripides, the writer of tragedies. The dates of his stay in Athens are disputed: it is perhaps most probable that he came to the city in 480 and remained there until about 430 when he was tried on trumped up charges and condemned. He fled Athens and settled in Lampsacus in the Troad where he died, an honoured guest, in 428.

Anaxagoras is said to have written only one book, which appears to have offered a complete account of the natural world on the old Milesian model. He was called a 'follower' of Anaximenes, and there can be little doubt that he was attempting to revive, in the post-Parmenidean period, the enterprise which the Milesians had carried out in the age of intellectual innocence.

The surviving fragments of Anaxagoras' book deal almost exclusively with the most general and abstract part of his thought. Anaxagoras' universe began as an undifferentiated mass of stuff. Mind then worked on the mass, and the articulated world developed. Anaxagoras' stuffs are continuous, not particulate. The cosmic development does not, and cannot, produce any 'pure' stuffs – every stuff always contains a 'portion' or 'share', however small, of every other stuff. Such is the general conception of things which the fragments convey. They can be supplemented from the doxography, which gives cursory information about Anaxagoras' more particular scientific theories.

Simplicius is again our chief source. Most of what currently pass as fragments of Anaxagoras are modern reconstructions based on distinct passages in Simplicius. Here the fragments are presented in the *disjointed form in which they are preserved. This introduces some repetitiveness, but it gives a proper picture of the evidence.*

In the first book of the *Physics* Anaxagoras says that uniform stuffs, infinite in quantity, separate off from a single mixture, all things being present in all and each being characterized by what predominates. He makes this clear in the first book of the *Physics* at the beginning of which he says:

> *Together were all things, infinite both in quantity and in smallness – for the small too was infinite. And when all things were together, none was patent by reason of smallness; for air and ether covered all things, being both infinite – for in all things these are the greatest both in quantity and in size.* [59 B 1]

And a little later:

> *For air and ether are separating off from the surrounding mass. And what surrounds is infinite in quantity.* [B 2]

And a little later:

> *This being so, one should believe that in everything that is combining there are present many things of every sort and seeds of all things having all kinds of shapes and colours and savours.* [cf B 4a]

> *But before they separated off,* he says, *when all things were together, not even any colour was patent; for this was prevented by the commixture of all things – of the wet and the dry and the hot and the cold and the bright and the dark and much earth present therein and seeds, infinite in quantity, in no way like one another. For of the other things too, none is like any other.* [B 4b]

He makes it clear that none of the uniform stuffs come into being or is destroyed but that they are always the same:

> *These things being thus dissociated, one should recognize that all things are neither fewer nor more numerous. For it is impossible for them to be more numerous than all, but all are always equal.* [B 5]

So much for the mixture and the uniform stuffs. On mind he has written as follows:

> *Mind is something infinite and self-controlling, and it has been mixed with no thing but is alone itself by itself. For if it were not by itself but had been mixed with some other thing, it would share*

*in all things, if it had been mixed with any. For in everything
there is present a share of everything, as I have said earlier,
and the things commingled with it would have prevented it from
controlling anything in the way in which it does when it is actually
alone by itself. For it is the finest of all things and the purest, and
it possesses all knowledge about everything, and it has the greatest
strength. And mind controls all those things, both great and small,
which possess soul. And mind controlled the whole revolution, so
that it revolved in the first place. And first it began to revolve in
a small area, and it is revolving more widely, and it will revolve
yet more widely. And mind recognizes all the things which are
commingling and separating off and dissociating. And mind
arranged everything – what was to be and what was and what
now is and what will be – and also this revolution in which revolve
the stars and the sun and the moon and the air and the ether
which are separating off. But the revolution itself made them
separate them off. And the dense is separating off from the rare,
and the hot from the cold, and the bright from the dark, and the
dry from the wet. And there are many shares of many things, but
nothing completely separates off or dissociates one from another
except mind. All mind, both great and small, is alike. Nothing
else is alike, but each single thing is and was most patently those
things of which it contains most.* [B 12]

That he supposes a two-fold world, one intelligible and the
other (derivative from it) perceptible, is clear both from what
we have already cited and from the following:

*Mind, *which always exists, now assuredly* is where all the other
things also are – in the surrounding mass and in the things that
have associated and in the things that have separated off.* [B 14]

Now having said that:

*There are present in everything that is combining many things of
every sort and seeds of all things having all kinds of shapes and
colours and savours, and men were compacted and the other
animals that possess soul,*

he continues:

*and the men possess inhabited cities and constructed goods, as
with us, and there is a sun present among them and a moon and
the rest, as with us, and the earth grows many things of every sort*

ANAXAGORAS

> *for them, the most useful of which they gather into their houses and use.* [B 4a]

The phrase 'as with us', which he uses more than once, shows that he is hinting at another world apart from ours. He does not think that it is perceptible and earlier than ours in time, as is shown by the sentence 'the most useful of which they gather into their houses and use' – for he said 'use', not 'used'. Nor is he referring to a present state of affairs similar to ours with other houses, for he said not 'the sun and the moon are present to them as they are to us', but 'a sun and a moon, as with us', as though he meant a different sun and moon. But whether that is so or not demands further enquiry.

> (Simplicius, *Commentary on the Physics* 155.21–157.24)

At the very beginning of his book [Anaxagoras] says that things were infinite:

> *Together were all things, infinite both in quantity and in smallness.* [cf B 1]

Among the principles there is neither a smallest nor a largest:

> *For of the small, he says, there is no smallest, but there is always a smaller. For what is cannot not be. And again of the large there is always a larger, and it is equal to the small in quantity. But in relation to itself each thing is both large and small.* [B 3]

For if everything is in everything and everything separates off from everything, then from what is taken to be the smallest thing something smaller will be separated off, and what is taken to be the largest has been separated off from something larger than itself. He says clearly that:

> *In everything there is present a share of everything except mind – and in some things mind too is present.* [B 11]

And again:

> *Other things possess a share of everything, but mind is something infinite and self-controlling, and it has been mixed with no thing.* [cf B 12]

Elsewhere he puts it like this:

> *Now since there are equal shares of the great and of the small in quantity, for this reason too all things will be in everything; nor can they be separate, but all things possess a share of everything.*

229

Since there cannot be a smallest, things cannot be separated or
come to be by themselves, but as they were in the beginning so too
now are all things together. In all things there are many even of
the things that are separating off, equal in quantity in the larger
and smaller. [B 6]

Anaxagoras also stipulates that each of the perceptible uniform stuffs comes about and is characterized in virtue of the
composition of similars. For he says:

But each single thing is and was most patently those things of
which it contains most. [cf B 12]

He seems, too, to say that mind attempts to dissociate them but
cannot do so.

(Simplicius, *Commentary on the Physics* 164.14–165.5)

Anaxagoras says at the beginning of his treatise:

Together were all things, infinite both in quantity and in small-
ness – for the small too was infinite. And when all things were
together, none was patent by reason of smallness. [cf B 1]

And:

One should believe that all things were present in the whole. [cf
B 4b]

Perhaps by 'infinite' he means what is ungraspable and
unknowable to us; for this is indicated by the phrase

so that we do not know the quantity either in word or in deed of
the things that are separating off. [B 7]

(That he thought them limited in *form* he makes clear by saying
that mind knows them all.)

(Simplicius, *Commentary on On the Heavens* 608.21–28)

[Aristotle] was not referring to Anaxagoras, according to Alexander, even though Anaxagoras placed mind among the first
principles – perhaps, he says, because he makes no use of it in
generating things. But it is plain that he *does* use it, since he
says that generation is nothing but separating out, that separating out comes about by motion, and that mind is responsible
for the motion. For this is what Anaxagoras says:

And when mind began to move things, things were separating off
from everything that was being moved, and everything that mind

*moved was dissociated. And as they were moving and dissociating,
the revolution made them dissociate far more.* [B 13]

[Aristotle] did not mention Anaxagoras because Anaxagoras
did not make mind an enmattered form (which is what he is
investigating here) but a cause of dissociation and arrangement, separate from the things that are being arranged and
belonging to a different order from the things being arranged.
For

*Mind, he says, is something infinite and self-controlling, and it
has been mixed with no thing, but is alone itself by itself.* [cf B 12]

And he adds the reason for this. Perhaps this is another reason
why [Aristotle] did not mention Anaxagoras – that his mind
seems not to make the forms but to dissociate them when they
exist.

(Simplicius, *Commentary on the Physics* 300.27–301.10)

Anaxagoras of Clazomenae seems to have conceived of all
the forms in three different ways. First, they are gathered
together in an intelligible unity – as when he says:

*Together were all things, infinite both in quantity and in small-
ness.* [cf B 1]

And again he says:

*But before these things separated off, when all things were
together, not even any colour was patent; for this was prevented
by the commixture of all things – of the wet and the dry and the
hot and the cold and the bright and the dark and much earth
present therein and seeds, infinite in quantity, in no way like one
another. This being so, one should believe that all things were
present in the whole.* [B 4b]

(And this totality will be the one existing thing of Parmenides.)

Secondly, he conceived of them in an intellectual dissociation on which the dissociation about us has been modelled. For in the first book of *On Nature*, shortly after the
beginning, Anaxagoras says this:

*This being so, one should believe that in everything that is combin-
ing there are present many things of every sort and seeds of all
things having all kinds of shapes and colours and savours, and
men were compacted and the other animals that possess soul. And*

the men possess inhabited cities and constructed goods, as with
us and they have a sun and a moon and the rest, as with us, and
the earth grows many things of every sort for them, the most use-
ful of which they gather into their houses and use. This I have said
about the separating off, because it will not have occurred with
us only but also elsewhere. [B 4a]

To some he will no doubt seem not to be contrasting a generat-
ive dissociation with an intellectual one but to be comparing
our habitation to other places on the earth. But he would not
have said of other places that they have a sun and a moon and
the rest, as with us, nor would he have called the things there
seeds of all things and shapes. Consider what he says a little
later on when he compares the two:

As these things thus revolve and are separating off by force and
speed (the speed produces the force), their speed is similar in speed
to none of the things that now exist among men, but is certainly
many times faster. [B 9]

And if this is his conception, he holds that all things are in all
things first in respect of intelligible unity, secondly in respect
of intellectual consubstantiality, and thirdly in respect of perceptible conjunctions and their generations and dissolutions.

(Simplicius, *Commentary on the Physics* 34.18–35.21)

When Anaxagoras says:

One thing neither separates off nor dissociates from another [cf
B 12]

because everything is in everything, and elsewhere:

They have not been cut off by an axe, neither the hot from the cold
nor the cold from the hot [B 8]

(for there is nothing pure by itself), this, says Aristotle, is not
based on knowledge.

(*ibid* 175.11–15)

In the first book of the *Physics* Anaxagoras plainly says that
generation and destruction are combination and dissociation.
This is what he writes:

The Greeks do not have a correct notion of generation and
destruction; for no things are generated or destroyed, but they are

commingled and dissociated from things that exist. And for this
reason they would be correct to call generation commingling and
destruction dissociation. [B 17]

All this – that 'together were all things' and that generation
takes place in virtue of alteration (or combination and dissociation) – was assumed in order to ensure that nothing comes
into being from what does not exist.

(ibid 163.18–26)

Perhaps Anaxagoras posited the compounds, and not the
simple and original qualities as elements when he said:

But the revolution itself made them separate off. And the dense is
separating off from the rare, and the cold from the hot, and the
bright from the dark, and the dry from the wet. [cf B 12]

And a little later he says:

The dense and the wet and the cold and the dark congregated here
where now is the earth, and the rare and the hot and the dry and
the bright moved out to the farther part of the ether. [B 15]

And he says that these original and very simple things are
separating off, and he says that other things, more compound
than these, sometimes become compacted like compounds and
sometimes separate off like the earth. For he says:

In this way from these as they separate off earth is compacted; for
water is separated off from the clouds, earth from the water, and
stones are compacted from the earth by the cold. [cf B 16]

(ibid 178.33–179.10)

Perhaps all the opposites are actually in the elements, if the
elements are first principles, but not directly (as in the case of
uniform stuffs). For sweet and bitter, e.g., on the hypothesis
of the elements do not inhere primarily in the elements, but
on the hypothesis of uniform stuffs they inhere primarily and
in their own right – as do the colour opposites. Or perhaps
even in the case of uniform stuffs some opposites are prior to
others, the secondary ones inhering because of the primary
ones. At any rate, Anaxagoras says in the first book of his
Physics:

For water is separated off from the clouds, earth from the water, and stones are compacted from the earth by the cold. And these move out further than the water. [cf B 16]

(Simplicius, *Commentary on the Physics* 155.13–23)

Some scholars have found a further fragment in the following text:

Anaxagoras hit upon the old doctrine that nothing comes into being from what is not, and did away with generation, introducing dissociation in its place. For he said that all things have been mixed with one another and that as they grow they dissociate. For in the same seed there are hairs and nails and veins and arteries and tendons and bones, and they are invisible because of the smallness of their parts; but as they grow they gradually dissociate. For how, he says, could hair come into being from what is not hair, or flesh from what is not flesh? [B 10] And he says this not only of bodies but also of colours; for black is present in white and white in black. And he posited the same for weights, believing that the light was commingled with the heavy and *vice versa*. All this is false – for how can opposites co-exist?

(Scholiast to Gregory of Nazianzus [*Patrologia Graeca* XXXVI 911 BC])

In fact, the only author apart from Simplicius who preserves any of Anaxagoras' words is Sextus Empiricus.

The distinguished natural scientist Anaxagoras, attacking the senses for their weakness, says:

We are not capable of discerning the truth by reason of their feebleness, [B 21]

and he offers as a proof of their untrustworthiness the gradual change of colours. For if we take two colours, black and white, and then pour from one to the other drop by drop, our sight will not be able to discriminate the gradual changes even though they exist in nature.

(Sextus Empiricus, *Against the Mathematicians* VII 90)

Diotimus said that [Democritus] supposed three standards: for the apprehension of what is unclear the standard is the apparent; for

> what appears is the sight of what is unclear, [B 21a]

as Anaxagoras says – and Democritus praised him for this.

(*ibid* VII 140)

One of the most celebrated parts of Anaxagoras' philosophy was his conception of the controlling power of mind in the universe. According to Aristotle,

someone said that just as in animals so in nature mind is present and responsible for the world and its whole ordering: he appeared as a sober man compared to his predecessors who spoke at random.

(Aristotle, *Metaphysics* 984b15–18)

Socrates had the same view when he first read Anaxagoras' book:

I once heard someone reading from a book of Anaxagoras and saying that it is mind which arranges and is responsible for everything. This explanation delighted me and it seemed to me somehow to be a good thing that mind was responsible for everything – I thought that in that case mind, in arranging things, would arrange them all, and place each, in the best way possible. So if anyone wanted to discover the explanation of anything – why it comes into being or perishes or exists – he would have to discover how it is best for it to be or to be acted upon or to act . . . Now, my friend, this splendid hope was dashed; for as I continued reading I saw that the man didn't use his mind at all – he didn't ascribe to it any explanations for the arranging of things but found explanations in air and ether and water and many other absurdities.

(Plato, *Phaedo* 97 B C, 98 B C)

Socrates' disappointment was echoed later by Aristotle and by Aristotle's pupil Eudemus.

On the details of Anaxagoras' views we are less well informed. Here

are, first, two short samples, and then the bulk of Diogenes Laertius'
life of Anaxagoras.

In all other respects we are more unfortunate than the beasts. But by experience and memory and wisdom and skill, according to Anaxagoras, we use them, taking their honey and their milk, herding them together and doing what we will with them, so that here nothing depends on fortune but everything on planning and foresight. [B 21b]

(Plutarch, *On Fortune* 98F)

Anaxagoras in his *Physics* says that what is called bird's milk is the white of the egg. [B 22]

(Athenaeus, *Deipnosophists* 57D)

Anaxagoras, son of Hegesibulus (or of Eubulus), of Clazomenae. He was a follower of Anaximenes, and was the first to put mind in charge of matter. His treatise, which is written in a pleasant and lofty style, begins as follows:

All things were together. Then mind came and arranged them.
[cf B 1]

Hence he was nicknamed 'Mind', and Timon in his *Silli* says this about him:

And there, they say, is Anaxagoras, a stout hero,
The Mind (for he had a mind), who suddenly rose up
and tied together all that had before been in disarray.

He was remarkable for his good birth and his wealth – and also for his generosity inasmuch as he ceded his inheritance to his friends. For when they accused him of neglecting it he said: 'Then why don't *you* look after it?' In the end he went into retirement and spent his time in scientific study, giving no thought to politics. When someone asked him if he had no care for his country, he replied: 'Be quiet – I have the greatest care for my country', pointing to the heavens.

He is said to have been twenty when Xerxes invaded Greece [480 BC], and to have lived to be seventy-two. Apollodorus in his *Chronicles* says that he was born in the seventieth Olympiad [500–497] and that he died in the first year of the eighty-eighth Olympiad [428]. He began to philosophize in Athens in the archonship of Callias when he was twenty, according to Demetrius of Phaleron in his *List of Archons*. They say that he stayed there for thirty years.

He said that the sun is a fiery lump, larger than the Peloponnese (but some ascribe this to Tantalus), and that the moon is inhabited and also contains hills and ravines. The uniform stuffs are first principles; for just as gold is compounded from gold-dust, so the universe is combined from small uniform bodies. Mind is the first principle of movement. Heavy bodies, like earth, occupy the lower regions, light bodies, like fire, the upper; water and air, the middle. For in this way the sea rests on the earth, which is flat, and its moisture is vaporized by the sun. At first the heavenly bodies moved as though in a rotunda so that the pole which is always visible was directly over the earth; later they acquired a tilt. The Milky Way is a reflection of light from stars which are not illuminated by the sun. Comets are conjunctions of planets which emit flames. Shooting stars are, as it were, sparks shaken from the air. Winds occur when the air is rarefied by the sun. Thunder is a clash of clouds. Lightning is friction in the clouds. Earthquakes are a subsiding of air into the earth. Animals were generated from the moist, the hot and the earthy; and later from one another. Males come from the right, females from the left.

They say that he predicted the fall of the meteorite which occurred at Aegospotami – he said that it would fall from the sun. That is why Euripides, who was his pupil, says in the *Phaethon* that the sun is a golden cloud. When he was going to Olympia he sat down under a mackintosh as though it were going to rain – and it did. When someone asked him if the mountains at Lampsacus would ever become sea, they say he replied: 'Yes, if time doesn't give out.' Asked for what end he had been born, he said: 'For the study of the sun and the moon and the heavens.' When someone said, 'You have been exiled from the Athenians,' he replied: 'No – they have been exiled from me.' When he saw the tomb of Mausolus, he said: 'A rich tomb is the image of a substance turned to stone.' When someone complained that he was dying in a foreign country, he replied: 'The descent to Hades is the same wherever you start from.'

He seems to have been the first – according to Favorinus in his *Miscellaneous Inquiries* – to have said that Homer's poetry is about virtue and vice. This theory was taken further by his friend, Metrodorus of Lampsacus, who was the first to occupy himself with the poet's ideas on natural science. Anaxagoras was also the first to publish a book with diagrams. Silenus says in the first book of his *Histories* that the meteorite fell from the sky in the archonship of Demulus, and that Anaxagoras said that the whole heavens were constituted of stones – they are held up by the rapid rotation and they fall to earth when it slackens.

Different stories are told about his trial. Sotion, in his *Succession of Philosophers*, says that he was condemned for impiety by Cleon because he said that the sun was a fiery lump, and that when his pupil Pericles conducted his defence he was fined five talents and exiled. Satyrus in his *Lives* says that the case was brought by Thucydides, Pericles' political opponent; that the charge was not only impiety but also Medism; and that he was condemned to death *in absentia*. When he was told both of the condemnation and of the death of his children, he said of the condemnation that 'Nature long ago condemned both them and me', and of his children that 'I knew they were mortal when I fathered them.' (Some ascribe this to Solon, others to Xenophon.) Demetrius of Phaleron, in his book *On Old Age*, says that he buried them with his own hands. Hermippus in his *Lives* says that he was incarcerated in the prison to await his death. Pericles arrived and asked them if they had any charge to bring against *him* for his way of life. They said they had none. 'Yet I am his pupil,' he said. 'Then do not yield to calumny and kill him, but listen to me and free him.' He was freed, but he could not bear the shame and killed himself. Hieronymus, in the second book of his *Miscellanies*, says that Pericles led him to the courtroom feeble and thin from disease, so that it was pity rather than judgement which freed him. So much for his trial.

He is thought somehow to have been hostile to Democritus

because he was not able to have conversation with him. In the end he retired to Lampsacus and died there. When the magistrates of the city asked him what he would like to be done for him, he said: 'Let the children have a holiday each year in the month of my death.' The custom is still observed.

(Diogenes Laertius, *Lives of the Philosophers* II 6–14)

19
ARCHELAUS

Archelaus was a minor figure in the history of Greek philosophy, and no fragment of his works has survived. Yet he deserves a brief mention: he was the first native-born Athenian philosopher; he was a pupil of Anaxagoras and a teacher of Socrates; and he made at least one striking, and apparently original, remark (on the subject of ethics). Here, then, are the two fullest ancient accounts of his thought.

Archelaus came from Athens or Miletus. His father was Apollodorus or, according to some, Midon. He was a pupil of Anaxagoras and a teacher of Socrates. He was the first to bring natural philosophy from Ionia to Athens, and he was called a natural philosopher – indeed natural philosophy actually ended with him, when Socrates introduced the subject of ethics. But he too seems to have touched upon ethics; for he philosophized about laws and about the noble and the just. (Socrates took this over from him and was supposed to have invented the subject because he developed it to its height.)

He said that there are two causes of generation, hot and cold, and that animals were generated from the mud. And that things are just or ignoble not by nature but by convention.

(Diogenes Laertius, *Lives of the Philosophers* II 16)

Archelaus was of an Athenian family, the son of Apollodorus. He spoke of the mixing of matter in the same way as Anaxagoras (and similarly with the first principles of things), but he maintained that there is a mixture present in mind from the start. The origin of motion is the separating off from one another of the hot and the cold: the hot is in motion, the cold at rest.

As water liquefies it flows into the middle where it burns and becomes air and earth, the former of which travels upwards while the latter remains below. Thus the earth is at rest and comes into existence for these reasons, and it lies at the middle, being the merest fraction of the universe. <The air> given off by the conflagration <supports the earth>; from it as it is first burned off comes the substance of the heavenly bodies, of which the greatest is the sun and the second the moon (of the rest some are greater, some smaller).

He says that the heavens are tilted, and that in this way the sun sheds light on the earth and makes the air transparent and the earth dry. For at first the earth was a marsh, high at the circumference and hollow in the middle. He offers as evidence for its hollowness the fact that the sun does not rise and set at the same time for everyone – something which would be bound to occur were the earth level.

On the subject of animals, he says that, as the earth grew warm, it was first in the lower part, where the hot and the cold were mixing, that many animals including men appeared, all of them having the same way of life inasmuch as they were nourished by the mud. They were short-lived. Later they came to reproduce from one another. Men were separated from the other animals and established leaders and laws and skills and cities and the rest. He says that mind is innate in all animals alike; for each of the animals uses its mind, some more slowly and others more quickly.

(Hippolytus, *Refutation of all Heresies* I ix 1–6)

20
LEUCIPPUS

Leucippus is a shadowy figure: his dates are not recorded, and even his birthplace is uncertain. He was the first to develop the theory of atomism, which was elaborated in far greater detail by his pupil and successor, Democritus of Abdera. Democritus overshadowed his master in the later tradition. The Greek historians of philosophy rarely distinguish between the views of the two men: they often refer, conjunctively, to 'Leucippus and Democritus'. We are rarely in a position to separate the contributions of Democritus from those of Leucippus.

The atomist philosophy, then, will be presented more fully in the next chapter under the name of Democritus. Here it is enough to cite one of the few doxographical passages which speak specifically of Leucippus, and to transcribe the one short fragment which is all that survives of Leucippus' writings.

Leucippus of Elea or of Miletus (both places are mentioned in connection with him) shared Parmenides' philosophy but did not take the same path as Parmenides and Xenophanes about the things that exist but rather, as it seems, the opposite one. For whereas they made the universe one and motionless and ungenerated and limited, and did not allow anyone even to inquire into what does not exist, he posited infinite and eternally moving elements, the atoms, and an infinite quantity of shapes among them (because there is no more reason for them to be thus than thus) supposing that generation and change are unfailing among the things that exist. Again, he held that being no more exists than non-being, and both are equally causes of the things that come into being. For supposing that the substance of the atoms is solid and full, he said that it was being and that it was carried about in the void, which he called non-being and which he says exists no less than being.

(Simplicius, Commentary on the Physics 28.4–15)

Leucippus: everything happens in accordance with necessity, and necessity is the same as fate.

Leucippus: he says in *On Mind*:

> *No thing happens in vain, but everything for a reason and by necessity.* [67 B 2]

(Stobaeus, Anthology I iv 7c)

21

DEMOCRITUS

Democritus was born in Abdera in the north of Greece. He was the most prolific, and ultimately the most influential, of the Presocratic philosophers: his atomic theory may be regarded from a certain point of view as the culmination of early Greek thought. Although Plato fails, remarkably, to mention his name, he was highly regarded by Aristotle, and his fundamental ideas were taken up and developed by Epicurus in the fourth century BC. None of Democritus' writings has survived intact, and there are, moreover, very few fragments bearing on what we now think of as the central and most important part of his thought. Much of Epicurus' work, however, was preserved, so that by way of Epicureanism Democritus has had a lasting effect on western science and philosophy.

Little is known of his life. He is said to have travelled to Egypt, to Persia, and to the Red Sea. He is supposed to have learned from Leucippus and from Anaxagoras and from Philolaus. In a fragment of uncertain authenticity he allegedly writes:

> I came to Athens and no-one knew me.
> (Diogenes Laertius, *Lives of the Philosophers* IX 36
> = 68 B 116)

He himself offered a little chronological information:

As to his dates, he was, as he himself says in *The Little World-ordering*, a young man when Anaxagoras was old, being forty years younger than him. And he says that *The Little World-ordering* was composed 730 years after the capture of Troy. So he was born, according to Apollodorus in his *Chronicles*, in the eightieth Olympiad [460–457 BC] – or, according to Thrasyllus in his work entitled *Prolegomena to the Reading of the Books of Democritus*, in the third year of the seventy-seventh Olympiad [470/469 BC], being, he says, one year older than Socrates. So he will have been a contemporary of Archelaus, the pupil of Anaxagoras, and of Oenopides (whom he mentions). He also mentions, in connection with their beliefs about the one, Parmenides and Zeno as being particularly celebrated in his time – and also Protagoras of Abdera, who is agreed to have been a contemporary of Socrates.

(*ibid* IX 41)

Some idea of Democritus' productivity, and of the breadth of his professional interests, may be gained from the list of his books which Diogenes Laertius preserves:

His books were catalogued and arranged in tetralogies by Thrasyllus in the same way as he arranged Plato's works. His ethical works are these:
Pythagoras, On the Disposition of the Wise Man, On the Things in Hades, Tritogeneia (so called because from her come three things which conserve all human affairs), *On Manliness* or *On Virtue, The Horn of Amaltheia, On Contentment, Ethical Commentaries*. (*Well-being* is lost.)
These are his ethical works; his works on natural science are:
The Great World-ordering (which Theophrastus says was written by Leucippus), *The Little World-ordering, Cosmography, On the Planets, On Nature* (one book), *On the Nature of Man* or *On Flesh* (two books), *On Mind, On the Senses* (some put these together under the title *On the Soul*), *On Flavours, On Colours, On Different Shapes, On Changing Shape, Buttresses* (which supports the previous works), *On Images* or *On Providence, On Logic* or *The Rule* (three books).
These are about nature. (Not integrated into the catalogue are the following:
Heavenly Causes, Atmospheric Causes, Terrestrial Causes, Causes Concerned with Fire and Things in Fire, Causes Concerned with

Sounds, Causes Concerned with Seeds and Plants and Fruits, Causes Concerned with Animals (three books), *Miscellaneous Causes, On Magnets*. These are the non-integrated works.)

The mathematical works are these:

On Different Angles or *On Contact of Circles and Spheres, On Geometry, Geometry, Numbers, On Irrational Lines and Solids* (two books), *Planispheres, On the Great Year* or *Astronomy* (a calendar), *Contest of the Waterclock, Description of the Heavens, Geography, Description of the Poles, Description of Rays of Light.*

These are the mathematical works; the literary works are the following:

On Rhythms and Harmony, On Poetry, On the Beauty of Verses, On Euphonious and Harsh-sounding Letters, On Homer or *Correct Language and Glosses, On Song, On Verbs, Names.*

Such are his literary works; his technical works are these:

Prognosis, On Diet or *Dietetics, Medical Judgement, Causes Concerning Appropriate and Inappropriate Occasions, On Farming* or *Farming, On Painting, Tactics* and *Fighting in Armour.*

Such are these. Some order separately the following works from the *Commentaries*:

On the Sacred Writings in Babylon, On Those in Meroe, Circumnavigation of the Ocean, On History, Chaldaean Account, Phrygian Account, On Fever and Coughing Sicknesses, Legal Causes, Artefacts or *Problems.*

The other books which some ascribe to him are either compilations of his works or else agreed to be by others.

(Diogenes Laertius, *Lives of the Philosophers* IX 45–49)

The remainder of this chapter is divided into four sections. First comes a selection of texts, none of them fragments of Democritus, which describe the atomic theory. Secondly come the texts which record Democritus' views on knowledge and scepticism. There follows a short section on Democritus' scientific and literary studies. Finally, the longest section is given to the ethical fragments. The relative lengths of the four sections are determined by the amount of available material: they do not reflect the importance which Democritus – or we – might ascribe to the different aspects of his thought.

I Atomism

*For Democritus' most celebrated doctrine, his atomism, we are obliged
to rely on second-hand reports.*

If the same atoms endure, being impassive, it is clear that [the
Democriteans] too will say that the worlds are altered rather
than destroyed – just as Empedocles and Heraclitus seem to
think. An extract from Aristotle's work *On Democritus* will show
what the view of these men was:

> Democritus thinks that the nature of eternal things con-
> sists in small substances, infinite in quantity, and for them
> he posits a place, distinct from them and infinite in extent.
> He calls place by the names 'void', 'nothing' and 'infinite';
> and each of the substances he calls 'thing', 'solid' and
> 'being'. He thinks that the substances are so small that they
> escape our senses, and that they possess all sorts of forms
> and all sorts of shapes and differences in magnitude.
> From them, as from elements, he was able to generate
> and compound visible and perceptible bodies. The atoms
> struggle and are carried about in the void because of their
> dissimilarities and the other differences mentioned, and
> as they are carried about they collide and are bound
> together in a binding which makes them touch and be
> contiguous with one another but which does not genu-
> inely produce any other single nature whatever from
> them; for it is utterly silly to think that two or more things
> could ever become one. He explains how the substances
> remain together in terms of the ways in which the bodies
> entangle with and grasp hold of one another; for some
> of them are uneven, some hooked, some concave, some
> convex, and others have innumerable other differences.
> So he thinks that they hold on to one another and remain
> together up to the time when some stronger force reaches
> them from their environment and shakes them and scat-
> ters them apart. He speaks of generation and of its con-
> trary, dissolution, not only in connection with animals but

also in connection with plants and worlds – and in general with all perceptible bodies. [Aristotle, fragment 208]
(Simplicius, *Commentary on On the Heavens* 294.30–295.22)

The excerpt from Aristotle's lost essay on Democritus can be supplemented from his extant Metaphysics:

Leucippus and his colleague Democritus say that the full and the void are elements, calling the one 'being' and the other 'non-being'; and of these the full and solid is being, the void non-being (that is why they say that being no more exists than non-being – because void no more exists than body), and these are the material causes of the things that exist. And just as those who make the underlying substance single generate other things by its properties, making the rare and the dense origins of the properties, so these men say that the differences [among the atoms] are the causes of the other things. They say that the differences are three in number – shape, order, and position. For they say that beings differ only by 'rhythm', 'contact' and 'mode' – where rhythm is shape, contact is order and mode is position. The letter A differs from N in shape; AN differs from NA in order; and N differs from Z in position. As for motion (whence and how existing things acquire it), they too, like the others, negligently omitted to inquire into it.

(Aristotle, *Metaphysics* 985b4–20)

Aristotle's final remark is echoed by Simplicius:

Democritus too, when he says that a whirl of every kind of forms was separated off from the whole [B 167] but does not say how and by what cause, seems to generate it spontaneously and by chance.

(Simplicius, *Commentary on the Physics* 327.23–26)

The same commentary contains a brief doxographical section which adds a little to what we learn from Aristotle.

In the same way [Leucippus'] associate Democritus of Abdera posited the full and the void as first principles, one of which he called being and the other non-being; for he posits the atoms as matter for the things that exist and generates everything else by their differences. These are three: rhythm, contact, mode – which is to say, shape and position and order. For by nature like is moved by like and things of the same kind are carried towards one another, and each of the shapes when arranged in a different compound produces a different condition. Thus since the principles are infinite, they reasonably undertook to account for all properties and substances and for how and by what cause they come into being. That is why they say that only those who make the elements infinite produce a reasonable account of things. And they say that the quantity of shapes in the atoms is infinite because there is no more reason for them to be thus than thus. They themselves give this as the explanation of the infinitude.

(*ibid* 28.15–27)

Democritus' idea that 'like is moved by like' is illustrated in the following passage:

There is an ancient opinion which, as I have already said, has long been current among the natural scientists to the effect that like recognizes like. Democritus is thought to have produced confirmation of this opinion and Plato to have touched on it in his *Timaeus*. Democritus bases his argument on both animate and inanimate things. For animals, he says, congregate with animals of the same kind – doves with doves, cranes with cranes, and so with the other irrational animals. Similarly in the case of inanimate things, as we can see from seeds that are being riddled and from pebbles on the sea-shore. For in the one case the whirling of the sieve separately arranges lentils with lentils, barley with barley, wheat with wheat; and in the other case, by the motion of the waves, oval pebbles are forced into the same place as oval pebbles, and round pebbles as round pebbles, as though the similarity in things contained some sort of force for collecting things together. [B 164] That is Democritus' view.

(Sextus Empiricus, *Against the Mathematicians* VII 116–118)

The texts so far cited do not explain why Democritus thought that the world consisted of atoms and void. The following Aristotelian passage does not purport to represent Democritus' actual arguments, but it is generally supposed to be an adaptation of Democritean material.

Democritus seems to have been persuaded by appropriate and scientific arguments. What I mean will be clear as we proceed.

There is a difficulty if one supposes that there is a body or magnitude which is divisible everywhere and that this division is possible. For what will there be that escapes the division? If it is divisible everywhere, and the division is possible, then it might be so divided at one and the same time even if the divisions were not all made at the same time; and if this were to happen no impossibility would result. So if it is by nature everywhere divisible, then if it is divided – whether at successive mid-points or by any other method – nothing impossible will have come about. (After all, if it were divided a thousand times into a thousand parts, nothing impossible would result, even though no-one would actually so divide it.)

Now since the body is everywhere divisible, suppose it to have been divided. What will be left? A magnitude? That is not possible; for then there will be something that has not been divided, but we supposed it divisible everywhere. But if there is to be no body or magnitude left and yet the division is to take place, it will either consist of points and its components will have no magnitude, or else they will be nothing at all so that it would come to be, and be composed, from nothing and the whole body would be nothing but an appearance.

Similarly, if it is made of points it will not be a quantity. For when the points were in contact and were a single magnitude and were together, they did not make the whole at all larger. For if it is divided into two or more parts the whole is no smaller or larger than it was before, so that even if all the points are put together they will not make any magnitude.

If some sawdust, as it were, is created when the body is being divided, and in this way some body escapes from the magnitude, the same argument applies: how is *this* body divisible?

Perhaps it is not a body but a separable form or property which escapes, and the magnitude consists of points or contacts with such and such a property? But it is absurd to think that a magnitude consists of what are not magnitudes.

Again, where will these points be, and are they motionless or moving?

And a single contact always involves two things, so that there is something apart from the contact and the division and the point.

If one posits that any body of whatever size is everywhere divisible, all these things follow.

Again, if I divide a log or anything else and then put it together, it is again a unit of the same size. This is so at whatever point I cut the log. So it has potentially been divided everywhere. Then what is there apart from the division? Even if it has properties, how is the body dissolved into these and how does it come into being from them? And how are they separated? So if it is impossible for magnitudes to consist of contacts or points, necessarily there are indivisible bodies and magnitudes.

(Aristotle, *On Generation and Corruption* 316a13–b16)

II Knowledge

Democritus' atomism was the framework within which he tried to understand the nature of the world. At the same time it was a theory which appeared to have strongly sceptical implications. It is best to approach this topic by setting down the passages in which Plutarch records and criticizes two objections made against Democritus by Epicurus' pupil Colotes.

[Colotes] first accuses [Democritus] of saying that each object is no more such-and-such than so-and-so, and thereby throwing life into confusion. But Democritus is so far from thinking that each subject is no more such-and-such than so-and-so that he attacked Protagoras the sophist for saying just this and wrote many persuasive things against him. Colotes, having not the slightest acquaintance with these writings, has misunderstood Democritus' words: when he lays it down that things no more exist than nothing, he means body by 'things' and the void by 'nothing', indicating that the latter too has a sort of nature and existence of its own.

(Plutarch, *Against Colotes* 1108F–1109A)

And even more in his second accusation [Colotes] fails to notice that he drives Epicurus out of life along with Democritus. For Democritus' claim – by convention colour and by convention sweet and by convention compounds, etc, in reality the void and the atoms [cf B 125] – was, he says, an attack on the senses; and he holds that anyone who sticks by this argument and uses it cannot even think that he is himself a man and alive.

But what does Democritus say? – That substances infinite in quantity, indivisible and indestructible, and also qualityless and impassive, are carried about scattered in the void. When they approach one another or collide or are entangled, the aggregates *appear* as water or fire or plants or men, but all things really *are* what he calls these indivisible forms and nothing else. For there is no generation from what does not exist, while from the things that exist nothing can be generated in virtue of the fact that, because of their hardness, the atoms neither are affected nor change. Hence no colour can emerge from things which are colourless, and no nature or soul from things which are qualityless and impassive.

(*ibid* 1110F–1111A)

The most important text is found in Sextus Empiricus. It contains most of the fragments which bear on the issue.

Democritus sometimes does away with what appears to the senses and says that nothing of this sort appears in truth but only in opinion, truth among the things that exist lying in the fact that there are atoms and void. For he says:

By convention sweet and by convention bitter, by convention hot, by convention cold, by convention colour: in reality atoms and void. [cf B 125]

That is to say, objects of perception are thought and believed to exist but they do not exist in truth – only atoms and void do.

In his *Buttresses*, although he undertakes to ascribe reliable power to the senses, he is found nonetheless condemning them. For he says:

We in reality know nothing firmly but only as it changes in accordance with the condition of the body and of the things which enter it and of the things which resist it. [B 9]

And again he says:

That in reality we do not know how each thing is or is not has been shown in many ways. [B 10]

And in *On Ideas* he says:

And a man must recognize by this rule that he is removed from reality; [B 6]

and again:

This argument too shows that in reality we know nothing about anything, but our belief in each case is a changing of shape; [B 7]

and again:

Yet it will be clear that to know how each thing is in reality is a puzzle. [B 8]

Now in these passages he does away in effect with all knowledge, even if it is only the senses which he explicitly attacks. But in the *Rules* he says that there are two forms of knowledge, one by way of the senses and the other by way of the understanding. The one by way of the understanding he calls genuine, ascribing reliability to it with regard to the discrimination of truth; the one by way of the senses he names dark, denying that it is unerring with regard to the discernment of what is true. These are his words:

There are two forms of knowledge, one genuine and the other dark. To the dark belong all these: sight, hearing, smell, taste, touch. The dark, separated from this <. . .>. [B 11a]

Then, setting the genuine above the dark, he continues thus:

> *When the dark can no longer see more finely or hear or smell or*
> *taste or perceive by touch, *but something finer* <. . .>.* [B 11b]

So according to Democritus, reason, which he calls genuine knowledge, is the standard of truth.

But Diotimus said that he supposed three standards: for the apprehension of what is unclear the standard is the apparent (for what appears is the sight of what is unclear, as Anaxagoras says [59 B 21a] – and Democritus praised him for this); for investigation, it is the concept ('for in every case, my friend, one principle is to know what the investigation is about' [Plato, *Phaedrus* 273B]); of choice and avoidance, it is the passions – for that which we find congenial is to be chosen and that which we find alien is to be avoided.

(Sextus Empiricus, *Against the Mathematicians* VII 135–140)

Diogenes Laertius expresses the same sequence of thoughts more briefly:

According to some, Xenophanes and Zeno of Elea and Democritus were sceptics . . . Democritus, who does away with qualities where he says:
> *By convention hot, by convention cold: in reality atoms and void.*
> [cf B 125]

And again:
> *In reality we know nothing – for truth is in the depths.* [B 117]
>   (Diogenes Laertius, *Lives of the Philosophers* IX 72)

Several other texts refer to Democritus' celebrated claim that 'by convention colour' etc.

Everyone knows that the greatest charge against any argument is that it conflicts with what is evident. For arguments cannot even start without self-evidence: how then can they be credible if they attack that from which they took their beginnings? Democritus too was aware of this; for when he had brought charges against the senses, saying:
> *By convention colour, by convention sweet, by convention bitter:*
> *in reality atoms and void,*

he had the senses reply to the intellect as follows:

Poor mind, do you take your evidence from us and then try to overthrow us? Our overthrow is your fall. [B 125]

So one should condemn the unreliability of an argument which is so bad that its most persuasive part conflicts with the evident propositions from which it took its start.

(Galen, *On Medical Experience* XV 7–8)

All these people presuppose that the primary element is qualityless, having no natural whiteness or blackness or any other colour whatever, and no sweetness or bitterness or heat or cold or in general any other quality whatever. For, says Democritus,

by convention colour, by convention bitter, by convention sweet: in reality atoms and void. [cf B 125]

And he thinks that it is from the congregation of atoms that all the perceptible qualities come to be – they are relative to us who perceive them, and in nature there is nothing white or black or yellow or red or bitter or sweet. For by the term 'by convention' he means something like 'by custom', 'relatively to us', 'not in virtue of the nature of the things themselves'. This in turn he calls 'in reality', deriving the word from 'real' which means 'true'. So the sense of his theory, taken as a whole, will be this: Men think that there are white things and black things and sweet things and bitter things; but in truth everything is things and nothing – this is just what he said himself, calling the atoms 'things' and void 'nothing'. Now all the atoms, being small bodies, lack qualities. The void is a sort of space in which all these bodies move up and down for the whole of time, and either entangle with one another or strike and rebound, and in these meetings they dissociate and again associate with one another and from this they make all compounds, including our own bodies and their properties and perceptions.

(Galen, *The Elements according to Hippocrates* I 417–418k)

Democritus went wrong in a manner unworthy of himself when he said that in truth only the atoms are existent, all the rest being by custom. For according to your theory, Democritus, not only shall we not be able to discover the truth, we

shall not be able to live, taking no precaution against fire or
death <. . .>

(Diogenes of Oenoanda, fragment 6 II)

*Aristotle offers a brief and puzzling analysis of what he took to be
Democritus' error:*

Many other animals receive contrary impressions to ours from
the same things, and indeed things do not seem always the
same to the perception of a single individual. So it is unclear
which of them is true or false; for there is no more reason for
this to be true than for that – they are on a par. That is why
Democritus says that either nothing is true or to us at least it
is unclear. In general, because they take understanding to be
perception and perception to be alteration, they say that what
appears in perception is of necessity true.

(Aristotle, *Metaphysics* 1009b7–15)

*Finally, it should be stressed that not everything in Democritus sits
well with the sceptical musings of the last pages.*

We know that what is hard to acquire is unnecessary and that
what is necessary God has generously made easy to acquire.
Hence Democritus well says that
> *Nature and teaching are similar,*
and he briefly adds the reason:
> *for teaching changes a man's shape and nature acts by changing
> shapes.* [B 33]

(Clement, *Miscellanies* IV xxiii 149.3–4)

*And the writings attacking Protagoras (to which Plutarch refers) con-
tained the first occurrence of an influential argument against relativ-
ism:*

You cannot say that every impression is true, because of the
reversal – as Democritus and Plato showed in their reply to
Protagoras. For if every impression is true, then it will also be

true that not every impression is true (since that is an impression), and thus it will be false that every impression is true.

(Sextus Empiricus, *Against the Mathematicians* VII 389–390)

III Scientific and Literary Studies

Democritus, so they say, used to claim that he would rather discover a single causal explanation than become king of the Persians [B 118] – although his explanations were futile and groundless inasmuch as he started from an empty principle and an erroneous hypothesis.

(Dionysius, in Eusebius, *Preparation for the Gospel* XIV xxvii 4)

Like his predecessors, Democritus was concerned to understand and explain the varied phenomena of the world of nature. As the catalogue of his writings shows, he wrote at length on scientific topics.

Given his views on knowledge and sensible qualities, we should not be surprised to find that he devoted much attention to the nature of sense-perception. His ideas on this subject were described in detail by Theophrastus. The following two passages are only a representative sample.

Democritus does not state whether perception takes place by opposites or by likes. If he makes perceiving come about by alteration, then he would seem to have it take place by things that are different – for like is not altered by like. But if perceiving – and alteration in general – takes place by being affected, and if, as he says, it is impossible for things that are not the same to be affected (even if things which are different have an effect, they do so not insofar as they are different but insofar as they have something the same in common), then it would seem to take place by likes. So we can take him in either way.

He attempts to account for each of the senses in turn. He has sight occur by reflection, but he talks of reflection in a special way. The reflection does not take place immediately in the pupil; rather, the air between the eye and the seen object is imprinted when it is compressed by what is seen and what sees (for there are always effluences coming off everything). Then this air, which is solid and has a different colour, is reflected in the eyes, which are moist. What is dense does not receive it, but what is moist lets it pass through. That is why moist eyes are better at seeing than hard eyes – provided that the external integument is extremely fine and dense, the internal parts are as spongy as possible and empty of any dense and strong flesh and also of any thick and oily liquid, and the vessels leading to the eyes are straight and dry so as to take the same shape as the objects imprinted – for each thing best recognizes what is akin to it.

(Theophrastus, *On the Senses* 49–50)

Flavours are sharp if their shapes [i.e. their constituent atoms] are angular and crinkled and small and fine. For because of their asperity they quickly pass through everywhere, and being rough and angular they gather and hold things together. That is why they heat the body, by making emptinesses in it – for what is most empty is most easily heated.

Sweet flavour is constituted by round shapes which are not too small. That is why they relax the body completely without doing so violently or quickly passing through all of it. They disturb the other shapes because as they pass through they make the others drift about and moisten them; and when these are moistened and move out of order, they flow together into the stomach – that is the most accessible part since it is the emptiest.

Sour flavour is constituted by large shapes with many angles and as little roundness as possible. For when these enter the body they clog and stop the vessels and prevent the shapes from flowing together. That is why they also settle the bowels.

Bitter flavour is constituted by small, smooth, rounded shapes, where the roundness also contains crinkles. That is why it is viscous and sticky.

Salty flavour is constituted by large shapes which are not

rounded *nor yet uneven but angular and crinkled* – he calls uneven those which entangle and intertwine with one another. They are large, because salt rises to the surface – if they were small and were struck by the shapes about them, they would mix with the whole. They are not round, because what is salty is rough while what is rounded is smooth. They are not uneven, because they do not entangle with one another – that is why it is friable.

Pungent flavour is small, rounded and angular, but not uneven. For the pungent, being angular, heats by its roughness, and it relaxes because it is small and rounded and angular. For that is what the angular is like.

He treats the other powers of each thing in the same way, reducing them to the shapes. Of all the shapes none is pure and unmixed with any others, but there are many in each – the same flavour contains smooth and rough, rounded and sharp, and the rest. The shape which preponderates has a very great influence with regard to our perception and its own effect – so too has the condition in which it finds us. For this too makes no little difference, since sometimes the same thing has opposite effects and opposites the same effect.

This is what he has said about flavours.

(*ibid* 65–67)

The next few pages contain one or two passages which testify to Democritus' other scientific and literary interests. These included mathematics, geography, and biology:

Consider the way in which [Chrysippus] answered the puzzle which Democritus stated in such a vivid and scientific fashion: If a cone is cut by a plane parallel to its base, what should we think of the surfaces of the segments – are they equal or unequal? If unequal, they will make the cone irregular, for it will acquire a number of step-like notches or roughnesses; if equal, the segments will be equal and the cone will plainly have acquired the properties of a cylinder, since it will consist of circles which are equal and not unequal – and that is utterly

absurd. [B 155] Here [Chrysippus] declares that Democritus is
ignorant . . .

(Plutarch, *On Common Notions* 1079E)

Later Democritus and Eudoxus and others wrote up circum-
navigations and journeys round the earth. The old thinkers
pictured the inhabited earth as round, placing Greece in its
centre and Delphi in the centre of Greece (for Delphi holds
the navel of the earth). Democritus, a man of wide experience,
was the first to appreciate that the earth is elongated, its length
being one and a half times its breadth.

(Agathemerus, *Geography* I 1–2)

The womb accepts the seed which has fallen into it and protects
it as it takes root – for first the navel grows in the womb, as
Democritus says [B 148], as an anchorage against rolling and
drifting, as a rope and a branch for the fruit which is being
generated and coming to be.

(Plutarch, *On Love for One's Offspring* 495E)

*Democritus also had a strong interest in his own species – in the
natural and social history of man. A late source contains a striking
passage which has generally been thought to reflect Democritean ideas
(even though it does not explicitly mention Democritus).*

They say that the first men lived an anarchic and animal sort
of life, going out to forage individually and living off the most
palatable herbs and the fruit which grew wild on the trees.
Then, since they were attacked by wild animals, they helped
one another (instructed by their own self-interest); and thus
gathering together because of fear, they slowly came to recognize one another's shapes.

The sounds they made had no sense and were confused; but
gradually they articulated their expressions, and by establishing symbols among themselves for every sort of object they
made the interpretation in each case intelligible to one
another. Such groups came into existence throughout the
inhabited world, and not all men had the same language, since

each group organized its expressions as chance had it. Hence there are languages of every type, and the groups who first came into existence were the founders of all the different races.

Now the earliest men lived laboriously, none of the utilities of life having been discovered: they wore no clothes, they knew nothing of dwelling-places or of fire, they had not the slightest conception of cultivated produce. And not knowing how to harvest wild produce, they did not lay aside any fruits against need. Hence many of them died in winter from cold and from lack of food. Later, gradually instructed by experience, they took refuge in caves during the winter, and stored those fruits that could be preserved. Once fire and other utilities were recognized, the crafts and whatever else can benefit communal life were slowly discovered. For in general it was need itself which instructed men in everything, appropriately introducing knowledge of each thing to a creature which was well-equipped and which had assistants for every purpose in its hands, its reason, and its keenness of mind.

(Diodorus, *Universal History* I viii 1–7)

The following texts represent different aspects of Democritus' anthropological studies.

Democritus, who is compared to the voice of Zeus and who speaks in this way about all things, tried to explain the concept [of man] but could get no further than an amateur assertion, saying:

Man is what we all know. [B 165]

(Sextus Empiricus, *Against the Mathematicians* VII 265)

Democritus rightly says that:

A few of the wise men, stretching up their hands to the place we Greeks now call the air, said: 'Zeus is held to be all things, and he knows everything and bestows and takes away, and he is king of everything.' [B 30]

(Clement, *Protreptic* VI lxviii 5)

It is absurd to pay careful attention to the cawing of rooks and the crowing of cocks and to pigs rooting among the rubbish, as Democritus puts it [B 147], and to treat these things as signs of wind and rain . . .

(Plutarch, *On Preserving Health* 129A)

Perhaps we are foolish to admire animals for their learning, although Democritus asserts [B 154] that we are their pupils in all the most important things – of the spider in weaving and healing, of the swallow in building, of the song-birds (the swan and the nightingale) in singing.

(Plutarch, *On the Intelligence of Animals* 974A)

Democritus, a man who was not only the most scientific of the ancients but also the most industrious of all those of whom we have report, says that music is a young art, and he explains this by saying that it was not separated off by necessity but came into being from superfluity.

(Philodemus, *On Music* IV xxxvi)

Democritus similarly says:
What a poet writes with enthusiasm and holy inspiration is very fine. [B 18]

(Clement, *Miscellanies* VI xviii 168.2)

Democritus says this about Homer:
Homer, having a divine nature, fashioned a world of words of every sort, [B 21]
implying that it is not possible to produce verses so fine and wise without a divine or superhuman nature.

(Dio of Prusa, *On Homer* [*Discourses* liii] 1)

Your sons should be kept away from bad language; for the word is shadow of the deed, according to Democritus.

(Plutarch, *On Educating Children* 9F)

Democritus said that names are conventional, and he tried to establish this by four arguments:

From homonymy: different things are called by the same name; therefore names are not natural.

From polyonymy: different names will fit one and the same thing, and *vice versa*, which is impossible if names are natural.

Thirdly, from the changes of names – why did we rename Aristocles 'Plato' ánd Tyrtamus 'Theophrastus' if names are natural?

From the absence of similar forms – why do we say 'to think' from 'thought' when we do not derive anything from 'justice'? Therefore names are due to chance, not to nature.

He calls the first argument *polysemy*, the second *equipoll-ence*, <the third *metonymy*>, and the fourth *anonymy*. [B 26]

(Proclus, *Commentary on the Cratylus* 6.20–7.6)

IV Moral Philosophy

Numerous purported fragments of Democritus' moral and political philosophy survive. They are puzzling on two counts. First, it is in many cases uncertain whether or not the ascription to Democritus is trustworthy. Secondly, it is not clear to what extent the fragments represent the remains of a systematic *moral theory, or to what extent that theory (if it existed) was connected to Democritus' atomism.*

Most of the fragments are preserved in two collections. I shall first set down the remaining scattered fragments and then transcribe the collected items.

The Abderites too say that there is a goal of action. Democritus, in his work *On the Goal*, says that it is contentment, which he also calls well-being; and he often remarks:

> For joy and absence of joy is the boundary <of advantage and disadvantage. [B 4; cf B 188]

This, he says, is the goal in life for men both young> and old. Hecataeus holds that the goal is self-sufficiency, Apollodotus

of Cyzicus that it is amusement, Nausiphanes that it is unruf-
fledness – and he says that this was called imperturbability by
Democritus.

(Clement, *Miscellanies* II xxi 130.4–5)

The dispute between body and soul over the passions seems
to be an old one. Democritus, ascribing unhappiness to the
soul, says:

> *If the body were to take the soul to court for the pains and suffer-
> ings it had endured throughout its life, then if he were to be on
> the jury for the case he would gladly cast his vote against the soul
> inasmuch as it had destroyed some parts of the body by negligence
> or dissipated them by drunkenness, and had ruined and ravaged
> other parts by its pursuit of pleasures – just as he would blame the
> careless user if a tool or utensil were in a bad condition.* [B 159]

([Plutarch], *On Desire and Grief* 2)

Democritus:

> *Men enjoy scratching themselves – they get the same pleasure as
> those who are having sexual intercourse.* [B 127]

(Herodian, *On Accentuation in General* 445.9–11)

Let us then say to ourselves that your body, O Man, produces
many diseases and afflictions by nature from within itself and
receives many that strike it from without, and that if you open
yourself up, within you will find a large and varied storehouse
and treasury of evils, as Democritus says [B 149], which do not
flow in from outside but have, as it were, internal and native
springs.

(Plutarch, *On Afflictions of Mind and Body* 500DE)

Democritus urges us to be instructed in the art of war, which
is of the greatest importance, and to seek out labour, which is
a source of great and glorious things for men.

(Plutarch, *Against Colotes* 1126A)

When a man lives in his own opinion and thinks not ill but well
of himself as a reliable witness and spectator of what is good,
then he shows that reason is already nourished and rooted

within him and, as Democritus says [B 145], is accustomed to take its pleasures from itself.

(Plutarch, Progress in Virtue 81A)

Medicine, according to Democritus, cures the diseases of the body, and wisdom clears the soul of passions.

(Clement, Pedagogue I ii 6.2)

   Stobaeus' Anthology *is the source for the first of the two collections of ethical fragments. I cite them in the order in which they appear in the* Anthology. *I cite all the texts which are ascribed to Democritus (or to 'Democrates' or to 'Democ'): many ascriptions are at best dubious.*

Democritus:
> *Do not be eager to know everything lest you become ignorant of everything.*

(II i 12 = B 169)

Democritus:
> *Reason is a powerful persuader.*

(II iv 12: cf B 51)

Democritus and Plato both place happiness in the soul. Democritus writes thus:
> *Happiness and unhappiness belong to the soul.* [B 170]
> *Happiness does not dwell in herds, nor yet in gold: the soul is the dwelling place of a man's lot.* [B 171]

He calls happiness contentment, well-being, harmony, orderliness, tranquillity. It is constituted by distinguishing and discriminating among pleasures, and this is the noblest and most advantageous thing for men.

(II vii 3i)

Democritus:

> Men fashioned the image of chance as an excuse for their own
> thoughtlessness; for chance rarely fights with wisdom, and a man
> of intelligence will, by foresight, set straight most things in his life.

(II viii 16 = B 119)

Democritus:

> From the same sources from which good things come to us we may
> also draw bad; but we may avoid the bad. For example, deep water
> is useful for many purposes, and then again it is bad – for there
> is danger of drowning. So a device has been discovered: teaching
> people to swim. [B 172]

idem:

> For men bad things spring from good, when one does not know
> how to manage the good or to keep it resourcefully. It is not just
> to count such things bad: they are good, but it is possible, for
> anyone who wishes, to use good things for bad ends too. [B 173]
> A contented man who is led to deeds which are just and lawful
> rejoices night and day and is strengthened and free of care; but
> the man who pays no heed to justice and does not do what he
> ought, finds all his deeds joyless when he remembers any of them,
> and he is afraid and he reproaches himself. [B 174]
> The gods, both in the past and now, give men all things except
> those which are bad and harmful and useless. Neither in the past
> nor now do the gods bestow these on men, but they come upon
> them themselves because of the blindness and folly of their minds.
> [B 175]
> Fortune offers many gifts, but is unstable: nature is self-sufficient:
> that is why, being smaller but stable, she conquers the greater
> forces of hope. [B 176]

(II ix 1–5)

Democritus:

> Many men perform the foulest deeds and practise the fairest
> words.

(II xv 33 = B 53a)

266

Democritus:
> *One must emulate the deeds and actions of virtue, not the words.*
>
> (II xv 36 = B 55)

Democritus:
> *Fine words do not hide foul actions nor is a good action spoiled by slanderous words.*
>
> (II xv 40 = B 177)

Democrates:
> *Indulgence is the worst of all things with regard to the education of youth; for it is this which gives birth to the pleasures from which badness originates.* [B 178]

idem:
> *<. . .> children who are given free rein will learn neither letters nor music nor gymnastics nor yet – what most sustains virtue – a sense of shame; for it is precisely from this that shame usually originates.* [B 179]

idem:
> *Education is an ornament for the fortunate, a refuge for the unfortunate.* [B 180]

idem:
> *The use of exhortation and the persuasion of reason will appear a stronger inducement to virtue than law and necessity. For one who has been kept from injustice by law is likely to do wrong in secret, while one who has been led to duty by persuasion is unlikely to do anything improper either in secret or in public. That is why a man who acts uprightly from wisdom and knowledge is at the same time both courageous and right-thinking.* [B 181]
>
> (II xxxi 56–59)

Democ:
> *Learning produces fine things by labour: foul things come to fruit spontaneously without labour. For even one who is unwilling is often prevented <. . .>*
>
> (II xxxi 66 = B 182)

Democ:
> *Neither skill nor wisdom is attainable unless you learn.* [B 59]

idem:

> There is surely intelligence among the young and lack of intelligence among the old; for it is not time that teaches good sense but timely upbringing and nature. [B 183]

idem:

> Those who contradict and babble on are ill-equipped for learning. [B 85]

(II xxxi 71–73)

Democ:

> Frequent association with the wicked increases a disposition to vice.

(II xxxi 90 = B 184)

Democ:

> The hopes of the educated are better than the wealth of the ignorant.

(II xxxi 94 = B 185)

Democritus:

> Similarity of mind makes friendship.

(II xxxiii 9 = B 186)

Democritus:

> It is fitting for men to set more store by their souls than by their bodies; for perfection of soul rights wickedness of body, but strength of body without reasoning makes the soul no better at all.

(III i 27 = B 187 = B 36)

Democritus:

> It is fitting to yield to the law, the rulers, the wiser. [B 47]

Democritus:

> The boundary of advantage and disadvantage is joy and absence of joy. [B 188]
>
> It is best for a man to live his life with as much contentment and as little grief as possible; this will come about if he does not take his pleasures in mortal things. [B 189]

(III i 45–47)

Democritus:

One should avoid even speaking of evil deeds.

(III i 91 = B 190)

Democrates:

One should refrain from wrong-doing not because of fear but because of duty.

(III i 95 = B 41)

Democritus:

For men gain contentment from moderation in joy and a measured life: deficiencies and excesses tend to change and to produce large movements in the soul, and souls which move across large intervals are neither stable nor content. Thus you must set your judgement on the possible and be satisfied with what you have, giving little thought to things that are envied and admired, and not dwelling on them in your mind; and you must observe the lives of those who are badly off, considering what they suffer, so that what you have and what belongs to you may seem great and enviable and, by no longer desiring more, you may not suffer in your soul. For one who admires those who possess much and are deemed blessed by other men and who dwells on them every hour in his memory is compelled always to plan something new and, because of his desire, to set himself to do some pernicious deed that the laws forbid. That is why you must not seek certain things and must be content with others, comparing your own life with that of those who do worse and deeming yourself blessed, when you reflect on what they undergo, in faring and living so much better than they do. For if you hold fast to this judgement you will live in greater contentment and will drive away those not inconsiderable plagues of life, jealousy and envy and ill-will.

(III i 210 = B 191)

Democritus:

To praise and to blame what one should not are both easy, but each is a mark of a wicked character.

(III ii 36 = B 192)

Democritus:

> It is the mark of good sense to guard against future injustice, and
> of insensibility not to defend oneself when it has occurred.
>
> (III iii 43 = B 193)

Democritus:

> Great joys come from contemplating noble works.
>
> (III iii 46 = B 194)

Democritus:

> Images are by their dress and adornment magnificent to observe,
> but they are empty of heart. [B 195]
> Forgetting one's own misfortunes generates boldness. [B 196]
> Fools are shaped by the gifts of fortune, those who understand
> such things by the gifts of wisdom. [B 197]
> *That which is in need knows how much it needs: he who needs
> does not recognize the fact.* [B 198]
> Fools, though they hate life, wish to live from fear of Hades.
> [B 199]
> Fools live without enjoying life. [B 200]
> Fools desire longevity but do not enjoy longevity. [B 201]
> Fools desire what is absent: what is present, although it is more
> beneficial than what is past, they squander. [B 202]
> In fleeing death men pursue it. [B 203]
> Fools give no pleasure in the whole of their lives. [B 204]
> Fools, fearing death, desire life. [B 205]
> Fools, fearing death, want to grow old. [B 206]
> Many who have learned much possess no sense. [B 64]
> Without intelligence, reputation and wealth are not safe pos-
> sessions. [B 77]
>
> (III iv 69–82)

Democritus:

> One should choose not every pleasure but that concerned with the
> noble. [B 207]
> Rightful love is longing without violence for the noble. [B 73]

A father's temperateness is the greatest precept for his children.
[B 208]
For those brought up in self-sufficiency there are never any short nights. [B 209]
Fortune provides a rich table, temperateness a self-sufficient one.
[B 210]
Temperateness increases joys and makes pleasure greater. [B 211]

(III v 22–27)

Democritus:

Some men rule cities and are slaves to women. [cf B 214]
Sleeping during the day indicates a diseased body or a troubled soul or idleness or lack of education. [B 212]
Coition is mild madness; for a man rushes out of a man. [B 32]

(III vi 26–28)

Democritus:

Courage makes misfortunes small.

(III vii 21 = B 213)

Democritus:

The courageous are not only those who conquer their enemies but also those who are superior to pleasures: some men rule cities and are slaves to women.

(III vii 25 = B 214)

Democritus:

The glory of justice is confidence of judgement and imperturbability: the prize of injustice is fear of disaster.

(III vii 31 = B 215)

Democritus:

Imperturbable wisdom, being most honourable, is worth everything.

(III vii 74 = B 216)

Democritus:

To be good is not to refrain from wrongdoing but not even to want to commit it. [B 62]

271

Democritus:

Only those who hate injustice are loved by the gods. [B 217]

(III ix 29–30)·

Democritus:

When wealth comes from bad activity it makes the disgrace more conspicuous.

(III x 36 = B 218)

Democritus:

It is a waste of labour to offer advice to those who think they possess sense. [B 52]

idem:

Desire for money, if it is not limited by satiety, is far heavier than extreme poverty; for greater desires create greater needs. [B 219]

Democritus:

Evil gains bring loss of virtue. [B 220]

(III x 42–44)

Democritus:

Hope of evil gain is the beginning of loss.

(III x 58 = B 221)

Democritus:

The excessive accumulation of money for one's children is an excuse for avarice which displays its peculiar character. [B 222]

idem:

Whatever the body needs can readily be found by everyone without trouble or misery: the things which need trouble and misery and make life painful are craved not by the body but by misapprehension of judgement. [B 223]

(III x 64–65)

Democritus:

The desire for more destroys what is present – like Aesop's dog.

(III x 68 = B 224)

Democritus:
> One should tell the truth, not speak at length.
>
> (III xii 13 = B 44 = B 225)

Democritus:
> It is better to examine your own mistakes than those of others.
> [B 60]

Democritus:
> Frankness is a mark of liberty, but discerning the right occasion
> is hazardous. [B 226]
>
> (III xiii 46–47)

Democritus:
> To praise someone for noble deeds is noble; for to praise for bad
> deeds is the mark of a cheat and a deceiver.
>
> (III xiv 8 = B 63)

Democritus:
> The thrifty behave like bees, working as though they are to live for
> ever. [B 227]

idem:
> The children of the thrifty who are ignorant are like those dancers
> who leap over knives — they are killed if they fail to land on the
> one place where they should rest their feet (and it is difficult to
> land on the one place, for there is only room for their feet there).
> In the same way they too, if they fail to acquire their father's
> careful and thrifty character, are likely to be destroyed. [B 228]

idem:
> Thrift and fasting are good: so too is extravagance on occasion:
> it is the mark of a good man to recognize the occasion. [B 229]
>
> (III xvi 16–19)

Democritus:
> A life without feasts is a long road without inns.
>
> (III xvi 22 = B 230)

Democritus:
> A man of sound judgement is not grieved by what he does not
> possess but rejoices in what he does possess.
>
> (III xvii 25 = B 231)

Democritus:

> *Of pleasant things those that occur most rarely give most joy.* [B 232]

idem:

> *If you exceed the measure, what is most enjoyable becomes least enjoyable.* [B 233]

(III xvii 37–38)

Democritus:

> *Men ask for health in their prayers to the gods: they do not realize that the power to achieve it lies in themselves: lacking self-control, they perform contrary actions and betray health to their desires.*

(III xviii 30 = B 234)

Democritus:

> *For those who get their pleasures from their bellies, exceeding the measure in food and drink and sex, the pleasures are brief and short-lived, lasting as long as they are eating or drinking; but the pains are many. For they always have the same desire for the same things; and when they obtain what they desire, the pleasure swiftly departs, there is nothing good in them but a brief joy, and they need the same things again.*

(III xviii 35 = B 235)

Democritus:

> *It is hard to fight against anger: to master it is the mark of a rational man.*

(III xx 56 = B 236)

Democritus:

> *Ambition is always foolish: with its eye on what harms its enemy it does not see its own advantage.*

(III xx 62 = B 237)

Democritus:

> *For one who compares himself to his betters ends with a bad reputation.*

(III xxii 42 = B 238)

274

Democritus:
> Oaths made under compulsion are not kept by bad men once they
> have escaped.
>> (III xxviii 13 = B 239)

Democritus:
> Voluntary labours make it easier to sustain involuntary labours.
> [B 240]

idem:
> Continuous labour becomes lighter by custom. [B 241]
>> (III xxix 63–64)

Democritus:
> More men are good by practice than by nature. [B 242]

idem:
> Actions always planned are never completed. [B 81]
>> (III xxix 66–67)

Democritus:
> All labours are more pleasant than rest when men achieve what
> they labour for or know that they will achieve it. *But if you shun
> them and fail, everything* is both painful and miserable.
>> (III xxix 88 = B 243)

Democritus:
> Even when you are alone, neither say nor do anything bad: learn
> to feel shame before yourself rather than before others.
>> (III xxxi 7 = B 244)

Democritus:
> It is greedy to say everything and to want to listen to nothing.
>> (III xxxvi 24 = B 86)

Democritus:
> One should either be or imitate a good man.
>> (III xxxvii 22 = B 39)

Democritus:

> *If your character is orderly, your life too will be well-ordered.*
>
> (III xxxvii 25 = B 61)

Democritus:

> *A good man pays no heed to the censures of the bad.* [B 48]

idem:

> *Envious men pain themselves as though they were their own enemies.* [B 88]
>
> (III xxxviii 46–47)

Democritus:

> *The laws would not forbid each of us to live at his own pleasure if one man did not harm another; for envy makes the beginning of strife.*
>
> (III xxxviii 53 = B 245)

Democritus:

> *Mercenary service teaches self-sufficiency in life; for bread and a straw mattress are the sweetest cures for hunger and exhaustion.* [B 246]

idem:

> *To a wise man the whole earth is accessible; for the home country of a good soul is the whole world.* [B 247]
>
> (III xl 6–7)

Democritus:

> *The law means to benefit the life of men: it can do so when they themselves mean to fare well — for to those who obey, it indicates their own virtue.* [B 248]

idem:

> *Internecine strife is bad for both parties; for victor and vanquished suffer the same destruction.* [B 249]
>
> (IV i 33–34)

Democritus:

> *From concord come great deeds, and from concord states can fight wars — and in no other way.*
>
> (IV i 40 = B 250)

Democritus:

> Poverty in a democracy is preferable to what is called prosperity among tyrants – by as much as liberty is preferable to slavery. [B 251]

> One should think it of greater moment than anything else that the affairs of the state are conducted well, neither being contentious beyond what is proper nor allotting strength to oneself beyond the common good. For a state which is conducted well is the best means to success: everything depends on this, and if this is preserved everything is preserved and if this is destroyed everything is destroyed. [B 252]

> It is not advantageous for good men to neglect themselves and look to other things; for their own affairs will go badly. But if anyone neglects public affairs he comes to have a bad reputation, even if he steals nothing and commits no injustice. For even if he takes care and does no wrong, there is still a danger that he will get a bad reputation – and indeed fare badly: wrong-doing is inevitable and forgiveness is not easy for men. [B 253]

> When bad men gain office, the more unworthy they are the more heedless they become and the more they are filled with folly and rashness. [B 254]

> When those in power take it upon themselves to lend to the poor and to aid them and to favour them, then is there pity and no isolation but companionship and mutual defence and concord among the citizens and other good things too many to catalogue. [B 255]

(IV i 42–46)

Democritus:

> It is better for fools to be ruled than to rule. [B 75]

idem:

> Justice is doing what should be done, injustice not doing what should be done but turning away from it. [B 256]

idem:

> In the case of certain animals, it stands thus with killing and not killing: one who kills those who do or wish injustice suffers no penalty, and to do so conduces more to well-being than not to do so. [B 257]

277

*One should kill at any cost anything that offends against justice;
and anyone who does this *will in every society have a greater
share of contentment and justice and boldness and property.**
[B 258]

*As I have written about dangerous beasts and animals, so I think
one should act in the case of humans too: one should kill an enemy
in accordance with the traditional laws in every society, in which
law does not prohibit it: it is prohibited by the sacred customs of
different countries, by treaties, by oaths.* [B 259]

*Anyone who kills a highwayman or a pirate should be free from
penalty, whether he does it by his own hand, by issuing an order,
or by casting a vote.* [B 260]

(IV ii 13–18)

Democritus:

It is hard to be ruled by an inferior.

(IV iv 27 = B 49)

Democritus:

*One should avenge injustices to the best of one's ability and not
pass them by; for to do so is just and good, not to do so is unjust
and bad.* [B 261]

Democritus:

*Those who do deeds worthy of exile or imprisonment or who are
worthy of punishment should be condemned and not acquitted;
anyone who acquits them contrary to the law, judging by gain or
by pleasure, acts unjustly – and this must lie heavy on his heart.*
[B 262]

idem:

*Those who *worthily fulfil the greatest offices* have the greatest
share of justice and virtue.* [B 263]

idem:

*Feel shame before others no more than before yourself: do wrong
no more if no-one is to know about it than if all men are: feel
shame above all before yourself and set this up as a law in your
soul so that you may do nothing unsuitable.* [B 264]

idem:

Men remember wrongs better than benefits. And that is just; for

278

*as those who repay their debts should not be praised whereas those
who do not should be blamed and suffer, so too is it with rulers.
For they were elected not to do wrong but to do right.* [B 265]
*There is no means, as things are now constituted, whereby rulers
may be protected from injustice, even if they are very good men.
<. . .> These things too, I think, should be so arranged that one
who commits no injustice, even if he severely examines doers of
injustice, should not come under their power: rather, a statute, or
something else, should protect those who do what is just.* [B 266]
(IV v 43–48)

Democritus:
Ruling is by nature appropriate to the superior.
(IV vi 19 = B 267)

Democritus:
Fear produces flattery: it does not gain good-will.
(IV vii 13 = B 268)

Democritus:
Boldness is the beginning of action: fortune controls the end.
(IV x 28 = B 269)

Democritus:
*Use servants like parts of your body, one for one task and another
for another.*
(IV xix 45 = B 270)

Democritus:
If a woman is loved she is not blamed for lust.
(IV xx 33 = B 271)

Democritus: Democritus said that one who is lucky in his son-
in-law gains a son, one who is unlucky loses a daughter.
(IV xxii 108 = B 272)

Democritus:

> *A woman is far sharper than a man when it comes to foolish counsels.*

> (IV xxii 199 = B 273)

Democritus:

> *To speak little is an adornment in a woman — and it is best to be sparing with adornments.* [B 274]

Democritus:

> *To be ruled by a woman is the final insult for a man.* [B 111]

> (IV xxiii 38–39)

Democritus:

> *Having children is dangerous: success is full of trouble and care, failure is unsurpassed by any other pain.*

> (IV xxiv 29 = B 275)

Democritus:

> *I think one should not have children; for in the having of children I see many great dangers, many pains, few advantages — and those thin and weak.* [B 276]

idem:

> *Anyone who has a need for children would do better, I think, to get them from his friends. He will then have a child of the sort he wishes — for he can choose the sort he wants, and one that seems suitable to him will by its nature best follow him. There is this great difference: here you may choose among many as you will and take a child of the sort you need; but if you produce a child yourself there are many dangers — for you must make do with the one you get.* [B 277]

idem:

> *Men think that, by nature and some ancient constitution, it is a matter of necessity to get children. And so, it is plain, do other animals too; for they all acquire offspring by nature and not with any useful end in view — when they are born, the parents suffer and rear each as best they can, and they fear for them as long as they are small, and if they are hurt they grieve. Such is the nature of all living creatures; but for men it has been made a custom that some gain actually comes from offspring.* [B 278]

> (IV xxiv 31–33)

Democritus:

> *You should share your goods with your children so far as possible, and at the same time care for them lest they do any mischief with what they have in their hands. For then they become at the same time far more thrifty with their money and keener to acquire it, and they compete with one another. For common expenditure does not grieve us as much as private, nor common acquisition content us — but far less.* [B 279]

idem:

> *It is possible, without spending much money, to educate your children and to build a wall and a protection about their goods and their persons.* [B 280]

(IV xxvi 25–26)

Democritus:

> *For beasts, good breeding consists in bodily strength: for men, in grace of character.*

(IV xxix 18 = B 57)

Democritus:

> *Just as among injuries cancer is the worst disease, so in goods <. . .>*

(IV xxxi 49 = B 281)

Democritus:

> *Money when used with sense promotes generosity and charity: when used with folly it is *a common expense*.* [B 282]

idem:

> *It is not useless to make money, but to do so as a result of wrong-doing is the worst of all things.* [B 78]

(IV xxxi 120–121)

Democritus:

> *Poverty and wealth are names for lack and satiety; so one who lacks is not wealthy and one who does not lack is not poor.* [B 283]

Democritus:

>If you do not desire much, a little will seem much to you; for a small appetite makes poverty as powerful as wealth. [B 284]
>
>(IV xxxiii 23–24)

Democritus:

>Those who seek good things find them with difficulty: bad things come even to those who do not seek them.
>
>(IV xxxiv 58 = B 108)

Democritus:

>All men, aware of the wretchedness of life, suffer for their whole lives in troubles and fears, telling false stories about fear after death.
>
>(IV xxxiv 62: cf B 297)

Democritus:

>You must recognize that human life is frail and brief and confounded by many plagues and incapacities: then you will care for moderate possessions and your misery will be measured by necessity.
>
>(IV xxxiv 65 = B 285)

Democritus:

>Fortune is being content with moderate goods, misfortune being discontent with many.
>
>(IV xxxix 17 = B 286)

Democritus:

>If you are to be content you must not undertake many activities, whether as an individual or in concert with others, nor choose activities beyond your own power and nature; but you must be on your guard so that even when fortune strikes you and leads you to excess by your beliefs, you put it aside and do not attempt more than you can. For a modest cargo is safer than a great.
>
>(IV xxxix 25 = B 3)

Democritus:

> Shared poverty is harder than private poverty; for no hope of relief remains. [B 287]
> Your house and your life, no less than your body, may suffer disease. [B 288]

(IV xl 20–21)

Democritus:

> It is irrational not to accommodate yourself to the necessities of life.

(IV xliv 64 = B 289)

Democritus:

> Drive out by reasoning the unmastered pain of a numbed soul. [B 290]

idem:

> It is important to think as you should in times of misfortune. [B 42]

idem:

> Magnanimity is bearing wrongs lightly. [B 46]

idem:

> It is a mark of the temperate to bear poverty well. [B 291]

(IV xliv 67–70)

Democritus:

> The hopes of those who think aright are attainable: the hopes of the unintelligent are impossible. [B 58]

Democritus:

> The hopes of the unintelligent are irrational. [B 292]

(IV xlvi 18–19)

Democritus:

> Those who take pleasure in the disasters of their neighbours do not understand how the affairs of fortune are common to all — and they lack any joy of their own.

(IV xlviii 10 = B 293)

Democritus:

> *Strength and shapeliness are the good things of youth: temperance
> is the flower of age*
>
> (IV l 20 = B 294)

Democritus:

> *Old men were once young, but it is uncertain if young men will
> reach old age. Now a completed good is better than one which is
> still to come and is uncertain.*
>
> (IV l 22 = B 295)

Democritus:

> *Age is a general mutilation: it retains everything but everything
> is defective.*
>
> (IV l 76 = B 296)

Democritus:

> *Some men who do not know how mortal nature dissolves but are
> aware of the wretchedness of life spend their whole lives in troubles
> and fears, fashioning false stories about the time after death.*
>
> (IV lii 40 = B 297)

*We also possess a long list of maxims ascribed in the manuscripts to
'Democrates'. Some of these are certainly Democritean and many others
may derive ultimately from Democritus. Although some are certainly
not by Democritus, it seems best to translate the list as a whole and to
let it stand as an Appendix to the fragments of Democritus.*

> If anyone listens to these maxims of mine with intelligence, he
> will do many deeds worthy of a good man and he will leave undone
> many bad deeds. [B 35]
> It is fitting for men to set more store by their souls than by
> their bodies; for perfection of soul rights wickedness of body, but
> strength of body without reasoning makes the soul no better at all.
> [B 36 = B 187]
> He who chooses the goods of the soul chooses the more divine:
> he who chooses the goods of the body, the human. [B 37]
> It is noble to prevent a wrong-doer; or if not, not to do wrong
> with him. [B 38]

One should either be a good man or imitate one. [B 39]

Men flourish neither by their bodies nor by their wealth but by uprightness and good sense. [B 40]

Refrain from error not out of fear but out of duty. [B 41]

It is important to think as you should in times of misfortune. [B 42]

Remorse for foul deeds is the salvation of life. [B 43]

One should tell the truth, not speak at length. [B 44]

A man who does wrong is more wretched than one who is wronged. [B 45]

Magnanimity is bearing wrongs lightly. [B 46]

It is fitting to yield to the law, the rulers, the wiser. [B 47]

A good man pays no heed to the censures of the bad. [B 48]

It is hard to be ruled by an inferior. [B 49]

A man completely enslaved to money will never be just. [B 50]

Reason is often a more powerful persuader than gold. [B 51]

It is a waste of labour to offer advice to those who think they possess sense. [B 52]

Many do not learn reason but live in accordance with reason. [B 53]

Many perform the foulest deeds and practise the fairest words. [B 53a]

The unintelligent come to their senses by suffering misfortune. [B 54]

One should emulate the deeds and actions of virtue, not the words. [B 55]

It is those well-equipped for it who recognize and emulate the noble. [B 56]

For beasts, good breeding consists in bodily strength: for men, in grace of character. [B 57]

The hopes of those who think aright are attainable: the hopes of the unintelligent are impossible. [B 58]

Neither skill nor wisdom is attainable unless you learn. [B 59]

It is better to examine your own mistakes than those of others. [B 60]

If your character is orderly, your life too will be well-ordered. [B 61]

To be good is not to refrain from wrong-doing but not even to want to commit it. [B 62]

To praise someone for noble deeds is noble; for to praise for bad deeds is the mark of a cheat and a deceiver. [B 63]

Many who have learned much possess no sense. [B 64]

One should cultivate much sense, not much learning. [B 65]

It is better to plan before acting than to repent after. [B 66]

Trust not everyone but the reliable: the former is foolish, the latter is the mark of a man in his senses. [B 67]

Men are reliable and unreliable not only on the basis of what they do but also on the basis of what they wish. [B 68]

Goodness and truth are the same for all men: for different men different things are pleasant. [B 69]

Immoderate desire is the mark of a child, not of a man. [B 70]

Inopportune pleasures give birth to pains. [B 71]

Violent appetite for anything blinds the soul to everything else. [B 72]

Rightful love is longing without violence for the noble. [B 73]

It is pleasant to get nothing which is not to your advantage. [B 74]

It is better for fools to be ruled than to rule. [B 75]

Silly people are taught not by reason but by misfortune. [B 76]

Without intelligence, reputation and wealth are not safe possessions. [B 77]

It is not useless to make money, but to do so as a result of wrong-doing is the worst of all things. [B 78]

It is wretched to imitate bad men and not even to wish to imitate good. [B 79]

It is disgraceful to busy yourself over the affairs of others and neglect your own. [B 80]

Actions always planned are never completed. [B 81]

Cheats and hypocrites are those who promise everything and do nothing. [B 82]

Happy is the man who has property and sense; for he uses it nobly on what he should.

The cause of error is ignorance of what is better. [B 83]

One who does shameful deeds should first be ashamed of himself. [B 84]

Those who contradict and babble on are ill-equipped for learning what they should. [B 85]

It is greedy to say everything and to want to listen to nothing. [B 86]

One should be on guard against bad men lest they take their opportunity. [B 87]

Envious men pain themselves as though they were their own enemies. [B 88]

Your enemy is not he who wrongs you but he who wishes to. [B 89]

Enmity among kin is far worse than enmity among strangers. [B 90]

Do not suspect everyone – but be prudent and safe. [B 91]

You should accept favours only if you expect to give greater favours in return. [B 92]

When doing a favour keep watch on the receiver lest he prove a cheat and return evil for good. [B 93]

Small favours at the right time are very great for those who receive them. [B 94]

Honours count much with the wise who understand that they are being honoured. [B 95]

A generous man is not one who looks to a return but one who has chosen to confer a benefit. [B 96]

Many who seem to be friends are not: many who do not seem to be are. [B 97]

The friendship of one intelligent man is better than that of all the unintelligent. [B 98]

A man who has not a single good friend does not deserve to live. [B 99]

A man whose well-tried friends do not long stand by him has a graceless character. [B 100]

Many avoid their friends when they fall from wealth to poverty. [B 101]

Equality is everywhere noble: excess and deficiency do not to me seem so. [B 102]

A man who loves no-one seems to me to be loved by no-one. [B 103]

Old men are charming if they are wily and earnest. [B 104]

Beauty of body is an animal attribute if there is no sense behind it. [B 105]

In times of good fortune it is easy to find a friend, in times of bad fortune nothing is harder. [B 106]

Not all our kindred are our friends, but those who agree with us over what is advantageous. [B 107]

Being men, it is fitting that we should not laugh at human misfortunes but weep at them. [B 107a]

Those who seek good things find them with difficulty: bad things come even to those who do not seek them. [B 108]

Those who like fault-finding are not well-equipped for friendship. [B 109]

Let not a woman argue: that is terrible. [B 110]

To be ruled by a woman is the final insult for a man. [B 111]

It is a mark of a divine mind to think always of what is fine. [B 112]

If you believe that the gods observe everything, you will err neither secretly nor in public.

Great harm is done to the unintelligent by those who praise them. [B 113]

It is better to be praised by another than by oneself. [B 114]

If you do not understand the praise, suppose that you are being flattered. [B 115]

The world is a stage, life is our entrance: you came, you saw, you went away.

The world is change: life is opinion.

A little wisdom is more honourable than a reputation for great folly.

(Democrates, *Maxims* 1–86)

22
DIOGENES OF
APOLLONIA

*The Presocratic Diogenes, the first of several ancient philosophers to
bear that name, came from a town called Apollonia – either Apollonia
in Crete or Apollonia on the Black Sea. He is said to have been the last
of the Presocratic natural philosophers: that remark, together with the
various parodies of his views found in the comic playwrights, suggests
that he was active in the 430s and 420s. (There is no evidence for a
more precise chronology.)*

*Theophrastus wrote a monograph on Diogenes. His general line of
interpretation emerges from the following short passage:*

Diogenes of Apollonia, perhaps the last of those who studied
these subjects, wrote for the most part in a muddled fashion,
sometimes following Anaxagoras and sometimes Leucippus.
He too says that the nature of the universe is air, infinite and
eternal, from which, as it condenses and rarefies and changes
its properties, the other forms come into being. That is what
Theophrastus says about Diogenes, and the book of his
entitled *On Nature*, which I have seen, clearly says that it is air
from which everything else comes into being. But Nicolaus
records that he posited as the element something between fire
and air.

(Simplicius, *Commentary on the Physics* 25.1–9)

The opening words of On Nature *are twice cited by Diogenes Laertius:*

This is how his book begins:

> When beginning any account it seems to me that one should make the starting-point incontrovertible and the style simple and dignified. [64 B 1]

(Diogenes Laertius, *Lives of the Philosophers* IX 57: cf VI 81)

Most of our information about Diogenes' thought derives from Simplicius, who describes it in the course of a long discussion of the disagreement among earlier interpreters of Diogenes.

Most scholars say that Diogenes of Apollonia, like Anaximenes, posited air as the primary element. But Nicolaus in his treatise *On the Gods* records that he declared the element between fire and air to be the first principle; and Porphyry, the most learned of philosophers, has followed Nicolaus. Now you should know that this Diogenes wrote several works, as he himself records in his book *On Nature*, where he says that he has written against the natural scientists (whom he himself actually calls sophists) and that he has composed a *Meteorology* (in which he says he has discussed the first principle and also the nature of man). In *On Nature*, which is the only one of his works which I have seen, he proposes to show in many ways that there is much intelligence in the first principle which he posits. Immediately after the preface he writes as follows:

> It seems to me, in a word, that all existing things are alterations of the same thing and are the same thing. This is quite clear. For if the things that now exist in this world – earth and water and air and fire and the other things that plainly exist in this world – if any one of them were different from any other, being different in its own peculiar nature, and were not the same thing changed in many ways and altered, then they could in no way mix with one another, nor could benefit or harm accrue to one from another; nor indeed could plants grow from the earth, or animals or anything else come into being, unless they were so constituted as to be the same thing. But all these things, altering from some one thing, become different at different times and return to the same thing. [B 2]

I too, when I read those first remarks, thought that he had in mind as the common substrate something other than the four elements, since he says that these would not mingle with or change into one another if some one of them, having a peculiar nature of its own, were the first principle, and if there were not some one thing underlying them all, of which all were alterations. But next, having shown that there is much intelligence in this first principle – for, he says,

> Without intelligence it could not have been so distributed as to preserve measures of all things – of summer and winter and night and day and rain and wind and good weather; and all other things, if you are willing to apply your intelligence, you will find to be disposed in the finest possible way [B 3]

– he continues by urging that humans and other animals depend for their life and their soul and their intelligence on this first principle which is air. He says:

> Again, in addition to these there are the following important indications. Humans and other animals, inasmuch as they breathe, live by the air. And this is for them both soul and intelligence, as will have been shown clearly in this treatise; and if this departs, they die and their intelligence is lost. [B 4]

Then a little later he adds clearly:

> And it seems to me that that which possesses intelligence is what men call air, and that by this everyone both is governed and has power over everything. For it is this which seems to me to be god and to have reached everything and to arrange everything and to be in everything. And there is not a single thing which does not share in it.
>
> But no one thing shares in it in the same way as any other: there are many forms both of the air itself and of intelligence. For it is multiform: hotter and colder, drier and wetter, more stable and with a swifter motion, and there are many – infinitely many – other alterations in it both of flavour and of colour.
>
> The souls of all animals are indeed the same – air hotter than the external air in which we exist but much colder than the air by the sun. But this heat is not similar in different animals (for it is not even so in different men) but it differs – not greatly, however, but to such an extent that they are still like one another. Yet none of the things that alter can become absolutely similar to any other

without becoming the same thing. Thus inasmuch as the alteration is multiform, so too are the animals multiform and many, and they resemble one another neither in shape nor in habits nor in intelligence because of the multitude of the alterations. Nevertheless, it is by the same thing that they all live and see and hear, and they all get the rest of their intelligence from the same thing. [B 5]

Next he shows that the seed of animals is also breath-like and that acts of intelligence occur when the air together with the blood pervades the whole body through the vessels (here he gives a precise anatomy of the vessels).

Here, then, he plainly says quite clearly that what men call air is the first principle. It is noteworthy that, while he says that other things come into being by virtue of alterations in it, he nevertheless asserts that it is eternal:

And this itself is an eternal and immortal body; but by it some things come into being and others disappear. [B 7]

And elsewhere:

But this seems to me to be clear – that it is great and strong, eternal and immortal, and knows many things. [B 8]

So much for Diogenes.

(Simplicius, *Commentary on the Physics* 151.20–153.22)

Aristotle preserves Diogenes' 'precise anatomy of the vessels'. (The text is in some places uncertain, and it is not clear whether Aristotle's quotation is always verbatim.)

Diogenes of Apollonia gives the following account:

The vessels in men are as follows. There are two very large ones. They extend through the belly along the backbone, one to the right and the other to the left, into the legs, each on its own side, and upwards into the head past the collar-bones through the throat. From these, vessels extend throughout the whole of the body, from the right vessel to the right and from the left to the left, the largest two passing into the heart near the backbone itself, and others, a little higher up, passing through the chest under the armpits, each into the hand on its own side. One of these is called the spleen-vessel, the other the liver-vessel. Each of them divides at its extremity, one branch going into the thumb, one into the palm;

and from them fine, many-branched vessels pass into the rest of the hand and the fingers. Other finer ones extend from the first vessels, from the right vessel into the liver and from the left into the spleen and the kidneys. Those which extend into the legs divide at the junction and extend throughout the thighs. The largest of them extends down the back of the thigh and is seen to be thick; another passes inside the thigh, a little less thick than the former. Then they extend past the knee into the shin and the foot (just like those which extend into the hands), descending in the direction of the sole of the foot and thence extending into the toes. Many fine vessels divide from them in the direction of the belly and the flanks. Those which extend into the head through the throat appear large in the neck. From each of them, where it ends, many vessels divide off into the head, those from the right towards the left and those from the left towards the right. Each ends at the ear. There is another vessel in the neck, next to the large vessel on each side and a little smaller than it, with which most of the vessels from the head itself connect. These extend through the throat inside. From each of them, vessels extend under the shoulder-blades and into the hands, and they are seen alongside the spleen-vessel and the liver-vessel, a little smaller in size. These are the vessels which are lanced when anything causes pain beneath the skin – it is the liver-vessel and the spleen-vessel which are lanced when anything causes pain in the belly. Others extend from these under the breasts. Other vessels extend from each of these through the spinal marrow into the testicles; these are fine. Others extend under the skin and through the flesh into the kidneys, and end in the case of males in the testicles and in the case of females in the womb. These are called the spermatic vessels. The vessels are broader as they first leave the belly, and then become finer until they change from the right to the left and vice versa. *The thickest part of the blood is absorbed by the fleshy parts; that which overflows into the regions just mentioned becomes fine and hot and frothy.* [B 6]

(Aristotle, *History of Animals* 511b30–512b11)

Finally, the way in which air affects our mental lives may be illustrated by a passage from Theophrastus' account of Diogenes' psychological views:

Pleasure and pain come about in the following way. When the air in considerable quantity mixes with the blood and lightens it, being in a natural condition and pervading the whole body, there is pleasure; when the air is in an unnatural condition and does not mix, and the blood settles and becomes weaker and thicker, there is pain. Similarly with courage and health and their opposites. The tongue is the best judge of pleasure, for it is very soft and rare and all the vessels lead into it. That is why the tongue provides a very large number of signs in the case of the sick – and indicates the colours of other animals (for their varieties and characters are all reflected in it) . . .

We think by air that is pure and dry; for moisture inhibits the mind. That is why when we are asleep or drunk or full we think less. There is a sign that moisture destroys the mind in the fact that the other animals have weaker intellects; for they breathe air from the earth and the food they take is moister. Birds breathe pure air, but their nature is like that of fish; for their flesh is firm and the breath does not pass through the body but comes to a stop in the belly. Hence they digest their food quickly but are themselves stupid. In addition to their food, their mouths and tongues contribute to this; for they cannot understand one another. Plants, because they are not hollow and do not take in air, are completely incapable of thinking.

The same cause accounts for the fact that infants are stupid. For they contain a great quantity of moisture with the result that [the air] cannot pass through the whole body but is secreted in the chest. Hence they are dull and stupid. They are prone to anger, and in general impetuous and volatile because the air is moved in larger quantities from small bodies.

That is also the cause of forgetting. For because the air does not go throughout the body we cannot understand things. A sign of this is the fact that when we try to remember something there is a constriction in the chest and when we succeed it is dispelled and we are relieved of the pain.

(Theophrastus, *On the Senses* 43–45)

Appendix
THE SOURCES

The following telegraphic notes are designed to convey some minimal idea of each of the authorities who are quoted in the course of this book. The list also includes the most important of the sources who are now available to us only indirectly through quotation in later authors. The notes generally give, first, the dates of the source; then his place of birth (preceded by the letter 'b.') and the location of his main activities (preceded by an arrow); thirdly, a hint of his intellectual allegiances; fourthly, an indication – where apposite – of those of his works which are most pertinent to the study of the Presocratics. The letter 'Q' in square brackets indicates that the source is himself known to us only indirectly; the letter 'L' in square brackets indicates that the source wrote in Latin (all sources not so stigmatized wrote in Greek).

The most important sources are introduced by bold type. The length of a note is not proportional to the importance of its subject.

The sources are listed in alphabetical order, anonymous and pseudonymous works being collected at the end.

Achilles: third century AD (?); astronomer

Aelian: second half of second century AD; b. Praeneste; → Rome; wrote *The Nature of Animals* and *Miscellaneous Inquiries*

Agathemerus: first century AD (?); geographer

Albert the Great: AD 1200–1280; theologian and scholar; teacher of Thomas Aquinas

Alexander of Aphrodisias: flourished *c.* 200 AD; → Athens; Peripatetic philosopher; author of acute commentaries on **Aristotle**

Ammonius; fifth century AD; → Alexandria; pupil of Proclus; commentator on **Aristotle**

Apollodorus [Q]: second century BC; b. Athens; → Alexandria; scholar and polymath, his lost *Chronicles* are a major source for Presocratic chronology

Apollonius: second century BC (?); compiler of *Marvellous Stories*

Aristotle: 384–322 BC; b. Stagira; → Athens (also worked at Assos, and at Pella, where he tutored Alexander the Great). Pupil of *Plato*; founder of the Peripatetic school of philosophy. An unsurpassed polymath – scientist, philosopher, historian, scholar. He was interested in the history of philosophy and science; several of his surviving works (notably the *Physics* and the *Metaphysics*) contain invaluable information about the Presocratics

Aristoxenus: fourth century BC; b. Tarentum; → Athens; associate of **Aristotle**; musical theorist, biographer, with interest in Pythagoreanism

Arius Didymus [Q]: first century BC/AD; b. Alexandria; friend of the Emperor Augustus, author of philosophical handbooks

Athenaeus: flourished *c.* 200 BC; b. Naucratis in Egypt; his *Deipnosophists – Professors at the Dining Table –* is an encyclopaedic farrago in the form of table-talk

Marcus *Aurelius* Antoninus: AD 121–180; b. Rome; Emperor and Stoic; his *Meditations* occasionally allude to the Presocratics

Caelius Aurelianus [L]: fifth century AD; b. Numidia; medical translator of Soranus (second century AD)

Calcidius [L]: fourth century AD; Christian philosopher and author of influential commentary on Plato's *Timaeus*

Callimachus: third century BC; b. Cyrene; → Alexandria; eminent poet and scholar

Censorinus [L]: third century AD; → Rome; grammarian, his *On Birthdays* was written in 238

Marcus Tullius *Cicero* [L]: 106–43 BC; b. Arpinum; → Rome; orator, politician, statesman; leading literary figure of his age; keen and learned philosopher

Clement of Alexandria: AD *c.* 150–*c.* 215; b. Athens (?). Educated as a Greek, he converted to Christianity and became the first Christian philosopher. His *Miscellanies* compares Greek and Christian thought, unsystematically but with a wealth of quotation

Columella [L]: first century AD; b. Cadiz; writer on agriculture

Lucius Annaeus *Cornutus*: first century AD; Stoic philosopher, scholar, friend of the poet Persius

Damascius: AD *c.* 458–*c.* 540; b. Damascus; → Athens; Neoplatonic philosopher

Dio of Prusa: AD *c.* 40–*c.* 120; b. Prusa in Bithynia; → Rome. Friend of the Emperor Trajan, leading orator, prolific author, many of whose writings are Stoic-Cynic homilies

Diodorus: first century BC; b. Agyrium in Sicily; → Alexandria and Rome; author of a *Universal History*

Diogenes Laertius: third century AD (?). Nothing is known of his own life, but he survives in his *Lives of the Philosophers*. The work, in ten books, is derivative; it contains simplifications, confusions and some nonsense. But it remains a valuable source, both for the Presocratics and for later Greek philosophy

Diogenes of Oenoanda: second century AD; Epicurean philosopher who had his views carved on stone

Dionysius [Q]: third century AD; Bishop of Alexandria

Eudemus [Q]: fourth century BC; b. Rhodes; → Athens; pupil of **Aristotle**; philosopher and historian of science; used by **Simplicius**

Eusebius: AD *c.* 260–*c.* 340; Bishop of Caesarea, political figure, voluminous author; his *Preparation for the Gospel* includes many quotations from otherwise lost works of pagan philosophy

Eustathius: twelfth century AD; b. Constantinople; Archbishop of Thessalonica; wrote, among much else, a commentary on Homer

Galen: AD *c.* 129–*c.* 200; b. Pergamum; → Rome; eminent doctor and medical writer who was trained as a philosopher; his numerous writings make frequent reference to earlier philosophy

Aulus *Gellius* [L]: second century AD; from Rome; his *Attic Nights*, written in Athens, is a miscellany of essays on literary, historical and philosophical subjects

Harpocration: second century AD (?); → Alexandria; literary scholar

Hephaestion: second century AD; → Alexandria; literary scholar

Heraclides [Q]: *c.* 390–*c.* 310 BC; b. Heraclea on the Black Sea; → Athens; pupil of *Plato*; *littérateur* and lightweight philosopher

Heraclitus: first century AD (?); author of allegorizing interpretations of Homer

Herodian: second century AD; b. Alexandria; → Rome; works on linguistics and literary theory

Herodotus: c. 485–c. 420 BC; b. Halicarnassus, travelled widely; the 'father of history'

Hierocles: flourished early fifth century AD; → Alexandria; Neoplatonist philosopher, author of commentary on the so-called 'Golden Verses' of Pythagoras

Hippolytus: AD c. 180–235; → Rome; Christian, fierce controversialist, chosen as 'anti-Pope', exiled to Sardinia. His *Refutation of All Heresies*, in ten books, contains much information about pagan philosophy

Hisdosus: flourished AD c. 1100; wrote on Plato's psychology

Iamblichus: AD c. 250–c. 325; b. Chalcis; → Syria; Neoplatonist philosopher, pupil of *Porphyry*. Wrote at length on Pythagoreanism

Isocrates: 436–338 BC; from Athens; leading orator, political commentator, educational figure

Lucian: AD c. 120–c. 185; b. Samosata in Syria; → Athens; prolific author of satirical sketches

Macrobius [L]: early fifth century AD; scholar, his *Saturnalia* contains literary, scientific and philosophical discussions

Nicolaus of Damascus: first century BC; scholar and author of commentaries on **Aristotle**

Numenius [Q]: end of second century AD; from Apamea in Syria; Platonico-Pythagorean philosopher

Olympiodorus: sixth century AD; → Alexandria; Neoplatonist philosopher, author of commentaries on *Plato* and **Aristotle**

Origen: AD c. 185–c. 250; b. Alexandria; → Caesarea; most influential of early Christian theologians; his *Against Celsus* contains frequent allusions to pagan philosophy

Philodemus: first century BC; b. Gadara; → Naples; Epicurean philosopher, many of whose works survive among the Herculaneum papyri

John *Philoponus*: flourished in the sixth century AD; → Alexandria; Christian Neoplatonist, author of commentaries on **Aristotle**

Plato: 428–348 BC; b. Athens; philosopher of all-pervasive influence; his works often allude to the Presocratics

Plotinus: AD *c.* 205–270; b. Egypt; → Rome; leading philosopher of his age (founder of Neoplatonism); his *Enneads* contain occasional allusions to Presocratic thought

Plutarch: AD *c.* 45–*c.* 120; b. Chaeronea; a man of learning and letters (history, biography, literary criticism, philosophy); several of his 'moral essays' contain quotations from and allusions to the Presocratics

Polybius: *c.* 200–*c.* 115 BC; b. Megalopolis; → Rome (as a prisoner of war); leading historian

Porphyry: AD 234–*c.* 305; b. Tyre; → Rome; pupil of *Plotinus*, whose works he edited; Neoplatonist philosopher and voluminous author

Proclus: AD 412–485; b. Constantinople; → Athens; Neoplatonic philosopher; his commentary on Euclid contains information about the early history of Greek mathematics

Sextus Empiricus: second century AD (?); major figure in sceptical philosophy; his *Outlines of Pyrrhonism* and *Against the Mathematicians* contain much information about earlier philosophers

Simplicius: flourished *c.* 500–540 AD; trained in Alexandria, → Athens (529–534 in Persia); pagan, Neoplatonist philosopher (an enemy of *Philoponus*). His commentaries on **Aristotle**, all written towards the end of his life, are remarkable for their learning; his commentary on the *Physics* is the single most important source for Presocratic philosophy

John **Stobaeus**: fifth century AD; from Stobi in Macedonia; his *Anthology*, in four books, is a collection of excerpts from earlier Greek authors arranged by subject-matter

Strabo: 64 BC–AD *c.* 25; b. Amasia in Asia Minor; → Rome; leading geographer

Themistius: AD 317–388; → Constantinople; renowned orator, commentator on **Aristotle**

Theo of Smyrna: early second century AD; Platonist and mathematician

Theodorus Prodromus: twelfth century AD; → Constantinople; novelist and multifarious author

Theophrastus: 371–287 BC; b. Lesbos; → Athens; **Aristotle**'s leading pupil and successor, matching his master in the range of his interests. Had a profound influence on the historiography of Greek philosophy. Most of his works are lost; the essay *On the Senses*, discussing various pre-Aristotelian theories, survives

Thrasyllus [Q]: first century AD; b. Alexandria; → Rome; astrologer to the Emperor Tiberius; catalogued the works of Plato and Democritus

Timon [Q]: *c.* 320–*c.* 230 BC; b. Phlius; satirical poet of sceptical bent

John *Tzetzes*; AD 1110–*c.* 1180; → Constantinople; scholar, polymath, prolific author

Anonymous works

Anecdota Graeca: title (*Unpublished Greek Texts*) given to various miscellaneous collections of often anonymous texts

Etymologicum Magnum: encyclopedic dictionary, compiled *c.* AD 1100

Herculaneum papyrus no. 1012: fragments of work by (?) Demetrius of Laconia, second century BC Epicurean

Anonymus Londinensis: 'name' given to the unknown author of a medical text, found on papyrus, the contents of which contain material from the fourth century BC

Theosophia: AD *c.* 500; Christian compilation of pagan material bearing on oracles, etc

Pseudonymous works

[*Alexander*], *Problems*: late compilation of ultimately Peripatetic material

[*Aristotle*], *On the World*: brief summary of Aristotelian philosophy, dating from first century BC (?)

[*Aristotle*], *On Melissus, Xenophanes, Gorgias*: essays of exposition and criticism; date unknown

[*Aristotle*], *Problems*: Peripatetic compilation of uncertain date

[*Iamblichus*], *Theological Arithmetic*: essay on number-mysticism, perhaps by a contemporary of *Iamblichus*

[*Olympiodorus*], *On the Divine and Sacred Art of the Philosopher's Stone*; late essay on alchemy

[*Philoponus*], *Commentary on the Generation of Animals*: perhaps written by Michael of Ephesus, eleventh century AD

[*Plutarch*], *Consolation to Apollonius*: date uncertain

[*Plutarch*], *Is Fire or Water the More Useful?*

[*Plutarch*], *Miscellanies*: fragmentary doxographical notes

[*Plutarch*], *On Desire and Grief*: fragment of uncertain origin

[Plutarch], *On the Scientific Beliefs of the Philosophers*: superficial but valuable compilation, probably from second century AD

Scholiasts

Scholia are notes. Many manuscripts of ancient authors have scholia in their margins. These notes vary greatly in value and in date. This book has cited scholia to:

Euripides, *Phoenician Women* [tragedy, *c.* 410 BC]
Gregory of Nazianzus [Bishop, AD 330–390]
Homer
Nicander [didactic poet, second century BC (?)]
Plato

FURTHER READING

The literature on the Presocratics is extensive, and much of it is formidably technical. This list mentions a few of the more accessible items.

The best brief and general introduction to the subject in English is
  E. Hussey, *The Presocratics* (London, 1972)
A larger and more philosophical treatment can be found in
  J. Barnes, *The Presocratic Philosophers* (London, 1982 [2nd edition])
A larger and more literary treatment can be found in
  H. Fraenkel, *Early Greek Poetry and Philosophy*, trans. M. Hadas and J. Willis (Oxford, 1975)
There is a learned and sane discussion of all aspects of Presocratic thought in the first three volumes of
  W. K. C. Guthrie, *A History of Greek Philosophy* (Cambridge, 1962, 1965, 1969)

Most of the Greek texts are collected in
  H. Diels and W. Kranz, *Die Fragmente der Vorsokratiker* (Berlin, 1952 [10th edition])
There is a useful anthology
  M. R. Wright, *The Presocratics* (Bristol, 1985)
and a selection of Greek texts, together with translations and commentary, is printed in
  G. S. Kirk, J. E. Raven, and M. Schofield, *The Presocratic Philosophers* (Cambridge, 1983 [2nd edition])

Much of the best work on the subject has appeared in article form. Some of this can be found in
  D. J. Furley and R. E. Allen (eds), *Studies in Presocratic Philosophy* (London, 1970, 1975)

A. P. D. Mourelatos (ed.), *The Presocratics* (Garden City N.Y., 1974)

On the Milesian philosophers there is an outstanding study
  C. H. Kahn, *Anaximander and the Origins of Greek Cosmology* (New York, 1960)
On Heraclitus see
  C. H. Kahn, *The Art and Thought of Heraclitus* (Cambridge, 1979)
For everything to do with Pythagoras and Pythagoreanism consult
  W. Burkert, *Lore and Science in Ancient Pythagoreanism* (Cambridge Mass., 1972)
There is a new edition, with commentary, of Parmenides
  D. Gallop, *Parmenides of Elea* (Toronto, 1984)
For Zeno see the various essays collected in
  W. C. Salmon (ed.), *Zeno's Paradoxes* (Indianapolis Ind., 1970)
There are helpful notes on Empedocles in
  M. R. Wright, *Empedocles – the Extant Fragments* (New Haven Conn., 1981)
For Anaxagoras see
  M. Schofield, *An Essay on Anaxagoras* (Cambridge, 1980)
On the Atomists it is still necessary to refer to
  C. Bailey, *The Greek Atomists and Epicurus* (Oxford, 1928)

Further bibliography can be found in Guthrie and Barnes.

SUBJECT INDEX

INDEX TO
QUOTED TEXTS

INDEX TO DIELS-KRANZ B-TEXTS

READ MORE IN PENGUIN

In every corner of the world, on every subject under the sun, Penguin represents quality and variety – the very best in publishing today.

For complete information about books available from Penguin – including Puffins, Penguin Classics and Arkana – and how to order them, write to us at the appropriate address below. Please note that for copyright reasons the selection of books varies from country to country.

In the United Kingdom: Please write to *Dept. JC, Penguin Books Ltd, FREEPOST, West Drayton, Middlesex UB7 0BR*

If you have any difficulty in obtaining a title, please send your order with the correct money, plus ten per cent for postage and packaging, to *PO Box No. 11, West Drayton, Middlesex UB7 0BR*

In the United States: Please write to *Penguin USA Inc., 375 Hudson Street, New York, NY 10014*

In Canada: Please write to *Penguin Books Canada Ltd, 10 Alcorn Avenue, Suite 300, Toronto, Ontario M4V 3B2*

In Australia: Please write to *Penguin Books Australia Ltd, 487 Maroondah Highway, Ringwood, Victoria 3134*

In New Zealand: Please write to *Penguin Books (NZ) Ltd,182–190 Wairau Road, Private Bag, Takapuna, Auckland 9*

In India: Please write to *Penguin Books India Pvt Ltd, 706 Eros Apartments, 56 Nehru Place, New Delhi 110 019*

In the Netherlands: Please write to *Penguin Books Netherlands B.V., Keizersgracht 231 NL–1016 DV Amsterdam*

In Germany: Please write to *Penguin Books Deutschland GmbH, Friedrichstrasse 10–12, W–6000 Frankfurt/Main 1*

In Spain: Please write to *Penguin Books S. A., C. San Bernardo 117–6° E–28015 Madrid*

In Italy: Please write to *Penguin Italia s.r.l., Via Felice Casati 20, I–20124 Milano*

In France: Please write to *Penguin France S. A., 17 rue Lejeune, F–31000 Toulouse*

In Japan: Please write to *Penguin Books Japan, Ishikiribashi Building, 2–5–4, Suido, Tokyo 112*

In Greece: Please write to *Penguin Hellas Ltd, Dimocritou 3, GR–106 71 Athens*

In South Africa: Please write to *Longman Penguin Southern Africa (Pty) Ltd, Private Bag X08, Bertsham 2013*

READ MORE IN PENGUIN